Plotting Your Course

Student Activity Workbook

Jerry Ryan
Career Education Consultant
Akron, Ohio

Roberta Ryan
Career Education Consultant
Akron, Ohio

National Textbook Company
a division of NTC/Contemporary Publishing Group
NTC
Lincolnwood, Illinois USA

ISBN 0-314-06792-2

Published by National Textbook Company, a division of
NTC/Contemporary Publishing Group, Inc.
4255 West Touhy Avenue, Lincolnwood (Chicago), Illinois 60712-1975
U.S.A.

Manufactured in the United States of America.

04 03 02 01 00 PA 8 7

Contents

Chapter Ten

Chapter Eleven

Chapter Twelve

Chapter Thirteen

Chapter Fourteen

Chapter Fifteen

Chapter Sixteen

Chapter Seventeen

Chapter Eighteen

Chapter Nineteen

Chapter Twenty

Chapter Twenty-One

Chapter Twenty-Two

Name ______________________________ Date ____________________

Checkpoint 1.1

When Our Cause It Is Just

Supporting a cause you consider to be more important than yourself allows you to display your cherished beliefs and establish your identity as a person. This isn't a new idea. Young adults have attached their loyalty to causes for many generations.

Review the following list of causes and the years when each cause was very popular. The causes listed are still major concerns for many individuals and organizations. The dates listed represent time periods of major public concern.

Cause	Popular Years
Worker's rights (unionism)	1920's – 1930's
Democracy vs. facism	1940 – 1945
Democracy vs. communism	1946s – 1960's
Civil Rights of minorities	1950's – 1970's
Protecting the natural environment	1960's – present
Preventing worldwide nuclear destruction	1950's – 1990's
U.S. involvement in the Vietnam War	1964 – 1973
Alcohol and drug abuse	1970's – present
Gender equity (the women's movement)	1980's – present

1. Each generation faces unique political, social, and economic problems.
   a. Which causes on the list would you support most? ____________________
   b. Explain your reasons for supporting this cause. ____________________

   ____

   ____

   c. What affect would your support for this particular cause have on your relationships with family and friends?

   Family ____________________

   Friends ____________________

2. a. Which cause on the list would you support least? ____________________
   b. Explain your reasons for not supporting this cause. ____________________

   ____

   ____

   c. What affect would your lack of support for this particular cause have on your relationships with family and friends?

   Family ____________________

   Friends ____________________

continued

3. a. Can you think of a cause you would like to add to this list? If so, write it here: ____________________

____

b. Why is this cause important? ____________________

4. Several of the causes listed in this activity may have a positive or negative influence on your future career. Select the three causes you think will influence your career success the most. Explain the influence you expect they would have.

a. Cause ____________________ Explanation ____________________

____

____

b. Cause ____________________ Explanation ____________________

____

____

c. Cause ____________________ Explanation ____________________

____

____

5. Interview a worker who is at least forty years old, asking the following questions.

a. Which cause listed in this activity was most important to you when you were between the ages of seventeen and twenty-four? ____________________

b. How did this cause influence your education, training, or career? ____________________

____

c. How did this cause influence your lifestyle? ____________________

____

d. What influences in your life were the source of your loyalty to this cause? ____________________

____

e. Now that you are older and have gained more life experience, which cause listed in this activity would you consider to be most important? Why? ____________________

____

____

f. Which cause do you think will have the most influence on the future career success of new workers? Why? ____________________

____

g. What advice would you offer teenagers concerning their involvement with the causes listed in this activity? ____________________

____

Name ______________________________ Date ______________

1.2 Checkpoint

How Would You Handle the Situation?

People react differently to life situations. Imagine that you are having dinner with a good friend in a very expensive restaurant. Suddenly, the waiter drops a dish, and a small amount of yellow sauce is splattered on the sleeve of your new jacket. In each of the following, circle the response (a, b, or c) that is closest to the response you would probably make.

1. How would you feel?
   a. Nervous or apologetic
   b. Confident that you can clean your sleeve
   c. Angry

2. What would you think?
   a. I should have pulled my sleeve out of the way.
   b. We all make mistakes, but the waiter is responsible for this situation.
   c. The waiter is incompetent. He should be reprimanded by the manger.

3. What would you say?
   a. Very little.
   b. How I feel and what we need to do about the situation.
   c. "This situation is inexcusable. I want to speak with the manager."

4. What would be the tone of your voice?
   a. Soft
   b. Normal
   c. Loud

5. How would you act?
   a. Avoid eye contact with the waiter or quietly leave the table.
   b. Maintain eye contact with the waiter and probably remain seated
   c. Stand up to face the waiter

6. How would you expect the waiter to act toward you?
   a. Apologetic and regretful
   b. Responsible and sincere
   c. Disrespectful and aloof

continued

A. Results

1. You have expressed six personal behaviors in this activity. Total your six responses.
   Total *a* responses: _____ (Submissive behaviors)
   Total *b* responses: _____ (Assertive behaviors)
   Total *c* responses: _____ (Aggressive behaviors)

2. a. Which type of behavior did you express most? Describe a situation you experienced during the past six months in which you expressed this type of behavior. ______________________________

   ____

   b. Are you pleased with the behavior you expressed in this situation? If so, why? If not, what behavior would you have liked to express? ______________________________

   ____

3. a. Describe a situation in which someone was unfair to you. ______________________________

   ____

   b. Was this person's behavior submissive, assertive, or aggressive? ______________________________

   ____

4. a. Describe a situation in which someone was fair but firm with you. ______________________________

   ____

   b. Was this person's behavior submissive, assertive, or aggressive? ______________________________

   ____

Name ______________________ Date ______________

Checkpoint 1.3

Planning for Success

1. List several events, activities, and situations you have been involved in during the past six months. Examples include a specific course of study you are taking, a job you acquired, a party you attended, or a vacation.

2. a. Which events, activities, and situations on your list did you plan or help plan?

   b. Which planned event, activity, or situation was most successful?

   c. Which specific parts of the plan were responsible for the successful outcome?

   d. If you were planning a similar event, what would you do differently?

3. a. Which events, activities, and situations on your list were unplanned?

   b. Which unplanned event, activity, or situation was least successful?

   c. How would planning have improved the outcome?

4. Name one future event, activity, or situation that will influence your career success.

Are you satisfied with the plans you have made for this event, activity, or situation? If so, why? If not, why not?

Helpful Hint: Review the section "Career Planning Is Important" in Chapter 1 of your textbook. Pay special attention to the components of a career plan.

Name ____________________ Date ____________________

Checkpoint 1.4

Developing Skills for the School-to-Work Transition

Whether you are in a tech-prep, traditional college prep, vocational, or work-study program, the skills you learn in high school will determine your level of entry into the world of work or your level of preparation for additional education and training beyond high school.

1. a. What is the highest level mathematics course you have completed? ____________________

   b. List two occupations you would be prepared to enter with this level of mathematics skill.

   ____

2. a. What is the highest level mathematics course you plan to complete during high school or college?

   ____

   b. List two occupations you would be prepared to enter with this level of mathematics skill.

   ____

3. a. What is the highest level English course you have completed? ____________________

   b. List two occupations you would be prepared to enter with this level of English skill.

   ____

4. a. What is the highest level English course you plan to complete during high school or college?

   ____

   b. List two occupations you would be prepared to enter with this level of English skill.

   ____

5. When you think of your future career, what are the two most important skills you will need?

   ____

   ____

6. Where do you expect to learn each of these skills? ____________________

   ____

Helpful hint: It is important to understand the relationship between academic skills and occupational choices. You may wish to repeat this activity on a separate sheet of paper, using other high school courses. Some examples are science, social studies, art, music, and vocational skills courses. Review the section "Developing Skills" in Chapter 1 of your textbook.

Name ______________________________ Date ______________

Checkpoint 1.5

Finding the Right Words

Chapter 1 of your textbook contains numerous terms that employers and workers use. Recognizing and understanding these terms will help you make the important career decisions you will soon face.

Unscramble the terms in column B, and match them with the definitions in column A. (Some terms may contain two words.)

Column A	Column B
Example: __a__ the paid and unpaid work you do during your lifetime	a. CAREER RAREEC
1. _____ being paid as much as co-workers in the same occupation	b. ______________ FELS-PETNOCC
2. _____ apologetic, indifferent, passive	c. ______________ RAVEYIT
3. _____ the amount of goods and services you can buy with your income	d. ______________ LEADY FATCATGRINIOI
4. _____ how people view their own skills, interests, and competence level	e. ______________ ISGREASEVG
5. _____ dull and tedious labor	f. ______________ QUALE APY
6. _____ personal connections people develop with others	g. ______________ RESTSAVEI
7. _____ a periodic change in the task, pace, or location of the work	h. ______________ LIVETEAR RISAGENN
8. _____ domineering, relentless, quarrelsom	i. ______________ NAMHU NATORIESLIPSH
9. _____ to postpone acquiring certain things	j. ______________ RUGREDDY
10. _____ goods and services you can buy with your earnings compared to your neighbor's earnings	k. ______________ LOSTBEAU RINGSANE
11. _____ persistent, understanding, cooperative	l. ______________ BUSVISISEM

Name ______________________________ Date ____________________

Checkpoint 1.6

Checking Your Location

1. For each of the following statements, circle **F** if the statement is more false than true. Circle **T** if the statement is more true than false.

T F a. As you grow older, the world of fantasy gives way to the real world.

T F b. Most teenagers dislike being placed in adult roles.

T F c. Developing a career plan now will help you achieve a higher level of success later in life.

T F d. Your parents and teachers are responsible for your career satisfaction.

T F e. Submissive people frequently have problems with everyday life situations because of their failure to communicate their beliefs honestly.

T F f. Assertive people express their feelings and values openly and honestly.

T F g. Psychological and social concerns are unimportant to a person who works with tools.

T F h. Work that is valued by the worker can be paid or unpaid.

T F i. Several things that are far more important than the size of your paycheck will determine your future lifestyle.

T F j. Regardless of their age, sex, or race, people expect to be paid as much as their co-workers.

T F k. Job security is largely determined by seniority, seasonal ups and downs, hard work, and thrift.

T F l. Human relationships are a very important work value for some people.

T F m. For some workers, having a variety of work tasks is directly related to job satisfaction.

T F n. It is a well known fact that the basic skills of reading, writing, and mathematics are related to success on the job.

T F o. Failure on the job may cause feelings of role confusion, anger, depression, and incompetence.

continued

2. Use the space below to rewrite the statements you marked **false** and make them **true**. Include the letter of each statement you rewrite.

Name ______________________ Date ______________

2.1 Checkpoint

What Makes You Different?

In Chapter 2 of your textbook, you learned about the interaction of your heredity, culture, environment, and life experiences. You learned how this interaction creates the unique traits and characteristics that are you. Increasing your level of self-understanding in each of these areas will help you gain further control over your life goals and personal choices as you prepare for career success.

A. Heredity

1. Think about your family members (living or dead). Which family member is (or was) most similar to you?

   Name ______________________ Relationship ______________________

2. What behaviors, talents, or physical features did you inherit from this person? Consider your size and temperament and traits such as musical or mechanical skills. ______________________

3. How are you different from the person you selected? ______________________

A. Life Experiences

1. Describe two or more life experiences of yours that are different from the life experiences of the family member you selected. ______________________

2. How did the life experiences you described influence the person you are? ______________________

3. Describe two or more life experiences of yours that are similar to the life experiences of the family member you selected. ______________________

4. How did the life experiences you described influence the family member you selected?

____

____

____

A. Culture

1. Think about the culture in which you live. Think about the way of life of the people with whom you interact. What important belief have you learned and accepted from the people

   In your home? ______________________

   In your school? ______________________

   In your house of worship? ______________________

   In your neighborhood? ______________________

B. Environment

1. Your surroundings influence your beliefs, attitudes, and lifestyle choices.

   a. Describe the environment in which you live (urban or rural, climate, geographic features).

   ____

   ____

   b. How has your environment influenced your beliefs, attitudes, or lifestyle choices?

   ____

   ____

"WHO AM I, AND WHERE AM I GOING?.."

Name ______________________ Date ______________

2.2

Checkpoint

Workers in Your Family Tree

1. Ask a parent, guardian, family friend, or agency worker to help you obtain information for the following chart.

Family Worker Chart

Relationship	**First and Last Name of Relative**	**Where Relative Lived**	**Occupation(s) of Relative**	**Personal Qualities**
Maternal grandmother				
Maternal grandfather				
Paternal grandmother				
Paternal grandfather				
Great-grandmother				
Great-grandfather				

2. Use the information from the Family Worker Chart to answer the following questions. Select any three of the workers listed in your family tree.
   - Has this relative's occupation changed greatly or disappeared? Explain.

     a. ______________ Name of relative ______________ Answer

     b. ______________ Name of relative ______________ Answer

     c. ______________ Name of relative ______________ Answer

   - Have the education and training requirements for this occupation changed? Explain.

     a. ______________ Name of relative ______________ Answer

     b. ______________ Name of relative ______________ Answer

     c. ______________ Name of relative ______________ Answer

3. Imagine that you lived during the time of your great-grandparents.

   a. What occupation would you probably have? ______________

   b. Would you have more or less freedom to choose your occupation than you do now? Explain your answer. ______________

Name ______________________________ Date ____________________

Checkpoint 2.3

Self-concept

Self is the part of your experience that you regard as essentially you. It is how you see yourself in the past, present, and future. Your attitude toward yourself determines whether you view yourself with pride or shame, as worthy or unworthy. It affects the attitude you have toward others.

1. Explore the past.
   a. What kinds of things could you do during your elementary school years? ____________________

   ____

   b. What difficulties did you have? ____________________

   ____

   c. What or who is most important in your past? ____________________

   ____

2. Explore the present.
   a. How do you see yourself now? Use at least fifty words to describe yourself. ____________________

   ____

   ____

   ____

   ____

   ____

   b. What commonalities in your past and present describe you? ____________________

   ____

3. Explore the future.
   a. What do you want to do with your life in the next fifty years? ____________________

   ____

   ____

   ____

Name ______________________________ Date ____________________

Checkpoint 2.4

Self-esteem

Many employers link an employee's effectiveness in the workplace directly to positive self-esteem and successful personal management. Employees with positive self-esteem recognize their current skill level on the job; are aware of their impact on others; understand their emotions and cope well with stress, change, and criticism; deal with their limitations by seeking and applying new information to solve problems; and take pride in their work.

1. Evaluate yourself in terms of some of these points as they relate to your "job" as a student.

   a. Do you recognize your current skill level in each of your school subjects? Explain your answer.

   b. Are you aware of your impact on others? Give an example.

   c. Do you understand your emotions and cope well with stress, change, and criticism? Give an example.

   d. Do you deal with your limitations by seeking and applying new information to solve problems? Give an example.

   e. Do you take pride in your school work? Give an example.

2. Positive self-esteem expresses an attitude of approval and positive evaluation. One indication of positive self esteem is the number of positive statements a person makes about self or others. People with low self-esteem tend to make many negative comments about their own behavior or that of others.

   a. How many positive (yes) statements did you make in this activity? __________

   b. How many negative (no) statements did you make? __________

3. a. With which negative statement are you most dissatisfied? __________

   b. What action could you take that would cause you to feel better about this situation?

Name ______________________________ Date ____________________

Checkpoint 2.5

Identifying Interests

Inventoried interests are estimates of interests based on responses to a set of questions concerning likes and dislikes. People and jobs reflect patterns of interest.

The following are activities that people do. Select *All* of the activities you are interested in now as well as those you would like to try. Write ***L*** (for Like) on the line next to the matching number in the answer box at the end of this activity.

1. Skiing or ice skating
2. Repairing things
3. Playing chess
4. Sketching or painting
5. Visiting friends
6. Being a club officer
7. Collecting special items
8. Fishing or hunting
9. Being athletic
10. Reading science fiction
11. Reading or writing poetry
12. Going to a party
13. Expressing my viewpoints
14. Keeping a diary
15. Farming or gardening
16. Working on cars
17. Writing computer programs
18. Doing art or photography projects
19. Caring for pets
20. Being a leader
21. Working crossword puzzles
22. Jogging or hiking
23. Building or making things
24. Building models
25. Writing stories
26. Caring for plants
27. Being a referee or umpire
28. Attending worship services
29. Playing outdoor games
30. Doing physical activities
31. Building science projects
32. Singing or dancing
33. Writing to a friend
34. Being a student leader
35. Selling items for school
36. Riding a bike
37. Doing hands-on class projects
38. Using a microscope
39. Playing a musical instrument
40. Talking with friends
41. Campaigning for class officers
42. Attending club meetings
43. Boating or swimming
44. Making things in shop class
45. Reading mystery stories
46. Being in plays
47. Doing volunteer work
48. Earning awards or certificates
49. Playing spelling games
50. Learning about the outdoors
51. Learning about machines
52. Learning about science
53. Learning about art or music
54. Learning about child care
55. Learning about politics
56. Learning about office work

Answer Box

1. ____	2. ____	3. ____	4. ____	5. ____	6. ____	7. ____
8. ____	9. ____	10. ____	11. ____	12. ____	13. ____	14. ____
15. ____	16. ____	17. ____	18. ____	19. ____	20. ____	21. ____
22. ____	23. ____	24. ____	25. ____	26. ____	27. ____	28. ____
29. ____	30. ____	31. ____	32. ____	33. ____	34. ____	35. ____
36. ____	37. ____	38. ____	39. ____	40. ____	41. ____	42. ____
43. ____	44. ____	45. ____	46. ____	47. ____	48. ____	49. ____
50. ____	51. ____	52. ____	53. ____	54. ____	55. ____	56. ____
☐	☐	☐	☐	☐	☐	☐
1	2	3	4	5	6	7

Total the number of ***L***s in each column. Enter your score in the correct box. Later you will learn how your interests match up with different occupations.

Name ______________________________ Date ______________

Checkpoint 2.6

Identifying Aptitudes

The occupational aptitudes listed in Chapter 2 are specific capacities and abilities required of an individual in order to learn or adequately perform a task or job duty. Different occupations require different amounts or levels of a specific aptitude. The following rating scale applies to all occupational descriptions of aptitudes. Number 1 is the highest level of the aptitude; number 5 is the lowest.

1 = The highest 10 percent of the population. An extremely high degree of the aptitude.
2 = The highest third of the population (not including the highest ten percent). An above-average or high degree of the aptitude.
3 = The middle third of the population. A medium degree of the aptitude, ranging from slightly below to slightly above average.
4 = The lowest third of the population (not including the lowest ten percent). A below-average or low degree of the aptitude.
5 = The lowest 10 percent of the population. A very low degree of the aptitude.

1. Think about the aptitudes you have turned into skills in each of the following areas, then compare your skill level in each area with those of a friend. Review the descriptions of each worker aptitude on pages 37 and 38 of your textbook before beginning the actitivy. Use the rating scale above as a guideline.

Activity or Skill	**My Friend's Performance Level (1–5)**	**My Performance Level (1–5)**	**Work-Related Aptitude Used in This Activity**
Getting good grades in school			(G) General learning ability
Playing competitive sports			(K) Motor coordination
Correcting a business letter			(Q) Clerical perception
Using a drawing to build a model			(P) Form perception
Playing a piano			(F) Finger dexterity
Expressing ideas with words			(V) Verbal ability
Working a jigsaw puzzle			(S) Spatial
Riding a bike			(E) Eye-hand-foot coordination
Creating art and designs			(C) Color discrimination
Solving algebra problems			(N) Numerical ability
Fixing or making things			(M) Manual dexterity

2. a. In what ways will your highest rated skills help you succeed in the world of work? ______________

____

b. In what ways will your friend's highest rated skills help him/her succeed in the world of work?

____

3. Here are examples of specific aptitude ratings for several occupations:

Fashion designer: G2, V2, N3, S2, P2, Q3, K3, F2, M3, E5, C2
Chemist: G1, V1, N1, S2, P2, Q2, K3, F3, M3, E5, C3
Dentist: G1, V2, N1, S1, P1, Q3, K4, F2, M2, E4, C4
Fast-Food worker: G4, V4, N4, S4, P4, Q3, K3, F4, M3, E3, C4
Police officer: G3, V3, N4, S3, P3, Q3, K3, F4, M3, E3, C4
Mechanical engineer: G2, V2, N2, S2, P3, Q3, K3, F3, M3, E5, C5
Automobile mechanic: G3, V3, N4, S2, P3, Q4, K3, F3, M2, E4, C4
Work-processor operator: G3, V3, N4, S2, P4, Q2, K2, F3, M3, E5, C5

a. Use the rating scale and the examples above as a guideline to help you complete the following chart.

Aptitudes: Strengths and Weaknesses			
Aptitude	**Experiences Demonstrating That I Am Strong in This Aptitude**	**Experiences Demonstrating That I Am Not Strong in This Aptitude**	**Rating of My Level of This Aptitude (1–5)**
(G) General learning ability	____________	____________	________
(V) Verbal ability	____________	____________	________
(N) Numerical ability	____________	____________	________
(S) Spatial	____________	____________	________
(P) Form perception	____________	____________	________
(Q) Clerical perception	____________	____________	________
(K) Motor coordination	____________	____________	________
(F) Finger dexterity	____________	____________	________
(M) Manual dexterity	____________	____________	________
(E) Eye-hand-foot coordination	____________	____________	________
(C) Color discrimination	____________	____________	________

b. Are your aptitudes a good match for the occupations you are presently considering? Explain.

____

c. What will you need to work on? ______________________________

____

Name ______________________________ Date ____________________

Checkpoint 2.7

Skills — Now and for Tomorrow

Skills are the competencies you have developed through education or training. All jobs require specific skills. When you have the ability to perform a task well, you are a skilled worker.

Review the following list, and select *All* of the skills you have now or plan to develop in the future. Write an ***S*** (for *Skill*) on the line next to the matching number in the answer box at the end of this activity.

1. Planting, cultivating, or harvesting a garden
2. Building things with tools
3. Understanding technical information
4. Playing, writing, or performing music
5. Taking care of people or animals
6. Being a leader
7. Keeping track of numbers, systems, people, or records
8. Developing outdoor survival skills
9. Repairing or using mechanical things
10. Observing, studying, or experimenting with scientific information
11. Finding new ways to do things
12. Using verbal skills to help people solve problems
13. Using verbal skills to influence others
14. Following directions from others precisely
15. Developing outdoor camping skills
16. Using tools and drawings to repair things
17. Solving math or science problems
18. Performing in dramas or dance
19. Planning social activities for groups of people
20. Organizing students for an activity
21. Keeping neat and accurate records
22. Observing behavior patterns of birds or animals
23. Making crafts or clothes
24. Knowing how computers work
25. Using imagination to write or draw
26. Getting along well with others
27. Being a good speaker
28. Keeping homework organized
29. Developing fishing or hunting skills
30. Driving or operating a vehicle
31. Figuring out problems
32. Visualizing objects and creating drawings
33. Explaining ideas to people
34. Setting and reaching goals
35. Keeping accurate records
36. Doing yard work
37. Operating machinery or equipment
38. Understanding good chess moves and strategy games
39. Expressing feelings or ideas through art, music, or writing
40. Teaching or instructing people
41. Convincing people to do things your way
42. Knowing and following correct rules and procedures

Answer Box

1	2	3	4	5	6	7
1. ____	2. ____	3. ____	4. ____	5. ____	6. ____	7. ____
8. ____	9. ____	10. ____	11. ____	12. ____	13. ____	14. ____
15. ____	16. ____	17. ____	18. ____	19. ____	20. ____	21. ____
22. ____	23. ____	24. ____	25. ____	26. ____	27. ____	28. ____
29. ____	30. ____	31. ____	32. ____	33. ____	34. ____	35. ____
36. ____	37. ____	38. ____	39. ____	40. ____	41. ____	42. ____
☐	☐	☐	☐	☐	☐	☐

Total the number of *S*s in each column. Enter your score in the correct box. Later you will learn how your skills match up with different occupations.

Name ______________________________ Date ______________________

Checkpoint 2.8

Data, People, or Things?

The following is a list of job activities. Place a check mark (✓) in front of *all* of the activities you would prefer. Some people will choose many activities, and others will choose only a few. Review page 33 of your text for a complete explanation of data, people, and things.

A

- _____ Giving professional advice to people
- _____ Resolving conflicts
- _____ Teaching or demonstrating
- _____ Directing or helping others
- _____ Entertaining others
- _____ Influencing others' opinions or use of services or products
- _____ Making yourself understood through speech
- _____ Serving or assisting others
- _____ Following verbal instructions

B

- _____ Putting new ideas and facts together
- _____ Deciding on and organizing projects
- _____ Solving problems with information
- _____ Collecting, arranging, and reporting information
- _____ Using mathematics for reports
- _____ Copying numbers or words precisely
- _____ Comparing likes and differences

C

- _____ Understanding, fixing, changing, and operating equipment
- _____ Choosing and using tools to exact standards
- _____ Operating complex equipment
- _____ Steering, operating, and guiding machinery
- _____ Using tools to move, guide, or place things
- _____ Starting, stopping, and watching machines
- _____ Filling or emptying automatic machinery
- _____ Moving or carrying things

1. a. Total your check marks in Column A. This represents your *people* score. _____ Total check marks

   b. Total your check marks in Column B. This represents your *data* score. _____ Total check marks

   c. Total your check marks in Column C. This represents your *things* score. _____ Total check marks

2. Using your scores from this activity determine which are most important to you; people, data, or things. If two scores are the same, determine their order of importance.

   a. Most important __________ b. Second most important __________ c. Least important __________

3. What skills do you need to acquire to be eligible for a job you would enjoy in the category you chose as "most important"? ____

   ____

Name ______________________________ Date ____________________

Checkpoint 2.9

Leisure Time — A Change of Pace

Leisure activities are what you do when you have time to do as you please. During your leisure time, you are free to choose activities that reflect your personal interests and skills. An analysis of your leisure-time preferences can indicate the kinds of work activities that you would enjoy.

1. In the chart below, list ten activities that you enjoy doing in your leisure time. In the spaces next to the activities you list, place a check mark (✓) under the columns that are true of that leisure activity.

	Activities I Enjoy Doing in My Leisure Time	I Am Active Outdoors and Enjoy Nature	I Am Physically Active and Use Things	I Am Analytical	I Am Creative and Self-expressive	I Am Social or Helpful to Others	I Am in Charge	I Am Organized
1.								
2.								
3.								
4.								
5.								
6.								
7.								
8.								
9.								
10.								
	______	______	______	______	______	______	______	______

2. Total the number of check marks in each column.

3. a. What are you doing in your favorite activity? (Look at your check marks.) ______________________

   b. How is this activity symbolic of you? What skill or talent does it represent? ______________________

   c. What clues to the kinds of work you might enjoy can you find in your responses? ______________________

Name ______________________________ Date ____________________

2.10 Checkpoint

Checking Your Location

1. For each of the following statements, circle **F** if the statement is more false than true. Circle **T** if the statement is more true than false.

T F a. From the day you were born, you have been influenced by your environment; in turn, your environment has been influenced by you.

T F b. Physcial features, intelligence, reflexes, and temperament are part of your heredity.

T F c. Your culture has little influence on your attitude toward education and training.

T F d. Most psychologists believe that personality is formed late in childhood.

T F e. It is possible to have high interest but low ability in certain areas, and vice versa.

T F f. Personality traits change a great deal as you get older, so the results of accurate testing are of very little use over a long period of time.

T F g. Self-concept can be thought of as your attitude toward your personality.

T F h. It is wise to compare interests, abilities, temperament, and character with the worker traits of an occupation before deciding to acquire the education and training needed to enter the occupation.

T F i. A person's self-concept is always accurate.

T F j. A person with a high level of self-esteem feels competent, of value to society, in control of most life events, important to other people, and useful.

T F k. Your interests are related to only one occupation.

T F l. People usually possess one or more aptitudes that haven't been developed to a high level of skill.

T F m. Once you have identified your strong aptitudes, it is important to use your potential and learn specific career skills.

T F n. Every occupation requires workers to spend some of their time performing tasks working with data, people, and things.

T F o. Leisure-time pursuits are poor ways to identify possible interests in certain career areas.

2. Use the space below to rewrite the statements you marked **false** and make them **true**. Include the letter of each statement you rewrite.

____

____

____

____

____

____

Name ______________________________ Date ______________

What's Most Important?

When you think about career goals, do you sometimes feel confused or lost? If this happens, use your values for a compass, and follow their direction.

1. Use the following rating scale to express the importance you place on the career goals listed in columns I and II. Rate each goal from 1 to 5. There are no right or wrong answers.

Rating Scale

1 = Very important to me
2 = Somewhat important to me
3 = Of average importance to me
4 = Not very important to me
5 = Unimportant to me

Column I

Your Rating	Career Goal
a. _____	Helping people
b. _____	Having the respect of your co-workers
c. _____	Having a very secure job
d. _____	Having a job where you can learn new skills
e. _____	Having a job you enjoy
f. _____	Being able to spend your life in one community
g. _____	Improving the life of less fortunate people
h. _____	Being allowed to make decisions about your work

Column II

Your Rating	Career Goal
i. _____	Earning a lot of money
j. _____	Owning a high-quality TV, sound system, and entertainment center
k. _____	Being able to afford nice vacations
l. _____	Owning a nice home
m. _____	Being able to afford nice clothes
n. _____	Owning a new automobile
o. _____	Dining in nice restaurants
p. _____	Being able to buy things for your family

2. Which three career goals are the most important to you? a. ______ b. ______ c. ______

3. Which three career goals are least important to you? a. ______ b. ______ c. ______

4. Column I lists nonmaterialistic career goals. Total the rating points you recorded for the career goals in column 1. Write the total here : ______

5. Column II lists materialistic career goals. Total the rating points you recorded for the career goals in column II. Write the total here: ______

6. Do your total scores for column I and column II indicate that you are more inclined toward materialistic or nonmaterialistic career goals? ______________________________

7. Review the three career goals you listed as most important in question 2. Next, review the three career goals you listed as least important in question 3. Do your selections indicate that you are more inclined toward materialistic or nonmaterialistic career goals? ______________________________

Helpful Hint: Review the section "Defining Goals" in Chapter 3 of your textbook. Pay special attention to materialistic and nonmaterialistic goals.

"I'm Not Going to school today... I've Accomplished All my CAREER GOALS!

Name ______________________________ Date ____________________

3.2 Checkpoint

Examining Your Work Values

When you think about work and careers, how do you decide what is right or wrong, wise or foolish? You can use the following work-related values to help make career decisions.

From each group of seven work values below, select the three that are most important to you by writing ***M*** (for most important to me) on the appropriate line in the answer box at the end of this activity. Select only three values from each group.

Group 1
1. Working in the outdoors
2. Working with tools
3. Working with numbers of facts
4. Developing new procedures
5. Showing concern for people
6. Influencing people
7. Having secure work during recessions

Group 2
8. Working with plants or animals
9. Using mechanical skills
10. Investigating information or data
11. Creating new products or services
12. Having good relations with co-workers
13. Leading other workers to achieve goals
14. Working with clearly defined tasks

Group 3
15. Preserving the natural environment
16. Using high-quality tools and machines
17. Analyzing problems with the work
18. Expressing my feelings through work
19. Helping my co-workers be successful
20. Having the respect of other workers
21. Working for a well-organized employer

Group 4
22. Doing work involving nature
23. Using my hands
24. Solving problems
25. Using my imagination
26. Helping people
27. Leading others
28. Checking accuracy

Group 5
29. Working in a natural setting
30. Keeping machinery working well
31. Working with scientific skills
32. Making my own work decisions
33. Making fellow workers happy
34. Being in charge of projects
35. Having a secure insurance plan

Group 6
36. Working with natural resources
37. Repairing mechanical devices
38. Understanding work facts
39. Creating new methods of working
40. Teaching job skills to others
41. Making decisions about the work
42. Having ethical, moral co-workers

Answer Box

1. ____	2. ____	3. ____	4. ____	5. ____	6. ____	7. ____
8. ____	9. ____	10. ____	11. ____	12. ____	13. ____	14. ____
15. ____	16. ____	17. ____	18. ____	19. ____	20. ____	21. ____
22. ____	23. ____	24. ____	25. ____	26. ____	27. ____	28. ____
29. ____	30. ____	31. ____	32. ____	33. ____	34. ____	35. ____
36. ____	37. ____	38. ____	39. ____	40. ____	41. ____	42. ____
1	2	3	4	5	6	7
☐	☐	☐	☐	☐	☐	☐

Total the number of ***M***'s in each column. Enter your score in the correct box and also where indicated in Checkpoint 3.2.

Helpful Hint: Review the section "Clarifying Values" in Chapter 3 of your textbook. Pay special attention to the topic "Work Values."

Name ______________________________ Date ____________________

Checkpoint 3.3

Lifestyle Options

The demands and rewards of your future occupation will place limits on certain lifestyle options and will open the door to others.

Occupational Choice

1. a. Write the name of an occupation you are seriously considering for your future career. ____________
   b. What are the education and training requirements for this occupation?
   ____
   c. What are the average annual earnings for this occupation? $____________

Lifestyle Options

2. a. What type of vehicle to you expect to own ten years from now? ____________
   b. What is the present market value of this type of vehicle? $____________
   c. Is this lifestyle option consistent with your occupational choice? Provide facts to support your answer. ____
   ____
3. a. What type of home do you expect to live in ten years from now? ____________
   b. What is the present market value or annual lease or rental payment for this type of home? $ ________
   c. Is this lifestyle option consistent with your occupational choice? Provide facts to support your answer. ____
   ____
4. a. Name two leisure-time activities you expect to be involved in ten years from now.
   (1) ____________________ (2) ____________________
   b. How many hours per week will you spend participating in these leisure activities? ____________
   c. What hours of the day, evening, or weekend will you be involved in these leisure activities?
   ____
   d. What will be the monthly cost of your activities? $____________
   e. Is this lifestyle option consistent with your occupational choice? Provide facts to support your answer. ____
   ____

Note: Accurate salary and training information for this activity is available in the *Occupational Outlook Handbook*. See your school counselor or librarian.

Name ______________________________ Date ____________________

3.4

Don't Look Now, but Your Attitude Is Showing

Your attitude is the way you think about things and act toward others. It reflects your feelings as you react to life situations. Consider the following situation

It is Friday evening, and you are working the evening shift. Saturday is your scheduled day off, and you plan to attend a friend's birthday party. One of your co-workers called in sick with the flu. Because of his absence, your entire team must work faster. Your supervisor is helping the team as much as possible, but she has work tasks of her own to complete.

Yesterday, the employee who called in sick told you he was invited to go away for the weekend, but he was scheduled to work. You question whether or not he really is ill. During your first break, your supervisor cancels your day off and tells you that she will need you to work Saturday evening.

How would you react to this situation?

1. List four of your immediate feelings (emotions).

   a. ______________________ b. ______________________

   c. ______________________ d. ______________________

2. List three things you would probably say to your supervisor or another person.

   a. ____

   b. ____

   c. ____

3. List three things you would do as a result of this situation.

   a. ____

   b. ____

   c. ____

4. Carefully consider each of your ten responses to this situation. Determine whether each response is more positive (constructive or helpful) or more negative (uncooperative). Place a plus sign (+) next to each positive response and a minus sign (–) next to each negative response.

5. a. How many of your responses were positive? _____
   b. Use the following table to identify the type of attitude you displayed in this particular situation.

Number of Positive Responses	Type of Attitude Displayed
1 – 3	Strong negative attitude
4	Weak negative attitude
5	Weak attitude
6	Weak positive attitude
7 – 10	Strong positive attitude

6. What probable influence would your ten responses have on your future promotions and pay increases?

____

____

Name ______________________________ Date ________________

Checkpoint 3.5

The Time Is Now!

A wristwatch, alarm clock, or calendar is a handy tool if you are measuring the passage of time. Tools, machines, instruments, books, paper, and pens are better tools if you are making wise use of the present. Once you establish an educational or occupational goal, you will need to make wise use of these every day.

1. a. How did you spend your waking hours yesterday? List your two most time-consuming accomplishments and the amount of time you spent on each.

   (1) Accomplishment: ______________________________ Time spent: __________

   (2) Accomplishment: ______________________________ Time spent: __________

   b. Will either of your accomplishments help you achieve an educational or occupational goal? If so, describe how. If no, describe a different accomplishment that would have made wiser use of your time.

   ____

   ____

2. a. List one or more activities that you currently accomplish at least three times a week as preparation for an educational or occupational goal. Circle the activity that you consider to be most important.

   ____________________ ____________________ ____________________

   b. When you are involved with the activity you circled, do you remove or avoid distractions? If so, what distractions, and how? If not, why not?

   ____

   ____

   c. How much time do you allow for this activity? ______________

   d. Is this enough time? If so, how are you measuring your success? If not, how could you readjust your schedule to acquire more time?

   ____

   ____

3. a. Each of the following pairs of choices is concerned with time. In each pair, circle the choice that is closest to your daily use of time.

(A)	I live for today.	(A)	I am frequently late.
(B)	I plan for tomorrow.	(B)	I am usually on time.
(A)	I worry about things I can't change.	(A)	I make excuses for not completing my work.
(B)	I don't let my fears get in my way.	(B)	My work is usually completed on time.

   b. How many A responses did you circle? _____ How many B responses? _____

   The A responses are more mature; The B responses are less mature.

Name ______________________________ Date ____________________

Checkpoint 3.6

Finding the Right Words

Chapter 3 of your textbook contains numerous terms that employers and workers use. Recognizing and understanding these terms will help you make the important career decisions you will soon face.

Unscramble the terms in column B, and match them with the definitions in column A. (Some terms may contain two words.)

Column A

Example: __a__ cherished ideas and beliefs

1. _____ opinions formed beforehand
2. _____ trial
3. _____ an attitude that refuses to change
4. _____ how you think about things and act toward others
5. _____ a goal that provides inner satisfaction
6. _____ the people you frequently come in contact with
7. _____ an aim or objective
8. _____ the way you live
9. _____ parts
10. _____ obtainable
11. _____ schedule
12. _____ anything you can touch

Column B

a. VALUES
SAVEUL

b. ______________________________
LATERISMOANTINIC

c. ______________________________
DEVINECORPEC FEELSBI

d. ______________________________
TUDATEIT

e. ______________________________
AVETITENT

f. ______________________________
REDJUPICE

g. ______________________________
BITANGLE

h. ______________________________
ITISREALC

i. ______________________________
MITE NILE

j. ______________________________
ALOG

k. ______________________________
MOON ENTSCP

l. ______________________________
FILETYLES

m. ______________________________
COALIS REMOVEITNNN

Name ______________________________ Date ____________________

3.7 Checkpoint

Checking Your Location

1. For each of the following statements, circle **F** if the statement is more false than true. Circle **T** if the statement is more true than false.

T F a. Values are "moral truths" that guide your life.

T F b. Choosing an occupation that is related to your values will increase your likelihood of career success.

T F c. The achievement of materialistic career goals provides a great deal of inner satisfaction.

T F d. High school students learn most of their values from other students, teachers, and their house of worship.

T F e. Work adds a sense of purpose to a person's values.

T F f. Setting realistic goals puts you in charge of the direction that your career takes.

T F g. For every short-term goal you achieve, you will need several long-term goals.

T F h. Some day-to-day tasks are not interesting, but all successful workers perform some tasks they dislike.

T F i. A prejudice is an attitude you have about people from a racial, religious, or ethnic background that differs from your own.

T F j. Your future lifestyle will be a compromise between the lifestyle options you select and the requirements and rewards of your future occupation.

T F k. Learning to make lifestyle adjustments and adapting to new and sometimes unwanted situations are necessary elements of every successful career.

T F l. Achieving a goal gives you a sense of accomplishment and raises your level of self-esteem.

T F m. Failing to achieve a goal will make you a better person. Failure will motivate you to try again and work harder.

T F n. People with well-defined values also have high levels of self-understanding and self-esteem.

T F o. Once you have a clear understanding of your values, interests, and aptitudes, it will be time to set career goals.

2. Use the space below to rewrite the statements you marked **false** and make them **true**. Include the letter of each statement you rewrite.

Name ______________________ Date ______________

Checkpoint 4.1

What's Your Style?

Every day, you face situations in which you must choose between two or more options. The choices you make influence the outcome of your daily activities and personal interactions. They also influence your future career and lifestyle. Five decision-making styles are described in your textbook. What's your style?

Authority	Intuitive	Fatalistic	Impulsive	Rational
Relies on a spouse, parent, or other person	Relies on values and personal feelings	Believes that outcomes are predetermined and unavoidable	Decides quickly before considering outcomes	Considers the values and feelings of the decision maker, facts, and possible outcomes.

1. Which decision-making style would you use in each of the following situations? Why would you use that particular style?

   a. Deciding which medicine to take for an illness. Style: ______________

   Reason: ______________

   b. Deciding which house of worship to attend. Style: ______________

   Reason: ______________

   c. Deciding which pair of shoes to buy at a sale. Style: ______________

   Reason: ______________

   d. Deciding which mathematics course to take. Style: ______________

   Reason: ______________

   e. Deciding which occupation to prepare for. Style: ______________

   Reason: ______________

2. a. Which decision-making style do you use the most? ______________

   b. Why do you prefer this style? ______________

   ____

   c. Describe a decision you made using this style. ______________

   ____

3. a. Which decision-making style do you use the least? ______________

   ____

   b. Why do you avoid using this style? ______________

   ____

continued

4. a. Which decision-making style does your parent or gurdian use the most? ______________________

____

b. Which style does your best friend use the most? ______________________

____

5. Which decision-making style is easiest for you to use? Why? ______________________

____

6. Which decision-making style is most difficult for you to use? Why? ______________________

____

Name ______________________________ Date ____________________

4.2 Checkpoint

Matching Yourself to Seven Orientations Toward Work

In Chapters 2 and 3 of this workbook, you completed three activities expressing personal preferences and perceptions about your interests, skills, and values. The following tabulation of your results will help you relate the preferences and perceptions you expressed toward seven groups of characteristics. Fill in the chart.

Record of My Personal Preferences and Perceptions

Scores for Each Activity

Activity	1	2	3	4	5	6	7
2.6: Identifying Interests							
2.8: Skills—Now and for Tomorrow							
3.2: Examining Your Work Values							
Total							

The seven categories of preferences and perceptions you have totaled in the above activity represent your personal characteristics. In general, personal characteristics can be divided into seven broad groups called *orientations* (unique individual directions). Review the following descriptions of the seven orientations. An understanding of how important these orientations are to you will help you explore careers in the twelve related occupational clusters.

(1) *Environmental*: People with this characteristic are physically active, are interested in nature, and enjoy outdoor activities.
(2) *Mechanical*: People with this characteristic are physically active and like using tools, machines, or instruments to build or repair things.
(3) *Scientific*: People with this characteristic like investigating information or data to help them understand ideas and the causes of events.
(4) *Creative*: People with this characteristic frequently enjoy music, art, or literature. They like to use new methods and ideas.
(5) *Sociable*: People with this characteristic enjoy helping people and discussing problems or situations.
(6) *Persuasive*: People with this characteristic like to organize groups of people to accomplish goals. They are skilled at convincing and persuading.
(7) *Structured*: People with this characteristic are skilled at organizing and categorizing information or numerical data. They prefer proven methods to new ideas.

Helpful Hint: Review the section "Knowing yourself and Career Decisions" in Chapter 1 of your textbook.

Name ______________________________ Date ______________

Graphing Your Personal Orientations

Checkpoint 4.3

Each bar on the graph on the next page represents one of the seven total scores you obtained from Checkpoint 4.2. For each orientation (Environmental, Mechanical, and so on) darken the bars up to the number that you wrote in the Total Score row for that orientation. For example, if you obtained a total score of 10 in column 1, darken the bar under "Environmental" from 0 to 10. Repeat this process for all seven orientations.

1. Which two orientations are most like you?
   a. My highest score was in the ______________________________ orientation.
   b. Which orientation is most unlike you?
2. Which orientation is most unlike you?
   a. My lowest score was in the ______________________________ orientation.

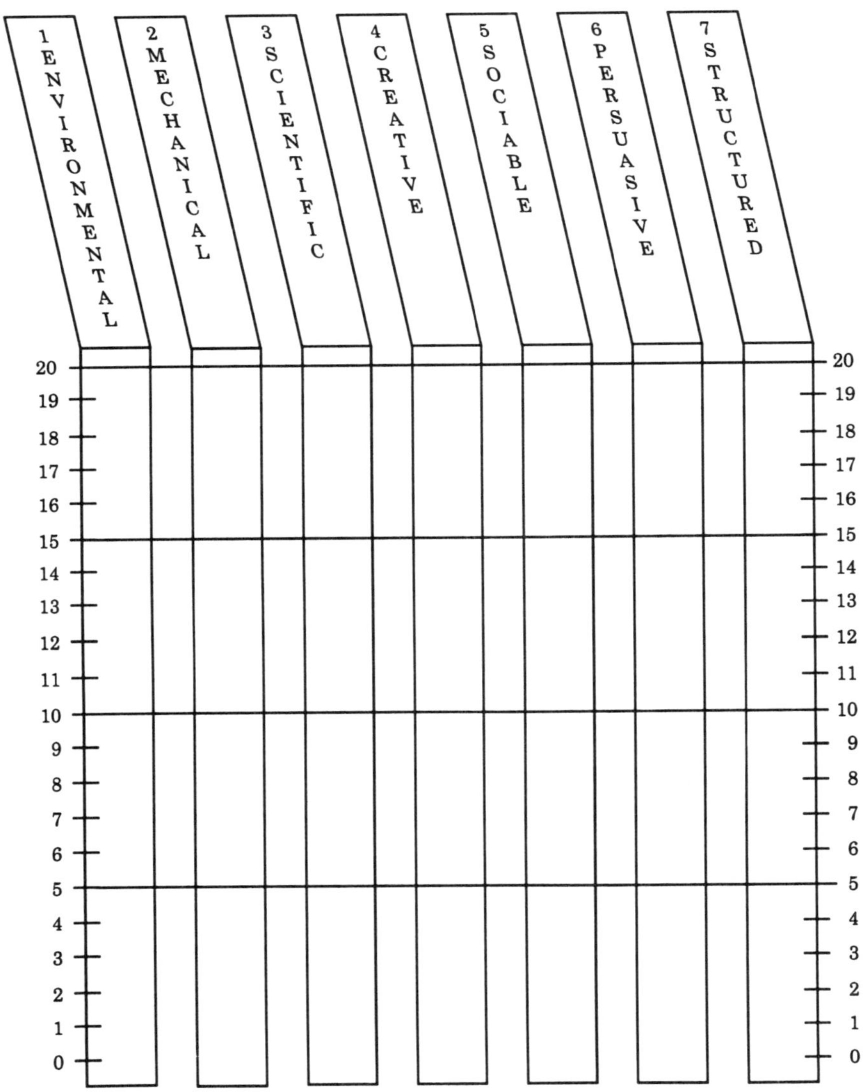

Name ______________________________ Date ____________________

Checkpoint 4.4

Matching Yourself to Twelve Occupational Clusters

The last section of your textbook is a handbook of twelve occupational clusters (groupings). The twelve clusters follow a system used by the U.S. Department of Labor.

Most occupations can be found to some degree in all of the twelve clusters. However, certain occupations are closely related to the work environment and the major job tasks and responsibilities found in specific job clusters.

1. The following list shows the twelve occupational clusters and the orientations to which they are closely related. As you review the list, keep in mind the orientations you identified in Checkpoint 4.3.

Occupational Cluster	Occupational Orientation
Executive, administrative, and managerial	Persuasive
Administrative support	Structured Sociable
Marketing and sales	Persuasive Sociable
Professional specialty	Scientific Sociable Creative Persuasive
Technicians and related support	Mechanical Scientific
Service	Sociable Environmental Structured
Agriculture, forestry, fishing, and related	Environmental Scientific Mechanical
Mechanics, installers, and repairers	Mechanical
Construction, trades and extraction	Mechanical Environmental

continued

Occupational Cluster (continued)	Occupational Orientation (continued)
Production	Mechanical Persuasive Structured
Transportation and material moving	Mechanical Environmental Structured
Handlers, equipment cleaners, helpers, and laborers	Mechanical Structured
Job opportunities in the armed forces	All orientations

2. Which clusters are related to the orientations with your two highest scores?

____

3. Which clusters are related to the orientation with your lowest score?

____

4. Which cluster interests you the most?

____

5. Which cluster interests you the least?

____

Name ______________________________ Date ____________________

4.5

Checkpoint

Deciding about the Education and Training You Need

It is important to take certain steps toward a future occupational goal while you are still a student. One of these steps is deciding what education and training you will need for the occupation you select.

Helpful Hint: Review "The Rational Decision-Making Process" in Chapter 4 of your textbook before beginning this activity.

Considering a Problem

1. You will probably have several jobs during your lifetime. What is the title of the highest level job you expect to achieve during the next ten years? ______________________________

2. Circle the level of education and training that is required for entry into the job you have selected.
   a. High School
   b. One-year technical school
   c. Two-year college
   d. Four-year college or higher

3. For the job you have selected, what will be the highest level course requirement in the following subject areas? (Be specific.)
   a. English: ____________________
   b. Mathematics: ____________________
   c. Science: ____________________
   d. An area of special training: ____________________

4. At the conclusion of the current school year, what will be the highest level course requirement you have successfully completed in the following subject area? (Be specific.)
   a. English: ____________________
   b. Mathematics: ____________________
   c. Science: ____________________
   d. An area of special training: ____________________

5. To become qualified for the job you have selected, what specific courses will you need to enroll in next? (Be specific.)
   a. English: ____________________
   b. Mathematics: ____________________
   c. Science: ____________________
   d. An area of special training: ____________________

Making a Decision

6. Now you must make a decision. Do you plan to continue your education and enroll in the next level of required courses to enter the job you have selected? If so, when will you enroll?

   ____

continued

7. List the facts you considered before you made this decision.

____

____

____

8. Could you have obtained additional facts before making your decision? If so, where? If not, why not?

____

____

9. Are you satisfied with your decision? If so, why? If not, why not? ______________

____

____

10. What course of action will you follow to carry out your decision? ______________

____

____

____

____

Name ______________________ Date ______________

Checkpoint 4.6

The Choice Is Yours

Imagine that you and two of your best friends are hiking in a large park. Write their first names here.

Friend 1: ______________ Friend 2: ______________

It is a sunny October day. The temperature is in the 70s, but it will drop into the 40s during the night. Friend 1 is carrying a knapsack containing two oranges, two sandwiches, a plastic rain poncho, and a box of matches. Friend 2 has a one-quart canteen of water and a liter bottle of pop. You have a wristwatch, a small pocketknife, and two candy bars. Each of you has a lightweight jacket and a hat. About four miles from the park entrance, you decide to follow an interesting trail with no directional signs. Within a few minutes your group is lost—no sign of a trail and no sound of people. Friend 2 slips on wet leaves and falls down a small hill. The result is a severely twisted ankle that might be fractured. Friend 2 is unable to walk. It is late afternoon, and friend 1 points out a bear on a hill about a half mile away. A mountain stream is flowing nearby. It is time to make some decisions.

1. a. What will you do first? ______________

2. a. How will your group select a leader? ______________

   b. Who will take charge? ______________

3. How will the three of you work together? ______________

   ____

4. What work tasks will need to be performed? Who will be responsible for each task?

	Work Task	Responsible Person
a.		
b.		
c.		

5. What are the two most important decisions you have made?

   a. ______________

   b. ______________

6. How did you make these important decisions? ______________

   ____

   ____

Name ______________________________ Date ______________

Checkpoint 4.7

Finding the Right Words

Chapter 4 of your textbook contains numerous terms that employers and workers use. Recognizing and understanding these terms will help you make the important career decisions you will soon face. Fill in the blank spaces in the vocabulary terms to complete the following sentences.

1. When a person acts on a decision, there are always c o ___ ___ e ___ ___ e ___ ___ e s.

2. Qualities that make an individual unique are called p ___ r s ___ n a ___ c ___ a ___ a ___ t ___ ___ i ___ t ___ c s.

3. Your unique individual direction is referred to as your ___ r ___ ___ n ___ ___ t ___ o n.

4. The ability to recognize forms in space and the relationships of plane and solid objects is called

   s ___ ___ t ___ a l ___ e ___ c e ___ t ___ o n.

5. Another term for decision making is p r ___ ___ ___ e m ___ o ___ v ___ n ___ .

6. A style of decision making that is based on personal feelings and values rather than facts is called

   i ___ ___ u ___ t ___ ___ e.

7. Believing that whatever you decide will happen anyway is known as the ___ a ___ a ___ i ___ t ___ ___ style of decision making.

8. The skill to examine your thoughts and feelings is called i ___ ___ r ___ s ___ e c ___ ___ v e a ___ i ___ i ___ y.

9. The word ___ o n ___ i ___ i a ___ i n ___ means bringing others together, pacifying, or winning them over.

10. Work settings are frequently referred to as w ___ ___ k ___ ___ v i ___ o ___ ___ e ___ t s.

11. When you share another person's thoughts and feelings, you are e ___ ___ a t ___ i ___ i ___ g.

12. People with a ___ ___ e a ___ i ___ e orientation tend to rely on their feelings and emotions more than on information or facts.

13. People with a ___ c i ___ n ___ i ___ i ___ orientation tend to use their intellect more than their social or physical skills to solve problems.

14. People with a ___ ___ c i ___ b ___ e orientation enjoy being helpful.

15. People with a ___ e ___ ___ a ___ i ___ a ___ orientation prefer work involving machines and tools.

16. People with a ___ e ___ s ___ a ___ i ___ e orientation enjoy sales and leadership roles.

17. People with a ___ ___ r ___ c ___ u ___ e ___ orientation are frequently skilled in coding, classifying, and computing information.

Name ______________________ Date ______________

Checkpoint 4.8

Checking Your Location

1. For each of the following statements, circle **F** if the statement is more false than true. Circle **T** if the statement is more true than false.

T F a. Every day, you face situations in which you must make choices.

T F b. Using the authority style of decision making makes a person feel very independent.

T F c. A rational style of decision making considers the feelings and values of the decision maker as well as the facts of the situation.

T F d. A decision isn't a decision until something happens.

T F e. The possibility of risk and failure can create feelings of confusion, conflict, and anxiety.

T F f. Once a decision is made, you shouldn't change it.

T F g. People with a strong scientific orientation enjoy working with tools and machines. They are usually skilled at repairing mechanical devices.

T F h. People with strong structured orientation solve problems using new ideas and the latest information.

T F i. As you grow older and gain career experience, your skill level will increase and your career hopes and goals will change.

T F j. As a responsible adult, it is very important to have an effective process for making decisions.

T F k. Understanding yourself and all of the facts of the situation will help you make realistic, acceptable decisions.

T F l. People with a strong creative orientation like to examine the rules of the organization and how society might react before they begin a project.

T F m. People with a strong mechanical orientation often develop their physical skills more fully than their human relation and verbal communications skills.

continued

T F n. When you make a decision, gather as much information as possible about the problem and each alternative for reaching an acceptable solution.

T F o. People with a strong sociable orientation rely more on their personal concern and emotion than on their intellectual ability.

2. Use the space below to rewrite the statements you marked **false** and make them **true**. Include the letter of each statement you rewrite.

____

____

____

____

____

____

Name ______________________ Date ______________

Checkpoint 5.1

What Must the Worker Know?

Some occupations require similar levels of skill but very different work tasks. For example, the mathematics skill level required for an engineering technician is the same as that for a dietitian. The language skill level required for an auto mechanic is the same as that for an ultrasound technologist.

The U.S. Department of Labor has developed six General Education Development Scales (GEDS) for measuring the mathematical and language skill requirements of occupations. Level 6 is the highest on the scale; level 1 is the lowest. Levels 1 to 3 span the skills taught in the primary grades through the 10th grade. Level 4 is taught in high school and advanced middle school courses. Level 5 is taught in advanced high school courses and college. Level 6 is taught in undergraduate and graduate college courses.

1. Read the list of occupations that follows. Estimate the levels of math and language skills you believe are necessary for success in each occupation using the GEDS levels (1 for the lowest and 6 for the highest). Write your estimates in the spaces provided. (Your teacher has the answers.)

What Must the Worker Know?

Occupation	Mathematics Level	Language Level
Dishwasher, kitchen helper	_____	_____
Bulldozer operator	_____	_____
Farm manager	_____	_____
Landscape architect	_____	_____
Range manager	_____	_____
Auto body repairer	_____	_____
Brickmason	_____	_____
Computer operator	_____	_____
Dental lab technician	_____	_____
Diesel mechanic	_____	_____
Electrician	_____	_____
Mechanical engineer	_____	_____
Numerical-control machine operator	_____	_____
Optician	_____	_____
Radiologic (X-ray) technician	_____	_____
Science technician	_____	_____
Telephone installer	_____	_____
Ultrasound technologist	_____	_____

Occupation	Mathematics Level	Language Level
Chemist	_____	_____
Computer programmer	_____	_____
Dentist	_____	_____
Dietician	_____	_____
Mathematician	_____	_____
Numerical tool programmer	_____	_____
Operations research analyst	_____	_____
Physical therapist	_____	_____
Physician	_____	_____
Chef	_____	_____
Writer or editor	_____	_____
Cosmetologist	_____	_____
Elementary school teacher	_____	_____
Airline flight attendant	_____	_____
Registered nurse	_____	_____
Social worker	_____	_____
Accountant	_____	_____
Bank teller	_____	_____
Paralegal	_____	_____
Secretary	_____	_____

continued

2. How many skills levels did you mark correctly? __________

3. What occupations require a higher level of math skills than you expected? ____________________

____

4. What occupations require a higher level of language skills than you expected? ____________________

____

5. What occupations require a lower level of math skills than you expected? ____________________

____

6. What occupations require a lower level of language skills than you expected? ____________________

____

"YOU'VE SEEN MY GRADES! IF I QUIT WATCHING TV, I WON'T BE ABLE TO PASS ANYTHING!!"

Name ______________________________ Date ____________________

Checkpoint 5.2

Broaden Your Opportunities in the World of Work

Rapidly changing job requirements mean that workers with outdated employment skills are likely to be laid off, whereas those with up-to-date employment skills can take advantage of new employment opportunities.

Interview a parent or family member about the effect education has had on his or her present career. Ask the following questions:

1. What is the title of your present position? ______________________________
2. How many years have you been in this position? ______________________________
3. What is the entry level of education required for this occupation?

_____ On-the-job training	_____ Apprenticeship program	_____ Military training
_____ High school graduate	_____ Community college	_____ Four-year college
_____ Graduate School	_____ Vocational high school training	_____ Other

4. What specific high school subjects have helped you in your work?

   a. ______________ b. ______________ c. ______________ d. ______________

5. What additional education and training have you needed since you started this job?

   ____

6. What specific skills and abilities do you need to succeed in your work?

   a. ____

   b. ____

   c. ____

   d. ____

   c. ____

7. What math skills do you use in your work?

_____ Algebra	_____ Shop math	_____ Multiplication	_____ Units of measure
_____ Calculus	_____ Addition	_____ Division	_____ Percents
_____ Statistics	_____ Ratios	_____ Fractions	_____ Spreadsheets
_____ Geometry	_____ Subtraction	_____ Graphs	_____ Other

continued

8. What language skills do you use in your work?

a. Reading:

_____ Journals _____ Financial reports _____ Correspondence _____ Legal documents
_____ Abstracts _____ Manuals _____ Diagrams _____ Other

b. Writing: _____ Articles _____ Reports _____ Proposals
_____ Editorials _____ Music _____ Business letters _____ Other
_____ Manuals _____ Memos

c. Speaking:

_____ Instructing _____ Persuasive speaking _____ Other
_____ Discussion/debate _____ Dramatization

9. What advances in technology have affected your job in the last ten years? ____________________

____

10. What do you believe the future of your job will be? ____________________

____

11. If you were my age and had it to do all over again, what would you do differently? What would you do the same?

Differently: ____

Same: ____

Name ______________________________ Date ________________

5.3 Checkpoint

The Best Time to Learn Is Now!

Education or training is usually required for jobs in the occupations with the highest earnings and the lowest unemployment rates. Between the years 1975 and 1990, the proportion of workers having at least one year of college increased from 33 to 47 percent. Currently, more than 25 percent of all U.S. workers have a four-year college education.

Despite these statistics, many U.S. companies insist they can't fill job openings because they can't find qualified, skilled, motivated workers. It's a matter of abilities, they say. Workers often lack adequate skills in reading, writing, and mathematics.

The grades you earn today will affect your future acceptance or rejection by postsecondary schools and employers. Employers and postsecondary school admissions staff will view your high school grades as an indicator of your commitment to hard work, your ability to learn certain skills, and your interest in specific subjects. They will consider your high school achievement an important predictor of what you will do in the future.

Evaluate your academic achievement by completing the following chart.

1. Place a check mark under the grades you earned in each subject during the last grade period.
2. Decide if these grades are a real evaluation of your ability in these subjects. Place a check mark (✓) in the appropriate column.

My grades

School Subject	**A**	**B**	**C**	**D**	**F**
English					
Science					
Math					
Social studies					
Foreign language					
Music					
Art					
Vocational education					
Physical education					
Other:					
Other					

Is this grade a real measure of my ability?

Yes	**No**	**Unsure**

continued

3. If you were an employer, what opinion would you have about *you* after reviewing your high school grades or transcript? ______________________________

____

4. How can you improve an employer's opinion of you? ______________________________

____

____

Name ______________________________ Date ____________________

5.4 Checkpoint

Learning How to Learn — Effective Study Skills

If you strive for high achievement in high school, you will be more likely to connect your education and training to employment opportunities. Knowing how to learn is the most basic of all skills.

1. Read the following learning techniques, then consider how helpful they are for you.
   a. Rank them in order from most helpful (1) to least helpful (10).

      _____ Reading the textbook
      _____ Listening to the teacher's lectures
      _____ Working on projects or units
      _____ Going over material often (drilling)
      _____ Studying alone
      _____ Memorizing information
      _____ Seeing movies or other visuals
      _____ Taking notes
      _____ Participating in a group or class discussion
      _____ Hands-on experience

   b. Which learning techniques have room for improvement? ______________________________

      ____

2. How much time do you spend on homework each day? (Include study halls)

   ____ Over two hours ____ Between one and two hours ____ Less than one hour _____ None

3. Rate your study skills on the following chart.

	My rating			I need . . .	
Study Skills	**Very Good**	**Average**	**Poor**	**Help**	**Practice**
Understanding what I read	______	______	______	______	______
Reading speed	______	______	______	______	______
Outlining	______	______	______	______	______
Taking notes	______	______	______	______	______
Listening and paying attention	______	______	______	______	______
Memorizing	______	______	______	______	______
Using reference materials	______	______	______	______	______
Scheduling study time	______	______	______	______	______
Preparing assignments	______	______	______	______	______
Getting ready for tests	______	______	______	______	______
Concentrating on the subject	______	______	______	______	______

4. Which study skills do you need to improve? ____

____

5. Select one study skill to improve for the following grade period. Work on it as you would a real job. Develop a schedule, take it one step at a time, and master the skill just as you would a job skill.

   a. Which study skill would you most like to improve? ______________________________

   b. Which subject would you most like to improve?__________________________________

   c. Who can help you if you need help? ____

   d. How much time will you spend each day on this project?___________________________

6. Use the following log to keep track of your efforts for one month. Mark each day that you meet your goal with an *X*.

Month _____ Date _____ Year_____

	Monday	Tuesday	Wednesday	Thursday	Friday	Saturday	Sunday
Week 1	________	________	________	________	________	________	________
Week 2	________	________	________	________	________	________	________
Week 3	________	________	________	________	________	________	________
Week 4	________	________	________	________	________	________	________

7. At the end of the grade period, evaluate your efforts.

   _____ I improved.

   _____ I did not improve.

   _____ I tried but did not improve.

   _____ I could do better.

Career Tip: Once you master one study skill, you can use the same techniques to improve another. This technique puts you in charge of *self*.

Name ______________________________ Date ____________________

5.5 Checkpoint

Education and Training after High School

One education or training program will not end your education. You may enter one now but in order to qualify for a better position, a new job, or to keep up with the skills demanded in your occupation, you may later continue your education and training in other programs. This activity will help you learn about the opportunities each educational and training program described in Chapter 5 offers.

1. Use your textbook and the resources listed to complete the following chart.

Education and Training Programs

	Apprenticeship	Vocational Training	Tech-Prep	On-the-Job Training	Military Training	Community, Junior, Technical College	Four Year College and University	Graduate and Professional
What occupation in this program interests me?								
What does this program offer?								
What are the requirements needed to complete the program?								
What are the admissions requirements?								
Where is the nearest program location?								
What are the advantages of the program?								
What are the disadvantages of the program?								
How does this program fit me in terms of personal values, interests, aptitudes, and goals?								

continued

	Apprenticeship	Vocational Training	Tech-Prep	On-the-Job Training	Military Training	Community, Junior, Technical College	Four Year College and University	Graduate and Professional
What high school program is needed to prepare for this program?								
What is the cost of this program?								
What financial resources are available to pay for this program?								

2. Rank the programs in the order that best fits your personal interests, aptitudes, values, occupational goals, and financial resources.

_____ Apprenticeship
_____ Vocational training
_____ Tech-prep
_____ On-the-job training
_____ Military training
_____ Graduate or professional school
_____ Community, junior, technical college
_____ Four-year college or university

3. Which program would be most satisfying to you? Why?

____

____

Name ______________________________ Date ____________________

Checkpoint 5.6

Getting More Information — Using a Directory

Visit your high school library, and use one of the directories mentioned in the "Getting More Information" features in Chapter 5 of your textbook to complete the following activity.

1. Select three postsecondary schools or programs that you would be interested in attending. Compare them according to the following factors, and rate each school according to how well it meets your requirements. Let 1 be the highest rating and 3 be the lowest rating.

Postsecondary School Comparison

Factors	**Your Requirements**	**Rating**		
		School 1 Name:	School 2 Name:	School 3 Name:
Tuition/fees for 1 year				
Room and board fees				
Admissions requirements: SAT verbal and math scores	(your scores)			
ACT scores				
Application deadline				
Number of freshmen applications				
Number freshmen accepted				
Students/faculty ratio				
Level of competitiveness				
Programs of study offered				
Financial aid available				
Location of class				
Total Enrollment				
Average class size				
Accreditation				
Public/Private School				

continued

2. a. Which school would you select on the basis of your requirements? ______________________

   b. Why?____

3. a. Based on your school achievement, which school would accept you? ___________________

   b. Why?____

Name ______________________________ Date ____________________

Checkpoint 5.7

Finding the Right Words

Chapter 5 of your textbook contains numerous terms that employers and workers use. Recognizing and understanding these terms will help you make the important career decisions you will soon face.

Unscramble the vocabulary terms, and complete the following sentences.

1. DAIOTNEUC Through _ _ _ _ _ _ _ _ _, students acquire knowledge in various subject areas.
2. INTRAGIN Through _ _ _ _ _ _ _ _, students learn specific occupational skills.
3. PTADA _ _ _ _ _ means to fit into.
4. PLOYEMNTME TURSCURET The type of jobs within an organization is known as its _ _ _ _ _ _ _ _ _ _ _ _ _ _ _ _ _ _ _.
5. PORTIOBAN A _ _ _ _ _ _ _ _ _ is a trail period.
6. PPATICESHIPREN An _ _ _ _ _ _ _ _ _ _ _ _ _ _ is a relationship between an employer and a worker during which the worker learns a trade.
7. ILDUGS _ _ _ _ _ _ are unions of craft workers.
8. TUREINDEN An _ _ _ _ _ _ _ _ _ is a legal contract for service.
9. JNEYOUR ERWORK A _ _ _ _ _ _ _ _ _ _ _ _ _ is a certified, experienced, skilled craft worker who has successfully completed his or her apprenticeship.
10. HCSOOL A _ _ _ _ _ _ _ _ _ _ _ _ _ _ _ _ _ is a school that is privately owned and operated for profit. oprirearyt
11. TECHLCANI OOHSCL A _ _ _ _ _ _ _ _ _ _ _ _ _ _ _ is a two-year institution that offers occupational programs intended to prepare students for immediate employment in fields related to engineering and the physical sciences.
12. FCCDDEETIA An _ _ _ _ _ _ _ _ _ _ college or educational program has met certain minimum standards for its program of study, and facilities.
13. RRESDENCECOPON COUSESR _ are also known as home study courses.
14. OBJ PCORS The _ _ _ _ _ _ _ _ is a federally administered, national employment and training program serving severely disadvantaged youth sixteen to twenty-one years of age.

continued

15. ECHT PPRE ___ ___ ___ ___ - ___ ___ ___ ___ programs coordinate the last two years of vocational high school training with two years of experience-based community-technical instruction.

16. NO HET OBJ INGTRAIN ___ ___ - ___ ___ ___ - ___ ___ ___ ___ ___ ___ ___ ___ ___ ___ ___ comprises a wide range of education and training provided by employers for their employees.

17. LAURBACCEATEA EREEGD ___ is sometimes called a bachelor's degree or an undergraduate degree.

18. VERUNTYSII A ___ ___ ___ ___ ___ ___ ___ ___ ___ ___ ___, the largest type of institution of higher learning, is composed of several undergraduate colleges and graduate schools for advanced study.

Name ______________________________ Date ____________________

Checkpoint 5.8

Checking Your Location

1. For each of the following statements, circle **F** if the statement is more false than true. Circle **T** if the statement is more true than false.

T F a. Job opportunities for highly trained and educated workers are increasing, as are those for unskilled workers.

T F b. Some form of postsecondary education and training will be required for 75 percent of all job classifications during and beyond the 1990s.

T F c. The risk of unemployment is higher for high school dropouts than for high school graduates.

T F d. Employers rarely contact a job seeker's high school to obtain information about grades and attendance.

T F e. An increasing number of employers are testing job seekers to determine their proficiency in basic high school skills.

T F f. Although English usage and reading comprehension are needed at some level in all occupations, mathematics is not.

T F g. Today's apprenticeship programs usually require about four years of training but may range from one to six years.

T F h. Tech-prep students are expected to graduate from high school prepared for both further training and work.

T F i. More than 90 percent of today's high school graduates enter some form of educational program after high school.

T F j. It is important to be very selective in choosing a postsecondary school because of the wide range of quality and the high cost of tuition.

T F k. The Job Corps is a federally administered employment and training program that serves severely disadvantaged young people aged sixteen to twenty-one.

T F l. A major share of postsecondary education is provided by public and private colleges that award associate degrees after two years of full-time study.

continued

T F m. There are more than thirty-three hundred accredited colleges, community colleges, and universities in the United States.

T F n. State universities are supported by public funding and are usually more expensive than private universities.

T F o. To obtain a graduate degree, a student must meet the requirements established by the college or school awarding the degree.

2. Use the space below to rewrite the statements you marked **false** and make them **true**. Include the letter of each statement you rewrite.

Name ______________________________ Date ____________________

Checkpoint 6.1

Encode, Decode

1. On the following chart, keep track of who you communicate with, how you communicate, and how much time you spend encoding (changing thoughts, feelings, and ideas into words) and decoding (interpreting symbols as the sender intended) messages from the time you get up in the morning until you go to bed that night. Include television, telephone, and computer use. A sample entry is provided.

A Day of Encoding and Decoding

Location and Time of Day	What Did You Read?	What Did You Write?	To Whom Did You Listen?	To Whom Did You Speak?
Sample: 7:00 a.m. at home				Mother, 15 min.

2. How much time did you spend reading? _______ Writing? _______ Listening _______ Speaking _____
3. Which did you do the most? ________________________ The least? ________________________
4. Which of the four was the easiest to understand? _______________ Most difficult? _______________

Name ______________________________ Date ____________________

Checkpoint 6.2

Do You Really Know Better?

Most of us use incorrect language as a habit. We know better, but we just do not pay attention to the correctness of how we are speaking.

1. Which of the underlined words is used correctly in each of the following sentences? Draw a circle around the correct word. (Your teacher has the answers.)

   a. You had ought to/should vote in the election.

   b. The reason is because/that it makes sense.

   c. The award must be acceped by whoever/whomever won the contest.

   d. Where did you find those/them books?

   e. This ice cream is different from/than the one we had yesterday.

   f. Just between you and I/me.

   g. I want that sweater regardless/irregardless of the price.

   h. We/us girls can swim much better than the boys.

   i. I wish this book had fewer/less pages than it does.

   j. The theater is a little farther/further down the highway.

   k. This data is/These data are very accurate.

   l. I'm eager/anxious for Christmas vacation.

   m. Wipe that off/from the chalkboard.

   n. I felt bad/badly about being late for school.

   o. Let/Leave us go to the shopping mall after school.

   p. Set/Sit the book in the desk.

   q. He sets/sits here most if the day.

2. How many were correct? ______________________________

3. How many were incorrect? ______________________________

Name ______________________________ Date ______________________

6.3 Checkpoint

Body Language — What does It Mean?

Effective oral communication skill requires an understanding of the importance of body language (kinesics) when communicating. Body language depends on the situation and must be interpreted in context with the situation.

1. Many nonverbal gestures have almost universal meanings. What do the following gestures mean to you?

Gesture	Meaning
a. Waving your hand	
b. Holding your nose	
c. Clapping your hands	
d. Crossing your fingers	
e. Holding your thumbs up	
f. Blowing a kiss	
g. Nodding your head up and down	
h. Shrugging your shoulders	
i. Tapping your fingers	
j. Clenching your fist	
k. Holding your thumb down	
l. Shaking your head sideways	
m. Hugging	

2. Body language must be interpreted as it relates to different situations. Observe someone using body language, and answer the following questions:
   a. What is the situation? ______________________________
   b. What is this person doing with his or her arms? ______________________________
   c. What is this person doing with his or her legs? ______________________________
   d. What is this person doing with his or her feet? ______________________________
   e. What is this person doing with his or her hands? ______________________________
   f. What is this person doing with his or her eyes? ______________________________
   g. How is this person postured? ______________________________

Name ______________________ Date ______________

6.4 Checkpoint

Are You a Good Listener?

When you have a full-time job, it will be important to listen to your boss and your co-workers. If you are a poor listener, you risk responding incorrectly, and you can come away with a very different message from the one intended. This can lead to misunderstandings, mistakes, and bad working relationships.

Evaluate yourself as a listener. Read "Listening" in "Important Facts for Chapter 6," then answer the following questions. There are no correct or incorrect answers. Your responses will help you understand yourself as a listener. When you've completed the questions, your teacher will give you the answers, and you can compare your score with those of thousands of others who have answered the same questions.

1. How would you describe yourself as a listener?
   ___ Superior
   ___ Excellent
   ___ Above average
   ___ Average
   ___ Below average
   ___ Poor
   ___ Terrible

2. How would the following people rate you as a listener on a scale of 0 (low) to 100 (high)?
   ___ Someone who tells you what to do
   ___ Your best friend
   ___ A Classmate
   ___ Your spouse or mother
   ___ Your brother or sister

DON'T ASSUME THAT EVERYTHING YOU SAY IS CLEARLY UNDERSTOOD...

continued

3. How often do you engage in the following bad listening habits? Put a check mark (✓) in the column that best describes how often you engage in each bad habit.

Listening Habit	Frequency				
	Almost Always	Usually	Sometimes	Seldom	Almost Never
a. Calling a subject uninteresting					
b. Criticizing a speaker's delivery or mannerisms					
c. Getting overly enthused by something a speaker says					
d. Listening primarily for facts					
e. Trying to outline everything					
f. Faking attention to a speaker					
g. Allowing distractions to interfere with communication					
h. Avoiding difficult material					
i. Letting emotion-laden words make you angry					
j. Wasting the advantage of thinking by daydreaming					
Total for each column	____	____	____	____	____

4. For every "Almost Always" checked, give yourself a score of 2. (2 X ______ = ______)
For every "Usually" checked, give yourself a score of 4. (4 X ______ = ______)
For every "Sometimes" checked, give yourself a score of 6. (6 X ______ = ______)
For every "Seldom" checked, give yourself a score of 8. (8 X ______ = ______)
For every "Almost Never" checked, give yourself a score of 10. (10 X ______ = ______)

5. How do your listening skills compare with those of others? (Your teacher will read these to you.)

____

____

6. Based on the results of this quiz, which areas need the most improvement? ____

____

____

7. What is one listing habit you would like to improve? ____

8. Use the method you learned in Activity 5.5 for improving your skills and keep a log to track your efforts.

Name ______________________________ Date ____________________

Checkpoint 6.5

Responding

When you have a full-time job, it will be important to listen to your boss and your co-workers. If you are a poor listener, you risk responding incorrectly, and you can come away with a very different message from the one intended. This can lead to misunderstandings, mistakes, and bad working relationships.

In your textbook, you learned that *paraphrasing* helps people communicate with one another. Paraphrasing is repeating the speaker's ideas or thoughts in your own words. It is a verbal reflection of what you heard the speaker say. You make no suggestions, give no advice, and ask no questions. You encourage the speaker to tell you more. It is useful when you want to help someone talk their way to the solution of a problem.

1. Ask two classmates or close friends to participate in this activity. Ask one person to be the observer and the other to be the speaker. You will be the listener who responds to the speaker.

   Speakers name: ______________________ Observer's name: ______________________

Speaker's role: The speaker talks to you for five minutes about what he or she hopes will happen in the next five years.

Listener's role: You respond to the speaker.

* Listen to the speaker with an open mind.
* Make a conscious effort to keep your own thoughts from interferring with attending to the speaker (we think much faster than we can talk.)
* Concentrate on what the speaker is saying, and pay attention to the speaker's nonverbal cues.
* Watch your own body language. Keep your hands and feet still.
* Look the speaker in the eye, do not stare.
* Encourage the speaker to keep talking. (Paraphrase, ask the speaker "Will you tell me more about that?", or say, I don't understand. Please clarify that for me.")

Observer's role: The observer gives you feedback on your use of communication helpers and stoppers, using the Observer's Record Sheet.

continued

Observer's Record Sheet

Did the listener	Yes	No	Sometimes
Paraphrase?			
Encourage?			
Probe question?			
Stay receptive?			
Interrupt the speaker?			
Judge the speaker?			
Communicate the message as received?			
Leave out part of the message?			
Add to the message?			
Seem attentive with good eye contact?			
Seem attentive with good body posture?			

2. At the end of the session, ask the speaker the following questions:
   a. What, if anything, did I do that made you feel as though I were listening to you? ____________________

   ____

   ____

   b. How did you feel as I paraphrased what you were saying? ____________________

   ____

   ____

3. Ask the observer to share his or her observations of you in your role as listener____________________

   ____

4. How did you feel as you tried to paraphrase the speaker? ____________________

   ____

   ____

5. Did you have the urge to say your own thoughts? ______ yes ______ no
6. Was it difficult to tune in to what the speaker was saying? ______ yes ______ no
7. Did you draw conclusions before listening to the speaker's entire message? ______ yes ______ no
8. What did you learn about listening and responding in this activity? ____________________

   ____

Name ______________________________ Date ____________________

Checkpoint 6.6

Conflict Resolution

In the workplace (as in any situation with personal interaction) there is a potential for conflict. Different priorities, biases, expertise, and interests can result in disagreements and opposition to issues. When anger or irritation are expressed, the conflict must be resolved.

The successful negotiation of conflict focuses on problems, not feelings or personalities. It relies on effective interpersonal skills and a clear understanding of the approach demanded by the circumstances. All beliefs, opinions, or viewpoints are in the open.

1. Assume the role of negotiator in the following situation.

   Rita and Betty live in the same neighborhood, own automobiles, and drive fifteen miles each way to work the evening shift at CDS Enterprises. Last month, Rita and Betty decided they could save considerable money by forming a car pool. Now they take turns driving to work.

   When Rita drives, they arrive at CDS only about five minutes before starting time. This caused them to be seven minutes late last Friday, and the supervisor gave them a warning.

   When Betty drives, they arrive at CDS about forty minutes before starting time. Betty enjoys drinking coffee with her co-workers in the employee lounge before her shift begins. Rita would rather drink coffee at home with her husband.

   The two women had an argument about this situation on the way to work this evening and didn't speak to each other on the way home.

   a. What is Rita's view of the conflict? (How does she feel, and what does she want?) ____________

   b. What is Betty's view of the conflict? (How does she feel, and what does she want?) ____________

   c. Why would agreement benefit both parties? ____________

   d. Identify a belief, opinion, or viewpoint on which both parties agree. ____________

   e. Idenfity beliefs, opinions, or viewpoints on which both parties disagree. ____________

continued

f. Offer a win-win solution or a compromise to the conflict.__________

g. How would your resolution of the conflict work in a real-life situation? __________

2. Think of a disagreement you have had with a friend or family member.

   a. What did you do to resolve the disagreement? __________

   b. How did you feel about the disagreement and the resolution. __________

3. Listen to a nightly news broadcast or scan the local newspapers for stories about conflict. Choose one conflict, and describe what could be done to resolve it.__________

Career Tip: When you have a disagreement with someone, focus on points of agreement before discussing your differences.

Name ______________________________ Date ____________________

6.7

Checkpoint

Checking Your Location

1. For each of the following statements, circle **F** if the statement is more false than true. Circle **T** if the statement is more true than false.

T F a. Communication is an integral part of every industry and business in the United States.

T F b. Job knowledge ranks slightly below communication skills as a factor in career success.

T F c. The average worker spends most of his or her time speaking.

T F d. Chinese is the most commonly used language in the international world of work.

T F e. Your recognition vocabulary will include at least eighty thousand words by the time you leave high school.

T F f. It is usually safer to begin using new words in your writing rather than in conversation.

T F g. Effective communication exists when the receiver interprets the sender's message as the sender intended.

T F h. Speaking is the most often used method of communicating policies, procedures, and concepts in the workplace.

T F i. The average employee spends one and a half to two hours each workday doing some form of reading.

T F j. Skimming material will never provide all that you need to completely understand printed material.

T F k. Successful interpersonal relationships are built on mutual trust, acceptance, empathy, and understanding.

T F l. Effective communication is important in all interpersonal aspects of life.

T F m. All groups have some form of organization, rules for establishing leadership, and expectations regarding member behavior.

T F n. In a democratic group, leadership rarely relies on the active participation of members in the decision-making process.

T F o. Each person involved in a conflict has personal biases, priorities, expertise, and interests that affect the points of agreement and create outright opposition on many issues.

2. Use the space below to rewrite the statements you marked **false** and make them **true**. Include the letter of each statement you rewrite.

Name ______________________________ Date ____________________

7.1 Learning How to Conduct a Successful Job Search

In your textbook, you have learned about several methods for finding a job.

1. Ask a parent or friend who is employed the following questions:

   a. What method did you use to get your present job? (Mark all that apply.)

   _____ Applied directly to the employer

   _____ Contacted professional or trade organizations

   _____ Responded to help-wanted ads

   _____ Used a private employment agency

   _____ Networked

   _____ Used school placement services

   _____ Used the State Bureau of Employment Services

   b. If you needed to look for employment again, which methods would you use? Why? ____________

   ____

   c. What did you do that made your job search successful? ____________

   ____

   ____

   d. What was the most difficult part about getting your present job? ____________

   ____

   e. Why do you believe you were selected over other applicants for your present job? ____________

   ____

2. Name one job you would like to have when you graduate from high school. ____________

3. List all of the requirements for the job you named. ____________

   ____

   ____

4. Think about the courses in which you receive the best grades, the courses you've taken that are job-related, school activities you like, tasks you have done well in the past, and good things people have said about you or your work. Now list the benefits you would offer an employer who hires you for the job you named in question 2.

   ____

   ____

5. Identify three employers in your area who would hire someone for this job.

   a. ____________ b. ____________ c. ____________

Name ______________________ Date ______________

7.2 Checkpoint

Telephone the Employer

Most successful job searches require careful planning. Review the case of Raymond Wilson.

Raymond is a senior at Martin Luther King High School. He would like to obtain part-time employment at a trucking company and eventually become a long-distance truck driver. Using the yellow pages of the telephone book, Raymond turns to the T's. He discovers sixty major headings from "Truck — Air-conditioning Equipment" to "Trucks — Motor." He turns to the heading "Truck —Motor Freight" and finds six trucking companies listed. Raymond decides to phone the J&R Transit Company. Listen to his conversation.

Raymond: Hello. I'm looking for a part-time job, and I would like to work for your company. Do you have any openings today?

Receptionist: I'm very sorry, but the person in charge of hiring is out of the office today.

Raymond: Thank you very much. I'll call back next week.

1. Raymond knows the career path he would like to follow, and he has used the job-search method of applying directly to the employer. He was very polite on the telephone, but he does not know anymore about who is responsible for hiring or what procedures the J&R Transit Company uses to hire employees than he did before he made the telephone call.

   a. What information should Raymond have sought from the receptionist? (Review "Applying Directly to the Employer" in your textbook.) ______________________

   b. What could Raymond have said to improve his telephone introduction? ______________________

   c. What are some questions he might have asked the receptionist? ______________________

   d. What personal information should Raymond have on paper when he calls back? Why? ______________________

2. Write a telephone introduction that you would use to introduce yourself to one of the employers you identified in question 5 of Checkpoint 7.1.

____

Name ______________________________ Date ____________________

Checkpoint 7.3

Network Your Way to a Job

Most jobs are not advertised, so it is important to use the process of networking to find job openings. Everyone you know who might have information about a job opening or who knows someone who might have a lead about a job opening, can be in your network.

1. From the following list, select three people who can give you information about potential job openings or can introduce you to others who have this information.

_____ Mother	_____ Father	_____ Mother's friend	_____ Father's friend
_____ Aunt	_____ Uncle	_____ Cousin	_____ Neighbor
_____ Friend	_____ Clergy	_____ Classmate	_____ Teacher
_____ Counselor	_____ Doctor	_____ Dentist	_____ Former employer

2. Contact the three people you chose, and tell them about the type of job you are interested in pursuing. Record below the information you receive from each person. If they know the names of people who are in charge of hiring new employees or whom you should contact, record that information. If they can point you to someone else to contact or if they tell you where to get more information, write that down.

   a. Name of person 1: ______________________ Phone Number: __________

   Address: ____

   Information received from this person: ______________________________

   ____

   ____

   a. Name of person 2: ______________________ Phone Number: __________

   Address: ____

   Information received from this person: ______________________________

   ____

   ____

   a. Name of person 3: ______________________ Phone Number: __________

   Address: ____

   Information received from this person: ______________________________

   ____

   ____

   ____

continued

3. Use the following outline as a guide to introduce yourself to one of the contacts suggested by your network. This technique will also enable you to expand your network.

a. Hello, Mr./Mrs.______________________________
[name of person you are calling.]

b. My name is ______________________________
[your name]

c. Mr./Mrs. ______________________ suggested that I talk with you about a job.
[name of person who gave you this person's name]

d. I am interested in a job as a ______________________________
[job you are interested in pursuing]

e. My qualifications for this job are ______________________________
[describe your qualifications for this job]

f. I would like to meet with you for about twenty minutes to get any advice you have to offer. When would be a convenient time to meet? ______________________________
[offer two different dates and times]

g. If you cannot help me, would you please give me the name and phone number of someone who might? ______________________________
[name and phone number of new contact]

h. Thank you for your time and advice.

Career Tip: Letters of introduction can be sent to contacts if calling is inappropriate. make certain that the letter is brief and to the point.

WANTING A JOB ISN'T ENOUGH... YOU HAVE TO FIND AN EMPLOYER!

Name ______________________________ Date ____________________

7.4

Checkpoint

Help-Wanted Advertisements

Almost 46 percent of job seekers use the advertisements in their local newspaper to find job leads. Although fewer than 25 percent of workers are actually hired through advertisements, this is still an effective method for finding employment.

1. Read the following classified advertisement, and answer the questions about it.

   a. Under what category of work does the ad appear? ____________

   b. Who is the employer? ____________

   c. What is the company's product or service? ____________

   d. What position or positions are open? ____________

   e. What do the abbreviations in the ad stand for? (Refer to page 136 of your text.) ____________

   f. What qualifications do you have for the position? ____________

   g. If you do not have relevant work experience for the job, what have you done that could substitute for that experience?

   ____

   h. What additional information would you need to have before deciding if you are qualified for this job? ____________

   i. What responsibilities would you have on this job?

   ____

   j. How do you apply for the job? ____________

   k. Whom do you contact at this company if you are interested in the position? ____________

   ____

> restaurant
>
> **BURGER DAYS**
>
> Now Hiring For All Shifts
> We Offer:
> • Free Meals
> • Free Uniforms
> • Opportunity for Growth
> • Flexible Hours
>
> Premium rate paid for day shifts and late night shifts. Minimum $3.65/hr. Apply Mon-Fri. between 2pm-4pm and after 7 pm or Call 614-4321. E.O.E. M/F/H/V/
> 325 State Road Mall

2. Select one job you would like to have from the classified advertisements in the Sunday edition of your local newspaper. Then answer the following questions:

   a. Under what category of work does the ad appear? ____________

   b. Who is the employer? ____________

   c. What is the company's product or service? ____________

   d. What position or positions are open? ____________

continued

e. What do the abbreviations in the ad stand for? (refer to page 136 of your text) ______

______

______

______

f. What qualifications do you have for the position? ______

______

______

g. If you do not have relevant work experience for the job, what have you done that could substitute for that experience? ______

______

______

h. What additional information would you need to have before deciding if you are qualified for this job? ______

______

______

i. What responsbilities would you have on this job? ______

______

______

j. How do you apply for the job? ______

______

______

k. Whom do you contact at this company if you are interested in the position? ______

______

______

Name ______________________________ Date ____________________

Checkpoint 7.5

Using State Employment Services

The U.S. Employment Service provides free employment assistance. Visit your local office, and ask to interview an employment counselor.

1. Name of employment counselor ______________________________
2. How do the counselors decide which employment candidates will be sent to interview for specific jobs?

   ____

   ____
3. What job openings are available in your job classification? ______________________________

   ____

   ____
4. What type of testing is available for job seekers at this agency? ______________________________

   ____

   ____
5. What special assistance does the agency offer to veterans? ______________________________

   ____

   ____
6. What special assistance does the agency offer to the physically challenged? ______________________________

   ____

   ____
7. What services does the agency offer to ex-offenders who are seeking to make the transition from prison to civilian life? ______________________________

   ____
8. What federally funded programs does the agency administer? ______________________________

   ____

   ____
9. Ask the employment counselor for an employment application. Fill it out and return it to the counselor.
   a. For what type of job did you qualify? ______________________________
   b. To what job classification did the employment counselor assign you? ______________________________

Name ______________________________ Date ____________________

Checkpoint 7.6

Private Employment Agencies

Private employment agencies placed 1.9 million workers in temporary jobs each day in 1994.

* Approximately 82 percent of temp workers have more than a high school education.
* 80 percent chose the job mainly for additional income.
* 44 percent of temps provide the main source of income for their families.
* Most temps have worked at least four weeks as a temporary.

Approximately 38 percent of workers who start out with a temporary-help firm are offered full-time jobs. For temp jobs, employers are interested in skills first and foremost; for full-time employment, they are more interested in the fit and personality of the workers.

Temporary Agencies

1. Use the yellow pages of the telephone book and select a temporary employment agency to contact.

   Name of Agency ______________________________ Phone number ______________

2. Contact the agency and ask to speak with an employment counselor.

   Name of the employment counselor ______________________________

3. Explain the purpose of your call and ask the employment counselor the following questions.

   a. How does a temporary agency operate? ______________________________

   b. How is a temporary agency different from a permanent placement agency? ______________________________

   c. In what employment fields does this agency specialize? ______________________________

   d. How do counselors decide which employment candidates will be sent to interview for specific jobs?

continued

e. What type of testing is available for job seekers at this agency? ______

______

______

f. How are employees paid? ______

______

______

g. What fringe benefits are offered? ______

______

______

4. Using your textbook, page 138 and the information above, list two advantages of using a temporary employment service.

   a. ______

   ______

   b. ______

   ______

5. List two disadvantages of using a temporary employment service.

   a. ______

   ______

   b. ______

   ______

Name ______________________ Date ______________

Checkpoint 7.7

Professional and Trade Associations

1. Use one of the following resources to learn more about job openings available from professional or trade associations. Mark the resource you decide to use.
   - _____ One of the resources mentioned in Getting More Information on page 137 of your textbook.
   - _____ The *Directory of Associations* available at your school or public library.
   - _____ The *Directory of National Trade and Professional Associations of the United States* available at your school or public library.
   - _____ A professional or trade association listed in the yellow pages of your telephone book.
   - _____ A professional or trade association recommended by a parent or friend.

2. Select one professional or trade association from the resource you selected to contact.

   a. Name of the association ______________________ Phone number ______________

   Address of the association ______________________

   Name of contact person ______________________

   b. Write a business letter to the association, and ask for information about the types of employment services they have that are available to their members. Write a draft of your letter on the following lines. Retype the corrected draft and send to the association. Be prepared to discuss the response from your letter in class.

Name ________________________ Date ________________

Checkpoint 7.8

Make Job lead Cards

Contact two of the companies you selected in Checkpoint 7.1, and gather the information you need to fill in the following job lead cards.

Job Lead Card

Company name: ________________ Company phone number: ________________

Company address: ________________

Job lead source: ________________ Position: ________________

Company business: ________________

Person to contact for hiring: ________________ Title of contact: ________________

Results of contact (include date): ________________

Other information: ________________

____

____

____

Job Lead Card

Company name: ________________ Company phone number: ________________

Company address: ________________

Job lead source: ________________ Position: ________________

Company business: ________________

Person to contact for hiring: ________________ Title of contact: ________________

Results of contact (include date): ________________

Other information: ________________

____

____

____

Name ________________________________ Date ____________________

Prepare Your Personal Data Sheet

Before you begin this activity, review the section, "Prepare a Personal Data Sheet," in your textbook. Then complete the following personal data sheet. Be thorough and careful as you fill in the information. Remember, a personal data sheet lists accurate information about you that is important to employers. You will be asked for this information when you fill out a job application or are interviewed for a job.

Personal Data Sheet

1. *Personal Information*

Your full name: ____________________ Social Security Number: __ __ __-__ __-__ __ __ __

Address: ____

Phone number: (______) __________ Date available for employment: ____________________

Date of Birth: Month _____ Day _____ Year 19___ Marital status: _____ Single _____ Married

Height: _____ Weight: _____lbs. Citizenship status: ____________________

Name and phone number of people to contact in an emergency:

a. Name: ____________________ Address: ____________________ ____

Phone number (_____) ______________ Relationship: ____________________

b. Name: ____________________ Address: ____________________

Phone number (_____) ______________ Relationship: ____________________

c. Name: ____________________ Address: ____________________

Phone number (_____) ______________ Relationship: ____________________

2. Educational Background

Name of high school: ____

School address: ____

School phone number: (_____)______________

Present status as a student: _____ Part-time _____ Full-time _____ Graduate

Grade point average: ____________________ Class rank: ______________

Dates of attendance: From: ____________________ To: ____________________

Course of study: _____ General _____ Vocational _____ College preparatory

continued

Extracurricular activities: (clubs, sports): ______________________________

____

Awards or honors: ______________________________

____

Favorite subjects: ______________________________

____

3. Part-time or Full-time Work Experience

a. Name of company: ______________ Dates employed: ______________

Your position: ______________________________

Your responsibilities: ______________________________

Wages or salary: Starting ______________ Final ______________

Reason for leaving: ______________________________

b. Name of company: ______________ Dates employed: ______________

Your position: ______________________________

Your responsibilities: ______________________________

Wages or salary: Starting ______________ Final ______________

Reason for leaving: ______________________________

4. Volunteer Work

a. Name of organization: ______________________________

Why you chose to volunteer for this organization: ______________________________

____

Your duties or responsibilities: ______________________________

____

b. Name of organization: ______________________________

Why you chose to volunteer for this organization: ______________________________

____

Your duties or responsibilities: ______________________________

____

5. **Future Educational Goals:** ______________________________

____

____

continued

6. **Career/job Goal:** ____

____

____

7. **References** (complete name, address, job title, and phone number)

   a. Name: ____________________ Address: ______________________________

      Job title: ____________________ Phone number: __________ Relationship: __________

   b. Name: ____________________ Address: ______________________________

      Job title: ____________________ Phone number: __________ Relationship: __________

   c. Name: ____________________ Address: ______________________________

      Job title: ____________________ Phone number: __________ Relationship: __________

8. **Major Qualifications for the Position** (Your skills, such as typing, operating equipment)

____

____

____

____

____

____

9. **Leisure-Time Activities and Hobbies**

____

____

____

____

Name ______________________________ Date ____________________

Checkpoint 7.10

Résumé Worksheet

Reread the section "Compose an Effective Resume" in your textbook, then complete the following chronological résumé. Refer to the information on your personal data sheet and in Figure 7.7 on page 144 as you work on this activity. Remember, your résumé is a portrait of you. It is a summary of your education, skills, and work history. Its content and appearance are very important. Employers will read only so far as their interest is maintained.

Revise your résumé until it is perfect. Retype it using Figure 7.7 on page 144 of your textbook as a guide.

Name: First ________________ Middle Initial ______________ Last __________________

Address: Street/Box Number __________________ City ______ State ______ Zip code ______

Phone number (include the area code) (________) - ___ ___ ___-___ ___ ___ ___

Career objectives: ____

____

Education

Name of high school: ____

Date (or anticipated date) of graduation: ____________________

Class rank: ____________________ Grade point average(optional): ____________________

Awards or honors: ____

____

____

____

Activities and work experience:

Begin with your most recent experience and work backwards. Include dates, job titles if employed, name of employer's business, and a full description of all jobs held. Always write in the first person.

____

____

____

____

____

continued

Personal information:

Include hobbies, special skills, extracurricular activities, and date of birth.

Date available for employment

State the earliest date you will be available. If you are a student seeking part-time employment, specify the hours and days of the week that you are available.

References

The names and contact information of references need not be included on your résumé. A statement like, "References are available on request," will do.

Reference 1: Name ___________________ Address ____

Job title _________________ Phone number (____) _____________ Relationship ________________

Reference 2: Name ___________________ Address ____

Job title _________________ Phone number (____) _____________ Relationship ________________

Reference 3: Name ___________________ Address ____

Job title _________________ Phone number (____) _____________ Relationship ________________

Name ______________________ Date ______________

7.11 Checkpoint

Write a Cover Letter

Write a cover letter responding to the ad you selected in checkpoint 7.4, question 2. Reread the section "Write a Successful Cover Letter" in your textbook. Refer to the example in Figure 7.8 on page 147 as you work on this activity. Remember that a cover letter introduces you to a specific employer regarding your interest in a specific job opening. A cover letter should accompany each résumé you send to an employer.

Your address ______________________

____

Date ______________________

Direct your letter to a particular person

Name: ______________________

Title: ______________________

Company name: ______________________

Company address: ______________________

Greeting. ______________________

Paragraph 1: Express your interest in the position. ______________________

Paragraph 2: Include a statement or listing of your qualifications for this particular job. ______________________

Paragraph 3: State your desire to work for the employer and ask for an interview. ______________________

continued

Salutation. ______________________________

Your signature. ______________________________

Your name typed. ______________________________

Enclosures that will be found in the envelope.
____
____
____
____

Revise the letter until it is perfect, then retype or rewrite it without the headings, just as you would if you were sending it to an employer. Single-space the paragraphs, but double-space between paragraphs. Sign your letter in ink, preferably blue.

Name ______________________________ Date ____________________

7.12 Checkpoint

Finding the Right Words

Decipher the Chapter 7 vocabulary terms hidden below, using the following key. The first one has been done for you.

KEY

a	b	c	d	e	f	g	h	i	j	k	l	m	n	o	p	q	r	s	t	u	v	w	x	y	z
1	2	3	4	5	6	7	8	9	10	11	12	13	14	15	16	17	18	19	20	21	22	23	24	25	26

Sample:

1. e m p l o y m e n t   s e r v i c e
   5 13 16 12 15 25 13 5 14 20   19 5 18 22 9 3 5

2. ___ ___ ___ ___ ___ ___ ___ ___ ___
   1 16 16 12 9 3 1 14 20

3. ___ ___ ___ ___ ___ ___
   18 5 19 21 13 5

4. ___ ___ ___ ___ ___ ___ ___ ___   ___ ___ ___ ___   ___ ___ ___ ___ ___
   16 5 18 19 15 14 1 12   4 1 20 1   19 8 5 5 20

5. ___ ___ ___ ___ ___ ___ ___ ___ ___ ___
   18 5 6 5 18 5 14 3 5 19

6. ___ ___ ___   ___ ___ ___ ___ ___
   10 15 2   12 5 1 4 19

7. ___ ___ ___   ___ ___ ___ ___ ___ ___
   10 15 2   19 5 1 18 3 8

8. ___ ___ ___   ___ ___ ___ ___ ___ ___
   10 15 2   10 1 18 7 15 14

9. ___ ___ ___ ___ ___   ___ ___ ___ ___ ___ ___
   3 15 22 5 18   12 5 20 20 5 18

10. ___ ___ ___   ___ ___ ___ ___
    10 15 2   6 1 9 18

11. ___ ___ ___   ___ ___ ___ ___ ___ ___
    10 15 2   13 1 18 11 5 20

continued

12. ___ ___ ___ ___ ___ ___ ___ ___ ___ ___ ___ ___ ___ ___ ___ ___
9 14 9 20 9 1 12 19 3 18 5 5 14 9 14 7

13. ___ ___ ___ ___ ___ ___ ___ ___ ___ ___
14 5 20 23 15 18 11 9 14 7

14. ___ ___ ___ ___ ___ ___ ___ ___ ___ ___ ___ ___ ___ ___ ___ ___ ___ ___ ___
3 8 18 15 14 15 12 15 7 9 3 1 12 18 5 19 21 13 5

15. ___ ___ ___ ___ ___ ___ ___ ___ ___ ___ ___ ___ ___ ___ ___ ___
6 21 14 3 20 9 15 14 1 12 18 5 19 21 13 5

Name ______________________________ Date ____________________

7.13 Checkpoint

Checking Your Location

1. For each of the following statements, circle **F** if the statement is more false than true. Circle **T** if the statement is more true than false.

T F a. The U.S. workforce will increase to 65 million by the year 2000.

T F b. The least successful method for a job search is networking.

T F c. The Sunday edition of most major newspapers carries advertisements about job openings from organizations and employment agencies.

T F d. Employment agency fees are always paid by the applicant.

T F e. It takes an average of six to eight weeks for an employer to fill a position.

T F f. You write a personal data sheet for your own use; you do not give it to an employer.

T F g. Employers thoroughly read all résumés sent to them by potential employees.

T F h. Cover letters should always be written for a specific employer and position.

T F i. The U.S. Department of Labor estimates that a bad hiring decision costs a company one-third of the new hire's annual salary.

T F j. State Bureaus of Employment Services provide no services to applicants with disabilities.

T F k. Job seekers are more likely to find the type of employment for which they are qualified if they learn specific job-search skills.

T F l. Having a personal data sheet will simplify the task of filling out job applications.

T F m. Job seekers with limited work experience should develop a functional résumé.

T F n. Using job lead cards and making a job file are effective methods for job seekers to organize their job-search information.

T F o. Nationwide, only 50 percent of all newly hired employees last more than six months.

continued

2. Use the space below to rewrite the statements you marked **false** and make them **true**. Include the letter of each statement you rewrite.

Name ______________________ Date ______________________

8.1 Checkpoint

Forms You Will Need for Employment

Employers must review certain documents before an employee is legally permitted to begin work.

1. If you do not have a Social Security card, you will need to apply for one. To receive the card, you must provide documents that show your age, citizenship or lawful alien status, and who you are — for example, a birth certificate and a school record. For practice, applying for a Social Security card, complete the following sample application. Follow the instructions exactly.

SOCIAL SECURITY ADMINISTRATION
Application for a Social Security Card

Form Approved
OMB No. 0960-0066

INSTRUCTIONS
- Please read "How To Complete This Form" on page 2.
- Print or type using black or blue ink. DO NOT USE PENCIL.
- After you complete this form, take or mail it along with the required documents to your nearest Social Security office.
- If you are completing this form for someone else, answer the questions as they apply to that person. Then, sign your name in question 16.

1 NAME To Be Shown On Card ▶ ______ FIRST ______ FULL MIDDLE NAME ______ LAST

FULL NAME AT BIRTH IF OTHER THAN ABOVE ______ FIRST ______ FULL MIDDLE NAME ______ LAST

OTHER NAMES USED ______

2 MAILING ADDRESS Do Not Abbreviate ▶ ______ STREET ADDRESS, APT. NO., PO BOX, RURAL ROUTE NO.

______ CITY ______ STATE ______ ZIP CODE

3 CITIZENSHIP (Check One) ☐ U.S. Citizen ☐ Legal Alien Allowed To Work ☐ Legal Alien Not Allowed To Work ☐ Foreign Student Allowed Restricted Employment ☐ Conditionally Legalized Alien Allowed To Work ☐ Other (See Instructions On Page 2)

4 SEX ☐ Male ☐ Female

5 RACE/ETHNIC DESCRIPTION (Check One Only—Voluntary) ☐ Asian, Asian-American Or Pacific Islander ☐ Hispanic ☐ Black (Not Hispanic) ☐ North American Indian Or Alaskan Native ☐ White (Not Hispanic)

6 DATE OF BIRTH ______ MONTH DAY YEAR

7 PLACE OF BIRTH (Do Not Abbreviate) ______ CITY ______ STATE OR FOREIGN COUNTRY ______ FCI ☐ Office Use Only

8 MOTHER'S MAIDEN NAME ______ FIRST ______ FULL MIDDLE NAME ______ LAST NAME AT HER BIRTH

9 FATHER'S NAME ______ FIRST ______ FULL MIDDLE NAME ______ LAST

10 Has the person in item 1 ever received a Social Security number before?
☐ Yes (If "yes", answer questions 11-13.) ☐ No (If "no", go on to question 14.) ☐ Don't Know (If "don't know", go on to question 14.)

11 Enter the Social Security number previously assigned to the person listed in item 1.
☐☐☐-☐☐-☐☐☐☐

12 Enter the name shown on the most recent Social Security card issued for the person listed in item 1.
______ FIRST ______ MIDDLE ______ LAST

13 Enter any different date of birth if used on an earlier application for a card. ______ MONTH ______ DAY ______ YEAR

14 TODAY'S DATE ▶ ______ MONTH DAY YEAR

15 DAYTIME PHONE NUMBER ▶ ( ) ______ AREA CODE

DELIBERATELY FURNISHING (OR CAUSING TO BE FURNISHED) FALSE INFORMATION ON THIS APPLICATION IS A CRIME PUNISHABLE BY FINE OR IMPRISONMENT, OR BOTH.

16 YOUR SIGNATURE ▶ ______

17 YOUR RELATIONSHIP TO THE PERSON IN ITEM 1 IS: ☐ Self ☐ Natural Or Adoptive Parent ☐ Legal Guardian ☐ Other (Specify) ______

DO NOT WRITE BELOW THIS LINE (FOR SSA USE ONLY)

NPN	DOC	NTI	CAN	ITV

PBC	EVI	EVA	EVC	PRA	NWR	DNR	UNIT

EVIDENCE SUBMITTED	SIGNATURE AND TITLE OF EMPLOYEE(S) REVIEWING EVIDENCE AND/OR CONDUCTING INTERVIEW
	DATE
	DCL DATE

Form SS-5 (9/89) 5/88 edition may be used until supply is exhausted

continued

2. The Immigration Reform and Control Act (IRDA) requires all employees hired after November 6, 1986, to show their employers documents that prove their identity and their eligibility to work in this country. Fill out Part 1 of the following sample Employment Eligibility Verification form (Form I-9) with the care and thoroughness you would use if you were submitting it to an employer.

U.S. Department of Justice
Immigration and
Naturalization Service
OMB No. 1115-0136

Employment Eligibility Verification

I-9

Please read instructions carefully before completing this form. The instructions must be available during completion of this form. ANTI-DISCRIMINATION NOTICE. It is illegal to discriminate against work eligible individuals. Employers CANNOT specify which document(s) they will accept from an employee. The refusal to hire an individual because of a future expiration date may also constitute illegal discrimination.

SECTION 1. EMPLOYEE INFORMATION AND VERIFICATION. To be completed and signed by employee at the time employment begins.

Print Name: Last	First	Middle Initial	Maiden Name
Address (*Street name and Number*)		Apt. #	Date of Birth (*month/day/year*)
City	State	Zip Code	Social Security #

I am aware that federal law provides for imprisonment and/or fines for false statements or use of false documents in connection with the completion of this form.

I attest, under penalty of perjury, that I am (check one of the following):

- O A citizen or national of the United States
- O A Lawful Permanent Resident (Alien #A ___________________________)
- O An alien authorized to work until ________/________/________ (Alien # or Admission # ________________________________)

Employee's Signature	Date (*month/day/year*)

Preparer and/or Translator Certification. *(To be completed and signed if Section I is prepared by a person other than the employee.) I attest, under penalty of perjury, that I have assisted in the completion of this form and that to the best of my knowledge the information is true and correct.*

Preparer's Translator's Signature	Print Name
Address *(Street Name and Number, City, State, Zip Code)*	Date *(month/day/year)*

continued

3. When you start any new job, you will need to complete a W-4 form. The W-4 is a legal document giving your employer permission to deduct taxes from your paycheck and to pay them to the government for you. If the information on your W-4 is accurate, the amount withheld each year will be very close to your annual tax bill. Fill out the following sample of a W-4 tax form.

Form W-4 (1995)

Want More Money In Your Paycheck? If you expect to be able to take the earned income credit for 1995 and a child lives with you, you may be able to have part of the credit added to your take-home pay. For details, get Form W-5 from your employer.

Purpose. Complete Form W-4 so that your employer can withhold the correct amount of Federal income tax from your pay.

Exemption From Withholding. Read line 7 of the certificate below to see if you can claim exempt status. *If exempt, complete line 7; but do not complete lines 5 and 6.* No Federal income tax will be withheld from your pay. Your exemption is good for 1 year only. It expires February 15, 1996.

Note: *You cannot claim exemption from withholding if (1) your income exceeds $650 and includes unearned income (e.g., interest and dividends) and (2) another person can claim you as a dependent on their tax return.*

Basic Instructions. Employees who are not exempt should complete the Personal Allowances Worksheet. Additional worksheets are provided on page 2 for employees to adjust their withholding allowances based on itemized deductions, adjustments to income, or two-earner/two-job situations. Complete all worksheets that apply to your situation. The worksheets will help you figure the number of withholding allowances you are entitled to claim. However, you may claim fewer allowances than this.

Head of Household. Generally, you may claim head of household filing status on your tax return only if you are unmarried and pay more than 50% of the costs of keeping up a home for yourself and your dependent(s) or other qualifying individuals.

Nonwage Income. If you have a large amount of nonwage income, such as interest or dividends, you should consider making estimated tax payments using Form 1040-ES. Otherwise, you may find that you owe additional tax at the end of the year.

Two Earners/Two Jobs. If you have a working spouse or more than one job, figure the total number of allowances you are entitled to claim on all jobs using worksheets from only one Form W-4. This total should be divided among all jobs. Your withholding will usually be most accurate when all allowances are claimed on the W-4 filed for the highest paying job and zero allowances are claimed for the others.

Check Your Withholding. After your W-4 takes effect, you can use **Pub. 919,** Is My Withholding Correct for 1995?, to see how the dollar amount you are having withheld compares to your estimated total annual tax. We recommend you get Pub. 919 especially if you used the Two Earner/Two Job Worksheet and your earnings exceed $150,000 (Single) or $200,000 (Married). Call 1-800-829-3676 to order Pub. 919. Check your telephone directory for the IRS assistance number for further help.

Personal Allowances Worksheet

A Enter "1" for **yourself** if no one else can claim you as a dependent . . . . A ______

B Enter "1" if:
- You are single and have only one job; or
- You are married, have only one job, and your spouse does not work; or
- Your wages from a second job or your spouse's wages (or the total of both) are $1,000 or less.

. . B ______

C Enter "1" for your **spouse.** But, you may choose to enter -0- if you are married and have either a working spouse or more than one job (this may help you avoid having too little tax withheld) . . . . C ______

D Enter number of **dependents** (other than your spouse or yourself) you will claim on your tax return . . . . D ______

E Enter "1" if you will file as **head of household** on your tax return (see conditions under **Head of Household** above) . E ______

F Enter "1" if you have at least $1,500 of **child or dependent care expenses** for which you plan to claim a credit . . F ______

G Add lines A through F and enter total here. **Note:** This amount may be different from the number of exemptions you claim on your return ▶ G ______

For accuracy, do all worksheets that apply.
- If you plan to **itemize or claim adjustments to income** and want to reduce your withholding, see the Deductions and Adjustments Worksheet on page 2.
- If you are **single** and have **more than one job** and your combined earnings from all jobs exceed $30,000 OR if you are **married** and have a **working spouse or more than one job,** and the combined earnings from all jobs exceed $50,000, see the Two-Earner/Two-Job Worksheet on page 2 if you want to avoid having too little tax withheld.
- If **neither** of the above situations applies, **stop here** and enter the number from line G on line 5 of Form W-4 below.

Cut here and give the certificate to your employer. Keep the top portion for your records.

Form **W-4**
Department of the Treasury
Internal Revenue Service

Employee's Withholding Allowance Certificate

▶ **For Privacy Act and Paperwork Reduction Act Notice, see reverse.**

OMB No. 1545-0010
1995

1 Type or print your first name and middle initial	Last name	**2** Your social security number
Home address (number and street or rural route)		**3** ☐ Single ☐ Married ☐ Married, but withhold at higher Single rate. Note: *If married, but legally separated, or spouse is a nonresident alien, check the Single box.*
City or town, state, and ZIP code		**4** If your last name differs from that on your social security card, check here and call 1-800-772-1213 for a new card . . . . . ▶ ☐

5 Total number of allowances you are claiming (from line G above or from the worksheets on page 2 if they apply) . **5** ______

6 Additional amount, if any, you want withheld from each paycheck . . . . **6** $ ______

7 I claim exemption from withholding for 1995 and I certify that I meet **BOTH** of the following conditions for exemption:
- Last year I had a right to a refund of **ALL** Federal income tax withheld because I had **NO** tax liability; **AND**
- This year I expect a refund of **ALL** Federal income tax withheld because I expect to have **NO** tax liability.

If you meet both conditions, enter "EXEMPT" here . . . . ▶ **7** ______

Under penalties of perjury, I certify that I am entitled to the number of withholding allowances claimed on this certificate or entitled to claim exempt status.

Employee's signature ▶ Date ▶ , 19

8 Employer's name and address (Employer: Complete 8 and 10 only if sending to the IRS)	**9** Office code (optional)	**10** Employer identification number

Cat. No. 10220Q

Name ______________________________ Date ______________________

Checkpoint 8.2

Working as Minor

Roberta Jones learned to paint the interior of houses when she was in the sixth grade. Her father taught her how to stir the paint, protect the furnishings with covers, and even trim around the windowpanes and doors. Now she is fifteen, and it seems sensible to take advantage of the offer Mr. Thompson has presented.

Mr. Thompson owns a small motel with eighteen individual units. Normally, half of the units are rented during the winter months. He has offered to let Roberta paint the units after school. He suggests that she work from 4:30 to 8:00 each evening. She can work as many hours as she wants on Saturday. The eight-foot-high walls would be easy for Roberta to paint with a six-foot stepladder.

Roberta is eager to earn money for her college education. She has told Mr. Thompson that she will apply for a work permit. When Roberta applies for a work permit, however, she learns that laws regulating the working hours and working conditions of employees fifteen years of age and younger prevent her from working for Mr. Thompson.

1. Review the federal laws governing fourteen- and fifteen-year-olds (see pages 152-154 in your text). Then answer the following questions.

   a. Which parts of the Fair Labor Standards Act prevent Roberta from getting the job?

   ____

   ____

   ____

   ____

   b. How could Roberta and Mr. Thompson adjust their plan so that she would be able to get a work permit? Explain your answer.

   ____

   ____

   ____

   ____

Name ______________________________ Date ____________________

8.3

Checkpoint

Filling in the Blanks

1. The following abbreviations are frequently found on job applications. Spell out each abbreviation in the space provided. (Your teacher has the answers.)

BD ____________________

Soc. Sec. ____________________

avg. ____________________

wt. ____________________

ave. ____________________

f. ____________________

tel. ____________________

yr. ____________________

co. ____________________

NA ____________________

WPM ____________________

yr. ____________________

col. ____________________

DOB ____________________

SS# ____________________

ht. ____________________

st. ____________________

zip ____________________

m. ____________________

dept. ____________________

mo. ____________________

ref. ____________________

ed. ____________________

sal. ____________________

HS ____________________

apt. ____________________

2. Some application forms require you to print information. Practice your printing skills using the following samples. Print as neatly as possible on the lines above the samples.

____

A a B b C c D d E e F f G g H h

____

I i J j K k L l M m N n O o P p

____

Q q R r S s T t U u V v W w X x

____

Y y Z z 1 2 3 4 5 6 7 8 9 0

3. To answer some questions, you may find that cursive writing is suitable. Practice your cursive hand writing skills using the following samples. Write as neatly as possible on the lines above the samples.

A a B b C c D d E e F f G g H h

I i J j K k L l M m N n O o P p

Q q R r S s T t U u V v W w X x

Y y Z z 1 2 3 4 5 6 7 8 9 0

Name ______________________________ Date ____________________

Checkpoint 8.4

Job Applications

What should Shonda Do?

Shonda knows that she can be a good salesperson at the mall. She likes to talk with people, enjoys helping them, and likes the idea of a job where she can dress well. Although she is only seventeen, people tell her that she is very mature and she relates well to adults.

Shonda spent the entire weekend going in stores at the mall and asking to speak with the person in charge of employment. She can hardly believe that she completed sixteen job applications. If being thorough, neat, and interested causes people to get jobs, she will have one soon.

Three days have gone by, and Shonda still hasn't heard back form any of the stores where she applied. She feels very discouraged.

a. What can Shonda do to follow up with the applications she made?

____

____

b. Do you think Shonda should wait for the employers she contacted to offer an interview or should she make additional applications? Why?

____

____

____

Practice filling our job applications before you begin submitting them to employers. Fill out the job application on the following pages with the care and thoroughness you would use if you were submitting it to an actual employer. Review the section, "Completing Job Applications," in your textbook before you begin.

1. Critique your job application after you have completed it. Answer **yes** or **no** to each of the following questions.
   a. Is your printing (or typing) neat and easy to read? ____________
   b. Did you spell all of the words correctly? ____________
   c. Is all of the information accurate? ____________
   d. Did you follow all of the directions? ____________
   e. Are the dates correct? ____________
   f. Does the information make you appear to be a good candidate for the job? ____________
   g. If you were an employer reading this application, would you interview the applicant? ____________

   If you filled in the application correctly and properly, all of your answers will be **yes**.

continued

Applicants are considered for all positions without regard to race, color, religion, sex, national origin, citizenship, age, marital or veteran status, or the presence of a non-job-related medical disability or handicap.

MUNICIPAL CIVIL SERVICE COMMISSION
APPLICATION FOR EMPLOYMENT

PERSONAL

Name: ______________________________ Today's Date: __________

Last First Middle

Present Street Address ______________________________ Telephone Number __________

Address City State Zip (Area Code)

Are you under 18? _____ Yes _____ No

For checking prior records, provide other names under which you are known. ______________________

Social Security No.

Are you legally authorized to work in the United States? _____ Yes _____ No
How? _____ U.S. Citizen? _____Visa/Work Permit?

How long have you lived in this city?

GENERAL

Position Desired: __________

Department: ____________

Have you previously taken a Civil Service Test? If so, which test? _________________ When? _______________
Will you need any accommodation to take a civil service test? If yes, specify .

Availability: ___Full-time _____Part-time _____Regular Basis _____ Temporary Basis

Have you ever applied to work here before?
_____ Yes _____ No When? _______________

Have you ever held a civil service position?
_____ Yes _____ No When? _____ Why did you leave? ____________________

Are you able to perform the required duties of the specific job for which you are applying with or without accommodation?
_____ Yes _____ No
If not, please explain: ________________________
____

Do you have any relatives currently employed here?
_____ Yes _____ No

Have you been convicted of a criminal offense? If yes, please give details?
____
____

EDUCATION

	Name and Location	Major Course of Study	Diploma/Degree	Did You Graduate?
High School	____________	____________	____________	____Yes ____No
College	____________	____________	____________	____Yes ____No
Graduate School	____________ ____________	____________ ____________	____________ ____________	____Yes ____No
Other: APPRENTICE, BUSINESS OR VOCATIONAL SCHOOL	____________	____________	____________	____Yes ____No

Are you now attending school? _____ Yes _____ No
__ Full-time __ Part-time

What courses are you taking? ______________________________

List other special training related to the position you are seeking.
____
____

MILITARY

Have you ever been in the U.S. Armed Services or Reserves? _____Yes _____No

Branch of Service: ______________

Discharged: _____Yes _____No

Are you applying for military credit? _____ Yes _____ No If so, please file a copy of your discharge/release with this application.

continued

EMPLOYMENT HISTORY: Beginning with your most recent employer, please list your last three (3) employers:

1. Name of Employer ______ Type of Business ______

Address ______ Phone ______

Dates Employed:
From ________ To ________ Position ______ Salary ______

Name of Supervisor ______ Reason for Leaving ______

Brief description of duties: ______

2. Name of Employer ______ Type of Business ______

Address ______ Phone ______

Dates Employed:
From ________ To ________ Position ______ Salary ______

Name of Supervisor ______ Reason for Leaving ______

Brief description of duties: ______

3. Name of Employer ______ Type of Business ______

Address ______ Phone ______

Dates Employed:
From ________ To ________ Position ______ Salary ______

Name of Supervisor ______ Reason for Leaving ______

Brief description of duties: ______

If you are applying for a police officer position, and you are currently certified as a police officer, please attach copies of your certification documents with this application.

Summarize period of unemployment or periods not accounted for above.

PERSONAL REFERENCES (Employment and School References Requested)

Name ______ Address ______ Occupation ______

Name ______ Address ______ Occupation ______

Name ______ Address ______ Occupation ______

Name ______________________________ Date ______________

8.5 Checkpoint

Being Informed About the Company

1. "Mrs. Stolz will see you now, Mr. Garcia," the receptionist says. Pete Garcia feels a little nervous as he walks into the interviewing office. He can only hope that Mrs. Stolz will be as pleasant as the receptionist in the outer office.

Mrs. Stolz stands up and walks around her large, mahogany desk to shake his hand. "Good morning, Mr. Garcia," she says. I'm looking forward to our interview. Let's sit at the table by the window. It's more comfortable than desk chairs."

As they sit down, Mrs. Stolz asks Pete, "Why would you like to work for our company, Mr. Garcia?" Pete tells her how he read about several insurance companies and talked with employees and customers of the different companies. This company was growing, the employees liked working there, and the customers were satisfied. As he continues talking, the words come more easily.

As Pete leaves the office to go home, he feels satisfied. He knows that it was a good interview.

a. What verbal messages did Pete send to Mrs. Stolz that indicated that he was informed about the company?

____

____

b. What verbal messages did Pete send to Mrs. Stolz that he had a positive opinion about the company?

____

____

2. Select one employer in your community that you might like to work for when you get a full-time job. Using one or more of the sources listed in Figure 8–2, on page 159 of your textbook, learn all you can about the company.

a. What is the name, address, and phone number of company you have selected? ______________

____

b. What is the company's product or service? ______________

c. What were the annual sales last year? ______________

d. How many employees does they company have? ______________

e. How long has the company been in business? ______________

f. Who owns the company? ______________

g. What is its financial standing? ______________

h. What is its reputation as an employer? ______________

i. How would this information help you in an interview and in making a decision about accepting a job offer? ______________

____

Name ______________________ Date ______________________

Checkpoint 8.6

Appearance Makes an Impression

Most companies are concerned about the image they wish to present to the public and about their employees' compatibility with that image. Most employers believe that employees that have pride in themselves will have pride in the company for which they work. When you go to an interview, be well groomed and neatly attired, and project an image of success. Consider the image each of the following job candidates project to potential employers.

Melissa who is seventeen is very nervous about her first important job interview with a large insurance company. She tries to overcome her youthful image with clothes and makeup that would be suitable for a rock star. She doesn't get the job. Once Melissa learns the true purpose of the job interview, she changes to a more conservative image and is successful.

Eugene, who is also seventeen, didn't find work as a data processor right away. Initially he dressed for interviews as he usually dresses—with an earring and a design shaved into his very short hair. He found that most hiring managers are conservative and have middle-class values, and he felt that they were uncomfortable with him. He did find success when dressed in a suit and tie, with the hairstyle and image of a well-groomed working man.

1. What opinion do you think the first interviewer had of Melissa? ______________________

   What opinion do you think the first interviewer had of Eugene? ______________________

2. People dress as they perceive themselves. Which of the two job seekers has the weakest self-image? What indications support your position? ______________________

3. Consider your present image. How would your appearance (hair, clothing, posture, fingernails, shoes, teeth, accessories) measure up in an employment interview? Explain your answer. ______________________

4. If you were a career counselor, what advice would you give Melissa? ______________________

   Eugene? ______________________

Name ______________________________ Date ____________________

8.7 Successful and Unsuccessful Job Interviews

1. Tyler Little is very excited about his interview with **Starworks**. He can imagine the car he will buy, the clothes he will have, and how his friends will look up to him when he gets the job. **Starworks** owns a very large factory complex, and the office where he will interview is located in a very modern high-rise building.

   "What time is your interview, Tyler?" His mom's voice interrupts his dream of success, and he realizes that the interview is in an hour. Tyler takes a quick shower, puts on the clothes he wore to the game last night, and hurries to the corner bus stop.

   A bright yellow customized car pulls over to the curb, and the driver waves. It is Tyler's friend, Sean, coming to his rescue. "Jump in, Tyler. I have my dad's wheels all day. You look cool, man, I like the chain. Where am I taking you?" Tyler explains where he is going and that he is already a couple of minutes late.

   Within ten minutes, Sean and Tyler walk in the door of **Starworks**' personnel office. Tyler tells the secretary who he is and asks if she would please let the boss know he is ready for the interview. Sean tells her that he wouldn't mind having an interview, also, if they have plenty of jobs.

   a. Review "Interviewing Tactics" in Chapter 8 of your textbook, and list all of the accepted interviewing tactics that Tyler violated. Explain how he violated each tactic you list.

   ____

   ____

   ____

   ____

   ____

2. The following lists of reasons people are hired or not hired after a job interview were taken from a publication by the Texas Advisory Council for Vocational Education. They reflect the survey responses of 1,695 employers.

Reasons People Are Not Hired	**Reasons People Are Hired**
Little interest or poor reasons for wanting a job	Interest shown in the job
Past history of job-hopping	Recommendations from previous employers
Inability to communicate during the job interview	Previous work experience
Inadequate health record	Adequate health record
Immaturity (other than chronological age)	Maturity (other than chronological age)
Sloppy personal appearance	Well-groomed personal appearance
Poor manners and mannerisms	Good manners and mannerisms
Unsuitable pesonality	Suitable personality
Lack of job-related skills	Strong education and training background
Poorly filled-out job application	High ambitions

continued

a. You will probably not be surprised to find out that Tyler was turned down for employment with **Starworks**. Review and compare Robert Castile's interview (he was hired) on page 164 of your textbook with that of Tyler.

b. What reasons might have influenced an employer's decision to hire Robert and not to hire Tyler?

____

____

3. Several reasons for hiring or not hiring one applicant over another are the same.

   a. What personality characteristics do you believe an employer would like in an employee? What personality characteristics would an employer probably dislike in an employee?

   ____

   ____

   b. What can an applicant do to demonstrate interest in the job for which he or she is being interviewed?

   ____

   ____

   ____

   c. What manners or mannerisms probabaly influence an interviewer positively? Negatively?

   ____

   ____

   d. What should a person do about personal appearance to impress a potential employer?

   ____

   ____

   e. What is meant by maturity and immaturity?

   ____

   ____

4. Of the reasons listed in question 2 for hiring an applicant, which two reasons would you select as most important?

   a. ____

   b. ____

5. Which two reasons from the first list would be most important to you in rejecting one applicant over another? Why?

   a. ____

   b. ____

Name ______________________________ Date ____________________

Checkpoint 8.8

Part-time and Summertime Jobs

Your first job will probably be a part-time or summer job. The job possibilities are more limited than they will be when you have more education and training, but what employers expect will not change. Use the information you have learned thus far when applying for part-time or summer employment.

1. Prepare for the interview as if it were the most important job of your life. The success of most interviews is determined by the skill demonstrated in communicating answers to specific questions. The interviewer will already have formed an opinion of you based on your job application or résumé. He or she will be looking you over and checking information about your school attendance, attitude, work values, goals, job experience, and job expectations.

   Imagine that the employer whose job application you completed in Checkpoint 8.4 has invited you to interview for the job. Write your responses to the following questions.

Employer's Questions	Your Response
a. Why do you want this job? Why do you want to work for our organization?	
b. What can you contribute to our company that would make us hire you over others?	
c. We need someone with experience. What kind of experience can you offer us?	
d. What high school courses have you taken that will help you on this job? What were your grades? What was your GPA?	
e. What are your strongest and weakest skills for this job?	
f. Tell me about yourself.	
g. How many days of school did you miss this year. What about last year?	
h. Do you prefer working closely with others or mostly by yourself?	
i. How did previous employers or teachers treat you?	
j. What would previous employers or teachers say about you?	

continued

2. What will your answer to question *(a)* tell the employer about your goals?

____

____

3. What will your answer to question *(g)* tell the employer about your reliability?

____

____

4. What will your answers to questions *(i)* and *(j)* tell the employer about your attitude?

____

____

5. What will your answer to question *(h)* tell the employer about your ability to get along with others in work relationships?

____

____

6. Which of the following would be ***easy*** for you in a part-time or summer job? Which would be ***difficult***? Write your answers (***easy*** or ***difficult***) in the space provided.

    a. Taking and following orders from supervisors ____________
    b. Expressing a positive attitude ____________
    c. Following instructions and handling criticism ____________
    d. Being responsible and using care in handling tools and equipment ____________
    e. Thinking before speaking ____________
    f. Listening carefully ____________
    g. Being courteous and respectful to customers at all times ____________
    h. Performing a full day's work ____________
    i. Responding to stress in an acceptable manner ____________
    j. Being reliable and on time ____________
    k. Being pleasant in appearance and personal hygiene ____________
    l. Keeping your personal life from interfering with the job ____________
    m. Cooperating with co-workers ____________
    n. Following policies and procedures ____________

continued

7. a. How many items in question 6 would you find easy?____________________

   b. How many would be difficult?____________________

   c. Look closely at those you marked difficult. What can you do to improve in these areas?

   ____

   ____

   ____

8. Read Checkpoint 2.5 on skills again. List four skills you will bring to a part-time or summer job.

   a. __________ b. __________ c. __________ d. __________

9. Read Checkpoint 3.2 on work values again. List four work values you will bring to a part-time or summer job.

   a. __________ b. __________ c. __________ d. __________

10. How could working at a part-time or summer job that closely matches your personal orientation help you make a long-term decision?

    ____

    ____

    ____

Career tip: Your search for summer work should be under way by spring break.

"SEND THE REST OF THE APPLICANTS HOME, MRS. JONES.. WE'VE FOUND THE RIGHT CANDIDATE FOR THE JOB!.."

Name ______________________________ Date ______________________

8.9 Checkpoint

Finding the Right Words

Chapter 8 of your textbook contains numerous terms that employers and workers use. Recognizing and understanding these terms will help you make the important career decisions you will soon face. Fill in the missing vowels in the vocabulary terms in column B, and match them with the definitions in column A.

Column A	Column B
1. _____ a statement containing information that employers require before hiring new employees	a. F___ ___r L___b___r St___nd___rds ___ct
2. _____ laws that protect all workers, including laws governing the employment of minors.	b. c___v___l s___rv___c___ ___x___m___n___t___ ___n
3. _____ a document that states that you don't have an infectious disease	c. h___ ___lth c___rt___f___c___t___
4. _____ a form from the Immigration and Naturalization Service or the Department of Labor	d. j___b ___ppl___c___t___ ___n f___rm
5. _____ a type of insurance that pays financial losses if an employee fails to perform his or her duty or is guilty of theft	e. ___mpl___ym___nt ___l___g___b___l___ty v___r___f___c___t___ ___n f___rm
6. _____ a serious crime	f. b___nd
7. _____ a government preemployment test	g. f___l___ny
8. _____ true and supported by facts	h. ___n___t___ ___t___v___
9. _____ readiness and ability to take the first steps in any undertaking	i. v___l___d
10. _____ the workers who are responsible for recruiting and hiring new employees	j. f___ ___r ___mpl___ym___nt pr___gr___m
11. _____ a program that helps employers actively seek to hire minorities	k. j___b ___ff___r
12. _____ an employer's formal proposal of employment	l. p___rs___nn___l d___p___rtm___nt

continued

13. _____ a position that provides you with an opportunity to assume adult responsibilities

14. _____ to contribute free labor

15. _____ a business that "rents" employees to employers

16. _____ a document required for employees under 18 in most nonfarm jobs

17. _____ an investigation of former employers, schools, and references

18. _____ a test that determines how well you are likely to perform in a certain area of work

19. _____ an opportunity to present yourself in person to an employer

20. _____ the lowest wage an employer may pay for certain types of work

m. w __ r k   p __ r m __ t

n. b __ c k g r __ __ n d   c h __ c k

o. p r __ __ m p l __ y m __ n t   t __ s t

p. t __ m p __ r __ r y   s __ r v __ c __

q. __ n t __ r v __ __ w

r. m __ n __ m __ m   w __ g __

s. v __ l __ n t __ __ r

t. f __ l l -t __ m __   j __ b

Name ______________________________ Date ____________________

Checkpoint 8.10

Checking Your Location

1. For each of the following statements, circle **F** if the statement is more false than true. Circle **T** if the statement is more true than false.

T F a. Job applications become legal documents once they are signed and dated.

T F b. You no longer need a work permit when you turn sixteen years old.

T F c. The applicant's skill in communicating answers to specific questions determines the success of most job interviews.

T F d. The Civil Rights Act of 1964 contains the Equal Employment Opportunity Law.

T F e. Some companies like to use temporary help because it saves them the expense of hiring full-time employees that they will only need for a short time.

T F f. Employers cannot use job applications to screen out unqualified applicants before job interviews are conducted.

T F g. The Fair Labor Standards Act protects most workers but does not include laws governing the employment of minors.

T F h. The federal government cannot limit or regulate the right of foreign citizens to be employed in the United States.

T F i. Most employers consider preemployment tests to be an objective and unbiased method for evaluating potential employees.

T F j. Learning all you can about an employer's business operations will help you make a wiser decision if you are offered a job.

T F k. The initial impression you communicate to an employer is regarded by many employers as a weak indication of what you will be like as an employee.

T F l. How effectively you present yourself in the interview will probably determine whether or not you get a job offer.

T F m. Being prepared for the interview is important because you have a limited amount of time to convince the interviewer why you should be hired.

continued

T F n. Affirmative Action and Fair Employment programs enable employers to identify minority group candidates so they can increase their numbers of minority employees.

T F o. It is good business manners to write a letter expressing your appreciation for time spent during an interview and to inform the interviewer whether you are interested in the job.

2. Use the space below to rewrite the statements you marked **false** and make them **true**. Include the letter of each statement you rewrite.

Name ______________________________ Date ______________________

Checkpoint 9.1

Attitude — The Great Communicator

You send attitude messages to people every day. Some of your messages are positive; others are negative. Your attitude can be revealed by what you say (verbally), by your appearance, or by your actions.

1. Imagine that you are the manager of a large department store. You have the authority to hire, fire, promote, and give raises to employees. For each of the following situations, mark the type of attitude message the employee is sending you.

Attitude Message Sent by Employee	Positive or Negative?	Verbal, Action, or Appearance?	Mature or Immature?
Example: Has a firm handshake	Positive	Action	Mature
1. Wears dirty clothing to work			
2. Arrives early for work			
3. Breaks expensive glass merchandise and laughs			
4. Tells a co-worker, "Do it yourself. It's not my job"			
5. Thanks a co-worker for a suggestion			
6. Listens patiently to an obnoxious customer			
7. Arrives late for work at least once a week			
8. Insults a customer			
9. Uses incorrect grammar when speaking to customers			
10. Gives co-workers a helping hand whenever possible			
11. Is frequently absent from work with very weak excuses			
12. Wears clean, appropriate clothing to work			

2. Imagine that you are selecting an employee for promotion or considering someone for a pay raise. Which three positive attitude messages from the preceding list would be most important to you? Write their numbers below, and explain the reason for each decision.

   a. Number: _____ Reason: ______________________________

   ____

   b. Number: _____ Reason: ______________________________

   ____

   c. Number: _____ Reason: ______________________________

   ____

Name ______________________________ Date ______________________

Checkpoint 9.2

What's Your Usual Attitude?

Your attitude is a reflection of your inner feelings. It influences your work, and your work influences your attitude.

1. How would you feel about and respond to the following situations?

   a. You are a salesperson in a clothing store. A customer yells at you because the dye in a shirt he purchased from you faded when he washed it. The customer slams the faded garment on your counter, demands his money back, and threatens to sue your store.

      How does this make you feel? ______________________________

      What do you say or do? ______________________________

      ____

   b. You are an airplane mechanic. The airplane you are working on is scheduled to fly in twelve more hours. You spent the first four hours of your shift finding an engine problem and acquiring the necessary parts. Your shift ends in four hours, and you will need about six hours to complete the repairs.

      How does this make you feel? ______________________________

      What do you say or do? ______________________________

      ____

   c. You are an accountant. It is Friday, and you are collecting information about production costs to help write a budget for your employer. You were told that the information would not be due for another week, but this afternoon your boss tells you that she needs it Monday morning. You will have to work all weekend to complete your assignment.

      How does this make you feel? ______________________________

      What do you say or do? ______________________________

      ____

2. In which situation did you maintain the most positive attitude? Why was this situation easiest for you?

   ____

   ____

3. In which situation were you least able to maintain a positive attitude? Why was this situation most difficult for you? ______________________________

   ____

4. *Career Tip:* As you consider future occupations, keep in mind the following:
   * Situation *a* entails working with people.
   * Situation *b* entails working with things (tools and machines).
   * Situation *c* entails working with data (information and numbers).

Name ______________________________ Date ____________________

9.3 Checkpoint

Rate Your Work Values

Consider the list of worker behaviors below. You may consider some of these behaviors to be very important and others to be less important. Use the following rating scale to rate each behavior from 1 to 5, according to your personal work values.

Rating Scale

5 = Very important	2 = Not very important
4 = Somewhat important	1 = Unimportant
3 = Of average importance	

	Worker Behavior	**Your Rating**
Example:	Always addresses a boss as "Sir" or "Ma'am"	3
1.	Spends additional time when necessary to complete a work task	_____
2.	Uses care in handling tools and equipment	_____
3.	Leaves his or her work area and equipment in good condition	_____
4.	Thinks before speaking and listens carefully	_____
5.	Is cooperative with supervisors, co-workers, and customers	_____
6.	Assumes responsibility for acquiring needed skills	_____
7.	Consistently arrives at work on time	_____
8.	Maintains a high level of personal cleanliness and grooming	_____
9.	Responds to stress in a mature, appropriate manner	_____
10.	Demonstrates an interest in learning new skills	_____

1. a. Total your score for the ten worker behaviors. Write the total here: _____

   b. Compare your total to the following guidelines.

Score	**Guidelines for Understanding**
50	Most employers would agree with you.
40 – 49	Your answers were thoughtful and positive. You have a good understanding of what employers expect.
30 – 39	Check the behaviors you rated lowest. Review the section "Beginning a New Job" in Chapter 9.
5 – 29	Your score indicates a very unrealistic understanding of what employers expect from employees. Discuss your answers with a successful worker. Review the section "Beginning a New Job" in Chapter 9.

Name ______________________________ Date ____________________

9.4 Checkpoint

Legitimate Absence or Not?

On the job, your supervisor and co-workers will depend on you. What are legitimate reasons for being absent from work?

Imagine that you are the assistant manager of a large grocery store. You are responsible for hiring and training employees and operating the store efficiently. How would you handle the following situation?

> You hired William three months ago as a part-time bagger. He works three hours each evening after school during the store's busiest time. When the cashier has to bag groceries, the checkout line slows, customers become angry, and business is lost. In fact, you must either pull another employee off of his or her job to bag groceries or do it yourself.
>
> William is a very efficient worker, displays a pleasant attitude, and had perfect attendance for the first two months. However, he has phoned in sick each of the past three Thursdays. He always phones your office at about 11:30 a.m. When you phoned the school attendance office, a worker there informed you that William wasn't absent from school on the days he missed work. When you phoned William's home, his mother told you he was at work.

1. It is Friday evening, and William has just arrived at work. He was absent yesterday, and you know he attended school and wasn't home sick. You ask William to report to your office. You very calmly tell William everything you know about the situation and ask him for an explanation. Use the following lines to write William's explanation.

   ____

   ____

   ____

   ____

2. a. Do you believe William's explanation? ____ Explain your answer. ______________________________

   ____

   ____

   b. Describe the course of action you will take. ______________________________

   ____

   ____

   c. Will your course of action cause the store to operate more efficiently? If so, how? If not, why are you following this course of action? ______________________________

   ____

   d. Will the other employees think you have treated William with fairness? How will your course of action influence your relations with the other workers? ______________________________

   ____

Name ______________________________ Date ____________________

Checkpoint 9.5

Finding the Right Words

Chapter 9 of your textbook contains numerous terms that employers and workers use. Recognizing and understanding these terms will help you make the important career decisions you will soon face.

Fill in the blank spaces in the vocabulary terms to complete the following sentences.

1. You demonstrate a (p __ s __ __ i __ e   a __ __ i __ u __ e) when you are courteous, cooperative, and considerate with your co-workers and superiors.
2. (C __ m p __ t __ n c __) is another word for "being capable."
3. People who help others project a desired image are called (__ __ a __ e   c __ n s __ __ t __ __ t __).
4. (S __ h e __ __ l __ __   __ r __ __ k __) are rest periods that employers provide so employees can take time out from the workday to relax, have refreshments, handle personal needs, or socialize with co-workers.
5. A (l __ g __ t __ __ __ t __   __ b __ __ n c __) occurs when an employee must miss work for a reason that is acceptable to the employer.
6. (__ n t __ r d __ p __ n d __ n c __) occurs when you depend on a group and the group depends on you.
7. (S __ __ __ s s) is another work for "tension."
8. Meetings or activities to acquaint you with the employer's purpose and organization are called (j __ b __ r __ __ n t __ t __ __ n) programs.
9. Training (__ a __ u a __ __) detail the use or repair of equipment or describe procedures to follow on the job.
10. (__ u __ __ e __ s) is a favorable result or a hoped-for ending.
11. All employers have a unique set of rules known as (p __ l __ c __ __ s) and (__ __ o __ e __ u __ e __).
12. The level of ethusiasm displayed by workers in the workplace is called their (m __ r __ l __).
13. The first few weeks and months on a new job make up an (__ r __ __ n t __ t __ __ n   p __ r __ __ d).
14. Your highest level of productivity is referred to as your (f __ l __   p __ t __ n t __ __ l).
15. A (p __ __ b __ t __ __ n __ __ y   p __ r __ o __) is a specific period of time in which you are expected to prove your ability to perform the job.
16. There is much to be said for "looking the part" in terms of success in a company. In Figure 9.1 in your textbook, (p __ r __ __ n __ l   __ p p __ __ r __ n __ e) ranked eighth out of eleven success factors.

Name ______________________________ Date ____________________

9.6 Checkpoint

Checking Your Location

1. For each of the following statements, circle **F** if the statement is more false than true. Circle **T** if the statement is more true than false.

T F a. Attitudes affect the way people get along at home, at school, and at work.

T F b. Many attitudes are learned in early childhood.

T F c. After you learn to be interdependent, your next step is to become a member of society at the highest level; independence.

T F d. Attitudes toward work and personal responsibility start at school

T F e. On a new job, you must learn the particular duties and responsibilities you were hired to perform, and your performance must meet your employer's expectations.

T F f. On a new job, you must learn the particular duties and responsibilities you were hired to perform, and your performance must meet your employer's expectations.

T F g. Motivation to succeed is frequently based on the need to survive, to gain social approval, or to obtain self-respect.

T F h. Successful people know their values and have learned to listen to them. Another word for the values that help us make decisions is *conscience*.

T F i. Once you have been hired, your supervisor and your closest co-workers will have considerable influence on your career success.

T F j. On the job, dress with enough fashion to be noticed. If you dress like a boss, you will be promoted much faster.

T F k. On the job, your supervisor and co-workers will depend on you. Your absence could affect other workers' ability to proceed with their jobs.

T F l. Your employer will expect you to be ready to work at starting time, stay until quitting time, and take no more than the allotted time for lunch and other scheduled breaks.

T F m. Many of your employer's policies and procedures will be confusing. Using your own judgment will eliminate most confusing situations.

continued

T **F** n. Much of your job success will depend on how well you follow your employer's policies and procedures.

T **F** o. Getting along well with others will help you enjoy your work, and your supervisor will appreciate your cooperative attitude.

2. Use the space below to rewrite the statements you marked **false** and make them **true**. Include the letter of each statement you rewrite.

____

____

____

____

____

____

"WHEN SHE SAID 'WE'RE ALL ONE BIG HAPPY FAMILY AT BIG BURGER', I DIDN'T REALIZE MY JOB WOULD BE TO TAKE OUT THE GARBAGE..."

Name ______________________________ Date ____________________

10.1 Fitting into the Corporate Culture

Understanding your employer's corporate culture will help you learn what personal behavior and job performance are expected.

1. Make an appointment to visit a local business workplace. A working parent, friend, or neighbor can probably give you the name of a contact person in the organization where he or she is employed. Record the following information:

   a. The name of the business you visited: ______________________________

   b. The product or service the business manufactures or provides: ______________________________

2. Observe the type (style) and purpose of clothing worn by specific workers.

Occupation of Worker	Type and Purpose of Clothing Worn
a.____________	______________________________
b.____________	______________________________
c.____________	______________________________

3. Observe the style (grammar) and purpose of verbal communication used by workers.

Occupation of Worker	Style and Purpose of Verbal Communication
a.____________	______________________________
b.____________	______________________________
c.____________	______________________________

4. Observe the form and purpose of written communication used by workers.

Occupation of Worker	Form and Purpose of Written Communication
a.____________	______________________________
b.____________	______________________________
c.____________	______________________________

5. Do the employees seem to get along with one another? ______________________________

   a. What specific employee behaviors did you observe that support your opinion? ____________

   ____

   ____

   ____

6. Based on your observations, describe the corporate culture of the organization you visited. (*Helpful hint*: Review the section "Conforming to the Organization" in Chapter 10 of your textbook).

7. Overall, would you fit in with the corporate culture of this employer? Explain your answer.

Name ______________________ Date ______________________

10.2 Checkpoint

Being Supervised

Imagine that today is your first day on the job and you are feeling nervous. Certain questions are going through your mind. What will your new boss expect? Will your job performance be acceptable? What will it be like to have a boss? It occurs to you that school and work are very similar. Having regular attendance, being on time, completing your assignments on schedule, getting along with co-workers, and following the supervisor's instructions are all part of being successful on the job.

Write your response to each of the following work situations.

1. It is your first week on the job. Your new boss is giving you directions. She speaks very rapidly, and you are not sure what she expects you to do.
   a. How do you handle the situation? ______________________
   b. What impression do you expect your response to have on your boss? ______________________
2. It is your second week on the job. You arrive twenty minutes late to work because of unusually heavy traffic. Your boss gives you a lecture and a warning.
   a. How do you handle the situation? ______________________
   b. What impression do you expect your response to have on your boss? ______________________
3. It is your third week on the job. You are doing household chores on your day off and plan to attend a movie with friends during the evening. The boss phones you at home. She is shorthanded and wants you to work this evening.
   a. How do you handle the situation? ______________________
   b. What impression do you expect your response to have on your boss? ______________________
4. It is your fourth week on the job. The boss calls you to her office. She is upset because the project you are working on is two days late and still unfinished. In fact, you are doing most of the work, and your two co-workers are not doing their share. Both of your co-workers have more than ten years of service.
   a. How do you handle the situation? ______________________
   b. What impression do you expect your response to have on your boss? ______________________

Name ______________________ Date ______________

10.3 Checkpoint

Getting Along with Co-workers

Building positive relationships with co-workers is an important part of career success. Whether or not you like certain co-workers, you must interact with them on the job. Consider the students in your class as co-workers as you complete the following activity.

1. *Be respectful and accept the differences of others.*

   a. Describe a situation in which a person didn't agree with your position and it turned out that he or she was right and you were wrong. ______________________

   b. What did you do when you discovered you were wrong? ______________________

   c. Did your action strengthen or weaken your relationship with the other person? ______________

   d. If you had it to do over again, how would you handle your behavior in this situation? ______________

2. *Don't start or repeat rumors.*

   a. Describe a time when you started or repeated a rumor about someone or when another person started or repeated a rumor about you. ______________________

   b. Were feelings or reputations injured by the rumor? ______________________

   c. Did you attempt to make the situation better? If so, how? If no, why not? ______________

continued

d. If you had it to do over again, how would you handle your behavior in this situation? ____________

3. *Give credit where credit is due.* People like recognition and appreciation

   a. Describe a situation in which another person praised your work or behavior or did something for you to demonstrate his or her appreciation. ____________

   b. How did you respond? How did you feel? ____________

   c. Describe a situation when you praised another person's work or behavior or did something to demonstrate your appreciation. ____________

   d. How did the other respond? How did he or she appear to feel? ____________

4. *Mind your own business.*

   a. Describe a situation in which someone asked you a question or interfered with a task you were performing that was clearly none of his or her business. ____________

   b. What feelings or emotions did you have as a result of the other person's interference? ____________

   c. How did you handle the situation? ____________

continued

5. *Be a good listener.*

   a. Describe a situation in which you were having an important conversation and the other person continually interrupted you. ______

   b. What feelings or emotions did you have as a result of the other person's continual interruption? ______

   c. At the conclusion of the conversation, did you understand the other person's point of view? ______

   d. Did the other person understand your point of view? ______

   e. Were you a good listener? ______

   f. Was the other person a good listener? ______

   g. If you had it to do over again, how would you have handled your behavior in this conversation? ______

6. *Don't make excuses.*

   a. Describe a situation in which another person was very late or didn't remember an important appointment with you. ______

   b. How did the other person's behavior influence your feelings toward him or her? ______

   c. If you were an employer, how would you handle the situation when a worker make excuses for failing to be on time or complete work projects on schedule? ______

continued

7. *Don't be a complainer.*

a. Describe a situation in which you took part in a group project and one person in the group complained, complained, complained. ______________________________

____

____

b. How did you react to the complainer? ______________________________

____

____

c. How did the complainer's behavior influence the outcome of the project? ______________________________

____

____

Name ______________________________ Date ______________

10.4 Checkpoint

Moving Up the Career Ladder

Career advancement is normally accompanied by increased income and prestige. Interview a friend, neighbor, or family member with twenty or more years of work experience. Ask the following questions.

1. What is the title of your present position? ______________________________

2. How long have you had this particular position? ______________________________

3. What was the title of your first full-time occupation? ______________________________

4. a. What was the most important or satisfying promotion you received during your career?

   ____

   From : ______________ To: ______________

   b. What factors caused you to receive this promotion? ______________________________

   ____

   ____

5. Did you ever find it necessary to acquire additional education or training to qualify yourself for a promotion? If so, what additional education or training did you acquire? If not, how did you qualify for the promotion? ______________________________

   ____

   ____

6. A mentor is a boss you admire who also serves as a role model. The mentor likes you, acts as an adviser, and helps you move up the career ladder. Did you ever have a mentor? If so, describe the situation and the effect your mentor had on your career. If not, what effect do you think the absence of a mentor had on your career? ______________________________

   ____

   ____

   ____

7. Based on your experience, do you think "who you know" is more or less important than "what you know"? Could you share an example? ______________________________

   ____

   ____

   ____

continued

8. a. Are the factors that cause workers to get promotions different for today's world of work than they were when you started your career? ______________________________

____

____

b. Please describe any factors that have changed. ______________________________

____

____

____

c. Please describe any factors that haven't changed. ______________________________

____

____

____

9. What advice would you give to beginning workers to help them move up the career ladder? ______

____

____

____

"I LIKE YOUR IDEAS, BUT I WISH YOU WOULD MAKE A LITTLE MORE EFFORT TO FIT IN..."

Name ______________________ Date ______________________

10.5 Checkpoint

Working Together

Helpful hint: Review the section "Labor Unions" in Chapter 10 of your textbook before beginning this activity.

> Tracy Ewing recently completed her tech-prep program earning an associate degree in electrocardiograph technology. After a job search of several weeks, two health-care organizations have offered her jobs. The jobs and the employers seem very similar, with one exception: The employees of one organization are represented by a union, and the employees of the other organization are not.

Imagine that Tracy has asked you to help her compare and evaluate the two job offers. In each of the following cases, circle the option that you prefer most.

1. I prefer that my wages and hours of employment be established by:

   a. bargaining between a union (including myself and my co-workers) and my employer.

   b. my employer.

   Briefly describe the reasons for your preference. ______________________

   ____

   ____

2. When a difference of opinion arises between workers and management, I would prefer:

   a. to accept the opinion of an impartial third party.

   b. to accept the decision of my employer or resign.

   Briefly describe the reasons for your preference. ______________________

   ____

   ____

3. When bargaining between my employer and union fails and my co-workers vote to strike, I would prefer:

   a. to strike until the employer agrees to an acceptable compromise.

   b. to accept the employer's terms and continue working.

   Briefly describe the reasons for your preference. ______________________

   ____

   ____

continued

4. During periods of recession or when work is slow, I would prefer that my employer lay off:

   a. employees with less service first.

   b. employees they consider to be less productive or less qualified first.

   Briefly describe the reasons for your preference. ______________________________

   ____

   ____

5. How many of your preferences were ***a***'s? _____ How many were ***b***'s? _____
   In general, the ***a*** preferences represent the position of most union members, and the ***b*** preferences represent the position of most employers.

6. Would you advise Tracy to accept the job with the unionized or nonunion employer? Briefly describe the reasons for your advice. ______________________________

   ____

   ____

   ____

Name ______________________________ Date ____________________

10.6 Checkpoint

Safety in the Workplace

Many of the factors involved in personal health and safety on-the-job can be controlled.

1. It was Tyrone's first day on the job with the E.W. Heslop Chair Company. The supervisor asked Tyrone if he knew how to operate a table saw. Tyrone explained that he had never used that type of tool. The supervisor demonstrated how to use a pattern and cut pieces of wood for a chair frame. Within twenty minutes, the supervisor returned to her office, and Tyrone was working alone. An hour later, Tyrone's scream pierced the air, louder than all of the noisy machines in the shop. Tyrone made one mistake, he forgot to use one safety device, and lost his right hand forever.

   a. What action could the supervisor have taken to prevent this accident? ____________________

   b. What action could Tyrone have taken to prevent this accident? ____________________

   c. Who is responsible for this accident? Explain your point of view. ____________________

2. Margo is a machinist employed by the West Shore Tool and Die Corporation. Frank operates an overhead crane. He moves large metal dies and lowers them to Margo's machine. When Margo is finished with a die, Frank uses the crane to remove it. Margo remains in the area under the crane to give Frank hand signals. Frank provides similar assistance to several machinists.

   Last week, Margo discovered that Frank has a drinking problem. While helping him lift a 50-lb tool by hand, Margo noticed the odor of alcohol on Frank's breath. During a break, she noticed the odor of alcohol coming from Frank's thermos bottle. Margo also noticed that Frank occasionally slurs his speech.

   Four days later, Frank's crane dropped a metal die on one of Margo's co-workers. The plant security officer proved that Frank was intoxicated at the time of the accident. The co-worker remains in critical condition.

   a. What action could Frank have taken to prevent this accident? ____________________

   b. What action could Margo have taken to prevent this accident? ____________________

   c. Who is responsible for this accident? Explain your point of view. ____________________

Name ______________________________ Date ____________________

10.7

Checkpoint

Finding the Right Works

Chapter 10 of your textbook contains numerous terms that employers and workers use. Recognizing and understanding these terms will help you make the important career decisions you will soon face.

Unscramble the terms in column B, and match them with the definitions in column A. (Some terms contain two words.)

Column A	Column B
1. Example: __a__ the paid and unpaid work you do during your lifetime	a. CAREER RAREEC
2. _____ differences of opinion over the interpretation of a labor contract	b. ____________________ TELLIVCECO GRAINGABIN
3. _____ the lowest level of job experience	c. ____________________ METI GAMETEAMNN
4. _____ the negotiating process between labor unions and employers	d. ____________________ ROPECORAT TRUELUC
5. _____ an organization that represents workers in negotiations with their employer	e. ____________________ VANRICESEG
6. _____ a member of the supervisor's staff	f. ____________________ KROW CITHE
7. _____ planning ahead to make the best use of your time	g. ____________________ RENTY VEELL
8. _____ the thoughts, feelings, manners, and sense of good taste each business or organization develops	h. ____________________ RABOL NUNIO
9. _____ the idea that through hard work individuals can make their own success	i. ____________________ BROADENSUIT
10. _____ workers who work as a group to identify and solve quality problems	j. ____________________ CORKSOWER
11. _____ people who work together and rely on one another to complete work assignments	k. ____________________ RISETINYO
12. _____ the supervisor in a team management system	l. ____________________ MEAT SAVERDI
13. _____ the length of time spent with an employer	m. ____________________ ITYALUQ RICECL

Name ____________________ Date ____________________

10.8

Checking Your Location

1. For each of the following statements, circle **F** if the statement is more false than true. Circle **T** if the statement is more true than false.

T F a. Unless you have previous experience, your first job with an employer will probably be at the entry level.

T F b. What is acceptable in one work setting may not be acceptable in another.

T F c. In a large organization, your immediate supervisor will have little influence on your future progress.

T F d. Traditional control-oriented management produces the highest levels of productivity.

T F e. Your ability to get along with your supervisor depends a lot on your attitude toward criticism and authority.

T F f. Sooner or later, you will probably have a boss you don't like or one who doesn't like you. The best solution is to quite the job and find a better boss.

T F g. Most full-time employees spend more of their waking hours with co-workers than with family and friends.

T F h. Having lunch or taking your breaks with the workplace gossips is a good way to find out what is going on in the organization.

T F i. Finding humor in a bad situation makes it less stressful.

T F j. The best predictor of future performance is past performance.

T F k. If you become the supervisor of your former co-workers, personal relationships will change.

T F l. The purpose of the National Labor Relations Board is to administer, interpret, and enforce the National Labor Relations Act.

T F m. Where management has been receptive and where workers' interests have been adequately reflected, unions have increasingly shown a willingness to work with management for the overall success of the enterprise.

continued

T F n. More than thirty-five hundred workers die each year in job-related accidents. More than six million lose time because of injuries that happen on the job.

T F o. In nearly every type of workplace injury studied, workers have accidents despite receiving safety training and information.

2. Use the space below to rewrite the statements you marked **false** and make them **true**. Include the letter of each statement you rewrite.

Name ______________________________ Date ____________________

Checkpoint 11.1

Self-Evaluation

Evaluators must be objective if they are to evaluate employees accurately. Be honest, objective, and accurate as you complete the following self-evaluation. Review each of the following situations. Then use the rating scale to rate how often you would probably respond in a certain way.

Rating Scale
1 = Almost always
2 = Usually
3 = About half of the time
4 = Not usually
5 = Almost never

Situation	Your Rating
Example: When I date a person for the first time, I feel very uncomfortable.	4
a. When I am with a group of friends and they ask for my opinion, I am able to speak clearly and present my views effectively.	______
b. When I am required to write information on a job application, a driver's license form, or other required applications or forms, my writing is neat and legible and presents information effectively.	______
c. When I take part in activities that require skill (sports, board games, musical performances, etc.) with my friends, I have the skills needed to be an effective participant.	______
d. When I am at home or involved with my friends, I am dependable and accurate in carrying out my responsibilities.	______
e. When I am involved in a disagreement with a friend or family member, I handle the situation in a calm, objective manner.	______
f. When I am involved in a group work activity with friends or family members, I am cooperative and open to suggestions from other members of the group.	______
g. When I belong to an athletic team, club, or other social organization, I have good attendance and show up on time for scheduled meetings or events.	______
h. When I am in a classroom and the teacher asks for my opinion, I am able to speak clearly and present my views effectively.	______
i. When I perform everyday written assignments at school, my writing is neat and legible and presents information effectively.	______

continued

j. When I take part in major academic classes at school (English, math, science, social studies), I have the skills needed to be an effective participant. ________

k. When I am at school, I am dependable and accurate in completing my assignments and other responsibilities. ________

l. When I am involved in a disagreement with a teacher or a student I dislike, I handle the situation in a calm, objective manner. ________

m. When teachers make group assignments, I am cooperative and open to suggestions from other members of the group. ________

n. I have good attendance at school. I am seldom late for classes. ________

2. a. In question 1, you rated yourself in fourteen situations. Each situation represents a major area of concern for employers. Expect to be in similar job situations when you join the work force. Now, total your fourteen scores, and write the total here: _____

b. Scores will range from a possible low of 14 to a possible high of 70. The following table will help you interpret your self-evaluation.

Your Score	A Career Counselor's Intrepretation of your Score
14	Three strong possibilities exist: (1) You are exceptional, (2) you avoided a decision by rating each item with a 1, or (3) you have difficulty accepting your weaknesses.
15 – 20	Are you closer to a score of 14 or 21? Check the advice for both. Employers will appreciate several of your positive, mature responses. Review the situations in which you gave yourself a score of two or higher. Work to improve in these areas.
21	Employers will expect you to display positive attitudes and mature behaviors and to perform at an expected skill level "almost always." They will expect you to be on time, be cooperative, be dependable, and be able to perform the job tasks every day. Rethink the situations in which you rated yourself 2 or higher. Work to improve yourself in these areas.
22 – 27	Are you closer to a score of 21 or 28? Check the advice for both.
28	Your average response was a 2, "usually," but this will not be good enough in the world of work. Review your ratings of two or higher. What can you do to improve?
29 – 41	Are you closer to a score of 28 or 42? Check the advice for both.
42	You react in a positive way and at an expected level about "half of the time." If you owned a business, would you hire or keep a worker, who followed instructions, showed up for work, was on time for work, and demonstrated adequate job skills only about half the time? Review the section "Employer's Evaluate Performance" in Chapter 11 of your textbook.
43 – 70	Are you serious about your future career and lifestyle? Do you expect to qualify for postsecondary education and training? Do you plan to have high-paying, steady employment throughout your career? If your answer to these questions is yes, it's time for a major reality check. You still have time to prepare for career success. However, the clock is ticking and the ball is in your court.

Name ______________________________ Date ______________________

Checkpoint 11.2

It's Legal, But Is It Ethical?

Ethics are the standards of conduct for what is believed to be right or wrong. Each day, you decide between actions that you consider to be right or wrong. Organizations do the same. Consider the following situation.

> In the early 1990s, a U.S. Senate report found that prescription drug manufacturers had increased prices an average of 152 percent in the preceding decade. The consumer price index had increased only 58 percent during the same time. This trend put pressure on Congress to regulate drug pricing for the first time and take away generous tax breaks for prescription drug makers. The Pharmaceutical Manufacturers Association's response was that prescription medicines are a bargain compared with other health-care costs and that a recent Medicaid law would cost prescription drug makers $3.4 billion in lost sales over a five-year period.
>
> One senator said that he planned to propose legislation directing the Department of Health and Human Services to study the feasibility of creating a price review board that would identify unreasonable price increases. In the meantime, one major prescription drug firm promised to keep prices at or below inflation rates and to help improve access to important medicines.

1. Do you think other prescription drug manufacturers will follow this example? Why or why not?

____

____

____

2. Does this situation require that price regulations be put into law? Why or why not? ______________

____

____

____

3. Would regulations lower the price of prescription drugs? Why or why not? ______________

____

____

____

continued

4. Would regulations lower the quality of prescription drugs? Why or why not? ______

5. Imagine that you have been appointed by the Pharmaceutical Manufacturers Association to write an ethical standard for the industry. In the space below, write an ethical standard that could be adopted and practiced that would eliminate the need for a governmental price review board.

Name ______________________________ Date ____________________

Checkpoint 11.3

Where Is the Limit of Honesty?

One value or ethic that's important to most individuals and organizations is honesty – the belief in truth and justice. Some questionable actions of workers and employers will never appear in a newspaper headline, but many people would consider them to be dishonest. Consider the following case.

> Leona needs to leave work thirty minutes early to keep a dental appointment. She asks Randy (a co-worker) if he will punch out her time card at the regular quitting time. Randy agrees. At the close of the shift, the supervisor discovers Randy punching out two time cards. After a short meeting in the office, the supervisor gives Randy a warning and two weeks off work to think about it. When Leona reports to work the next day, the supervisor fires her. This was the second time Leona had left early without permission.

1. Would you consider Leona's behavior to be dishonest, unethical, or acceptable? (Circle one.) Explain the reasons for your answer. ______________________________

2. Would you consider Randy's behavior to be dishonest, unethical, or acceptable? (Circle one.) Explain the reasons for your answer. (Circle one.) Explain the reasons for your answer. ______________________________

3. Would you consider the supervisor's behavior to be dishonest, unethical, or acceptable? (Circle one.) Explain the reasons for your answer. ______________________________

4. a. If you were the supervisor, how would you have handled the problem with Randy? ______________________________

   b. How would you have handled the problem with Leona? ______________________________

continued

5. If you were Randy, what response would you have made when Leona asked you to punch out her time card?

____

____

6. If you were Leona, how would you have handled the need to leave work early? ____________________

____

____

Name ______________________________ Date ____________________

11.4 Checkpoint

Is It a Violation of Your Legal Rights?

Congress has enacted many laws protecting the rights of workers that employers must follow. Many states offer additional protection. Consider the following situations.

1. Chris is the assistant manager of a large supermarket. He is paid a monthly salary. Based on a forty-hour week, his hourly wage is more than that of the workers he supervises. However, the workers receive a premium pay of one and a half times their regular rate for hours they work over forty, and Chris is expected to work extra hours without additional pay. As a result, Chris sometimes works longer hours than the workers he supervises and earns less.

   a. Is Chris's employer violating his legal rights as a worker? ____________________

   b. Which federal law covers this situation? (See page 240 of your textbook) ____________________

   ____

   c. What provision of the law covers this situation? ____________________

   ____

   ____

   ____

   d. If you were Chris, would you arrange a meeting with the store manager to discuss this situation? If so, what action would you expect from the manager? If not, why not? ____________________

   ____

   ____

2. Paul graduated from a community college program with a machinist/machine technologist certificate. Although Paul is hearing-impaired, he graduated first in a class of eighty-four students. He applied for an entry-level machinist job with a large tool and die manufacturer. A week later, Paul received a rejection letter from the employment manager. The manager thanked Paul for considering his company for employment and congratulated him on his skills and high level of achievement. However, the manager felt that Paul's hearing impairment would be a safety hazard in the machine shop.

   a. Is the employment manager violating Paul's legal rights as a worker? ____________________

   b. Which federal law covers this situation? ____________________

   ____

   c. What provisions of the law covers this situation? (See page 244 of your textbook) ____________________

   ____

   ____

   ____

Name ______________________________ Date ____________________

Checkpoint 11.5

Fringes — What Are They Worth to You?

Because your fringe benefits are not received directly as wages, they are usually not subject to taxes. In fact, they are hidden income. However, there is no legal obligation requiring employers to provide most of the fringe benefits that workers receive.

1. Imagine that you are employed full-time and pay income taxes of 1 percent to the local government, 4 percent to the state government, and 20 percent to the federal government. Unfortunately, your employer doesn't provide medical insurance. The monthly premium for the basic medical insurance you have purchased is $75.

   a. How much money must you earn each month in order to pay your medical insurance premium?

   ____

   b. Imagine that you have changed jobs. One of the fringe benefits your new employer provides is a health insurance policy that is similar and in some ways better than yours. Your earnings on the new job are $100 per month more than your earnings on the previous job. Has your actual spending power increased by $200 per month, decreased by $100 per month, or stayed the same?

   ____

2. a. Consider the following fringe benefits offered by some employers. Then rank them in terms of their importance to you, with **1** being *most important* and **8** being *least important*.

   ______ Partially paid medical insurance (employer pays 70 percent)
   ______ Wellness program
   ______ Paid vacation plan
   ______ Parenting leave
   ______ Fully paid pension plan
   ______ Disability insurance plan
   ______ Excellent child-care program
   ______ Fully paid life insurance plan

   b. What are your reasons for your number 1 selection? ______________________________

   ____

   ____

   c. What are your reasons for your number 8 selection?

   ____

   ____

   ____

"WHEN I HIRED IN, THE PERSONNEL MANAGER GUARANTEED ME A MAXIMUM AMOUNT OF FRINGES.."..."HE WASN'T KIDDING.."

Name ______________________________ Date ____________________

11.6 Checkpoint

A Schedule That Works

Take a moment to think about your ideal job. Factors to consider include wages, job tasks, the work environment, and of course, the work schedule. A work schedule that fits your general lifestyle will increase your level of job satisfaction.

1. When you are at work, it is important to feel alert and ambitious. Would you describe yourself as a morning person or a night owl? ______________________________

2. List your three favorite leisure activities. (Examples include camping, sports such as basketball or baseball, music, or hanging out with friends.) Then list the day of the week and the time of day that you prefer to be involved in each activity.

	Leisure Activities	Day of Week	Time of Day
a.	______________________	________	________
b.	______________________	________	________
c.	______________________	________	________

3. Imagine that it is ten years from now. Consider whether you will be married, have children, own or rent a home, or be responsible for certain family members. List the four most important family and household responsibilities you expect to have. Then list the day of the week and the time of day you prefer or need to be involved with each responsibility.

	Family and Household Responsibilities	Day of Week	Time of Day
a.	______________________	________	________
b.	______________________	________	________
c.	______________________	________	________
d.	______________________	________	________

4. a. Review your answers to questions 1, 2, and 3. How many of the activities and responsibilities on your lists would you prefer doing during the morning? ________ The afternoon? ________ The evening? ________ At night? ________

   b. Now that you have reviewed your personal time priorities, which of the following work schedules would fit your planned lifestyle? (Choose one.)

   _____ A fixed day shift　　_____ A split shift　　_____ A fixed evening shift
   _____ A swing shift　　_____ A fixed night shift

5. Review the days of the week that the activities and responsibilities on your list occur. List the two days of the week that you would prefer to be off work.

   a. ______________________________

   b. ______________________________

Name ______________________________ Date ____________________

11.7 Checkpoint

Career Training and Education — It Never Ends

Imagine that you are a training specialist employed by a large corporation. This morning, your manager gave you a list of sixteen new employees. Each of the new employees recently graduated from high school, a one-year technical school, a two-year community college, or a university. This is their first full-time work experience, and you are responsible for the organizational training and education they receive. You begin by reviewing a list of the new employees' occupations.

Occupations of New Employees

Carpenter	Electrical engineer	Machine operator	Truck driver
Machinist	Receptionist	Chemical technician	Word processor
Plumber	Bricklayer	Sales trainee	Secretary
Electrician	Painter	General office clerk	Commercial artist

1. You are planning a one-day training session to discuss employee fringe benefits and personnel policies (work rules). You will also demonstrate the organization's products and lead an orientation tour of the factory, office, and laboratory areas. Corporate policy requires that you involve no more than ten employees in a training session at a time. You have decided to present two training sessions and have eight new employees attend each session.
   a. Which eight employees will you involve in the first group? ____________________
   b. What are your reasons for selecting these particular employees? ____________________

2. Your company offers a tuition reimbursement plan as a fringe benefit. A two-year community college is located nearby.
   a. Which two of the sixteen new employees would benefit most from this program? ____________________
   b. Why? ____________________
   c. Which two of the sixteen would benefit lease from this program? ____________________
   d. Why? ____________________

Name ______________________________ Date ____________________

Checkpoint 11.8

Finding the Right Words

Chapter 11 of your textbook contains numerous terms that employers and workers use. Recognizing and understanding these terms will help you make the important career decisions you will soon face.

Unscramble the terms in column B, and match them with the definitions in column A. (Some terms contain two works.)

Column A

Example: __a__ cherished ideas and beliefs

1. _____ the federal law that established a national social insurance program
2. _____ the quantity of work you produce
3. _____ leave taken by mothers or fathers when a child is born or adopted
4. _____ standards of conduct for what is believed to be right
5. _____ a formal, periodic, written evaluation of your job
6. _____ Title VII of this 1964 law protects workers against discrimination
7. _____ one-day training courses offered by employers
8. _____ forms of compensation other than salary or wages
9. _____ nonprofit banking services that employees may join
10. _____ temporary, contractual, and leased employees
11. _____ an acronym for the act that regulates minimum wage, overtime pay, and record-keeping procedures
12. _____ an acronym for the act that protects qualified indivduals with a disability from discrimination
13. _____ a daily work schedule that's divided into two or more parts
14. _____ to make laws
15. _____ the amount of an expense that the beneficiary of an insurance policy must meet
16. _____ agreement between competitors to establish specific price ranges for products or services

Column B

a. VALUES
SAVEUL

b. ______________________
THESIC

c. ______________________
TIMER GINRAT

d. ______________________
SAILCO RICEYUTS CAT

e. ______________________
REDUSEAM TOPTUU

f. ______________________
GREATPINN VEALE

g. ______________________
CITRED NOSUNI

h. ______________________
PORKSHOWS

i. ______________________
TENTINCGNO ROSEKRW

j. ______________________
LIIVC SIGHTR CAT

k. ______________________
EFRING FINEBSET

l. ______________________
LISTP TFISH

m. ______________________
FLAS

n. ______________________
AAD

o. ______________________
CUTLIBDEED

p. ______________________
LATEISGEL

q. ______________________
ECIRP NIXFIG

Name ______________________________ Date ____________________

11.9

Checkpoint

Checking Your Location

1. For each of the following statements, circle **F** if the statement is more false than true. Circle **T** if the statement is more true than false.

T F a. Employers have the right to evaluate the work performance of their employees.

T F b. How the information in a performance appraisal will be used is determined by the employer or, in the case of a union shop, by a contract between the workers and the employer.

T F c. It is not your supervisor's role to evaluate your performance; it is your responsibility to perform at or above minimum standards.

T F d. The Fair Labor Standards Act (FLSA) limits the hours of work for employees who are sixteen years or older.

T F e. The 1971 Fair Credit Reporting Act (FCRA) requires employers to tell rejected job applicants if they are denied a job based on credit information.

T F f. About nine out of ten workers, including household employees and the self-employed, are covered by Social Security.

T F g. Once ethical standards are established and agreed on, all members or employees of the organization are expected to practice them.

T F h. Ethical behavior is a matter of personal values. Although points of view may vary, little harm can be traced to unethical behavior.

T F i. An employer has the right to take action against an employee for good cause.

T F j. Employers are required by law to provide a minimum package of fringe benefits for their workers.

T F k. Health maintenance organizations (HMOs) are expensive and provide a very limited range of health services.

T F l. Leave time is excused time away from work; it may be paid or unpaid.

continued

T **F** m. Most pension plans require that you work five years, with a minimum of one thousand hours of service each year, before you earn pension rights.

T **F** n. Employers lose millions of dollars annually from work-family conflicts caused when a child is sick, when day-care arrangements fall through, or when on-the-job time is spent worrying about a child's well-being.

T **F** o. To remain efficient and competitive in rapidly changing markets, an increasing number of employers are using contigent workers.

2. Use the space below to rewrite the statements you marked **false** and make them **true**. Include the letter of each statement you rewrite.

____

____

____

____

____

____

Name ______________________________ Date ____________________

12.1 Checkpoint

The Wise Old Owl

Imagine that you are the author of a career advice newspaper called "The Wise Old Owl." What career advice would you offer the following workers?

> Dear Wise Old Owl:
>
> I graduated from high school four years ago and acquired a full-time job as a machine operator in a plastics molding factory. My car is paid for, and I have a small savings account. However, I would have trouble meeting all my bills if I didn't live with my parents. Many of my friends have just graduated from two-year colleges and already earn more money than I do. What should I do?
>
> Disappointed in Atlanta

Dear Disappointed:

____

____

____

____

____

____

> Dear Wise Old Owl:
>
> I am a secretary working for the vice-president of a small factory. She is a very pleasant and considerate boss. I enjoy the work and feel that I have learned a great deal since I graduated from high school three years ago. The company seems to be doing very well, but I haven't received a pay increase for almost two years. I hate to quit my job, but I need to earn more money. What should I do?
>
> Need More Money in Boston

Dear Need More:

____

____

____

____

____

____

Name ______________________________ Date ____________________

Checkpoint 12.2

What Is Career Success?

What will it take to make you feel successful? The success you feel in your future role as a worker won't exist separately from your life outside the job.

1. Review the career success factors below. Using the following rating scale, rate them in order of importance from 1 to 5, according to your career ambitions.

Rating Scale

5 = Very important to me
4 = Somewhat important to me
3 = Of average importance to me
2 = Not very important to me
1 = Unimportant to me

Career Success Factors	**Your Rating**
Job Status Having rank and prestige within the organization	____
Job Security Feeling confident about job stability and layoffs	____
Advancement Opportunities Knowing you have a good chance for promotion within the organization	____
Potential Income Being certain you will have enough money to pay for your lifestyle	____
Work Environment The quality and type of surroundings (indoor or outdoor, new or old)	____
Education and Training The amount of education and training you achieve (high school, technical school, two-year degree, four-year degree, graduate school)	____
Work Schedule The required shift and hours of work the flexibility to establish your own hours of work	____
Job Responsibilities Being responsible for the job performance of others or having others responsible for your job performance (supervising or being supervised)	____
Leisure Time Having enough paid vacation time, holidays, and weekly hours away from the job to enjoy your personal lifestyle	____

continued

2. Review your responses to question 1, and write the titles of the three success factors that are most important to you.

   a. ______________________ b. ______________________ c. ______________________

3. What occupation are you presently considering for your future career?

   ____

4. Will the occupation you are presently considering satisfy the three success factors that are most important to you? If so, describe how the occupation will satisfy each factor. If not, what other occupations could you consider that would satisfy your important success factors?

   a. Success factor number one:______________________________________

   ____

   b. Success factor number two:______________________________________

   ____

   c. Success factor number three:____________________________________

   ____

"I'VE HAD IT UP TO HERE WITH FRANK.. TELL HIM I QUIT RIGHT NOW!"

Name ______________________________ Date ____________________

12.3 Checkpoint

The Process of Resigning

Don't make the mistake of being angry and creating bad feelings when you resign from a job. At some future date, you may want a reference. Consider the case of Carl.

> Carl graduated from President's High School last June. He is starting his third week as a driver-salesperson for the Sunrise Bakery Company. It is 5:30 a.m., and Carl is preparing to load his delivery van. It will be another ten hours before he returns to the bakery, sweeps out the inside of his van, and goes home. Carl is thinking about the long hours, low pay, and exhausting work load. The supervisor looks in the back of Carl's van. "Sweep it out" she says. "Don't load your van until it's spotless." Carl looks his supervisor in the eye and replies, "You sweep it out. I quit."

1. Is Carl a responsible employee? What evidence can you show to support your position?

____

____

____

2. Imagine that it is fifteen years later, and Carl needs a job. The supervisor of all of Carl's co-workers have left the Sunrise Bakery Company or retired. Do you think a new supervisor would hire Carl? Why or why not? ______________________________

____

____

____

3. Good business etiquette requires you to give a two-week advance notice to your employer before you resign.

   a. Why is an advance notice important to the employer? ______________________________

   ____

   ____

   ____

continued

b. How could giving advance notice be important to you? ______

______

______

______

4. If you were Carl, how would you have handled this situation? Be specific ______

______

______

______

5. Can you think of a time when you started something important and then quit? It might have been a course of study, private lessons, or a part-time job.

   a. What did you start? ______

   b. What were your reasons for starting? ______

   ______

   c. What were your reasons for quitting? ______

   ______

   d. Did you act in a responsible, mature manner in this situation? What evidence can you describe to support your position? ______

   ______

   ______

Name ______________________________ Date ____________________

Checkpoint 12.4

Losing Your Job

Millions of U.S. workers are laid off or fired from their jobs every year. Once they are over the shock, disbelief, and anger, most of them make a new beginning. Every unemployed worker's situation is different.

Imagine that you are an employment counselor asked for advice in the situations described below. Use the following list of options (A to E) to make your recommendations. You may suggest more than one option. In each case, describe the reasons for your advice.

Options for Unemployed Workers

A = Seek employment locally in the same occupation.
B = Seek employment in a different region of the country.
C = Seek education and training to update your skills in the same occupation.
D = Seek education and training to become qualified for a different occupation.
E = Seek personal career counseling before you attempt to become reemployed.

1. Charles is a diesel engine mechanic with six years of experience. He was fired today for having excessive absences. Recommended options: ______________________________

   Reasons for your recommendations: ______________________________

   ____

   ____

   ____

   ____

2. Bret was laid off today from his position as a general office worker. He has a high school education and one year of experience. Bret works in a large urban area. Employment is very good in the region. Bret's employer has installed a computer system and no longer needs workers to perform general tasks such as typing and filing. Recommended options: ______________________________

   Reasons for your recommendations: ______________________________

   ____

   ____

   ____

   ____

continued

3. Tricia, a legal administrative assistant, was laid off today. She is a tech-prep graduate with an associate degree. Her job was in the small town where she grew up. Tricia's employer retired, and the other lawyer has a legal assistant. Tricia loved her career. She will receive six months of severance pay and an excellent letter of recommendation. Recommended options: ______________________________

Reasons for your recommendations: ______________________________

____

____

____

____

Name ______________________________ Date ____________________

12.5 Checkpoint

Finding the Right Words

Chapter 12 of your textbook contains numerous terms that employers and workers use. Recognizing and understanding these terms will help you make the important career decisions you will soon face.

Fill in the blank spaces in the vocabulary terms to complete the following sentences.

1. A (s ___ l ___ r___) is employee compensation that is calculated weekly, biweekly, monthly, or annually.
2. (___ a___ e ___) are employee compensation that is calculated hourly.
3. When a worker is not employed and is looking for work, he or she is (___ n ___ m ___ l ___ y ___ d).
4. (___ e t   ___ a ___) is the amount of earnings that an employee receives after deductions are taken.
5. Compensation at greater-than-regular rates, such as overtime pay, is referred to as (p r ___m ___ ___m ___ a ___).
6. Incentive compensation in which a percentage of company profits is distributed to the employees involved in producing those profits is called (___ r o ___ i ___   s ___ a ___ i ___ g).
7. (___ o ___ m i ___ s ___ ___ n ___) are compensation to salespeople based on a predetermined percentage of the salesperson's sales value.
8. (D ___ ___ c ___ a ___ g ___) of an employee means dismissal from employment.
9. A (m ___ r i ___   i ___ ___ r ___ ___ s e) is an increase in a worker's pay rate, usually given on the basis of efficiency or performance.
10. A (___ a ___ o ___ f) is an involuntary separation of an employee from an employer for a temporary or indefinite period, through no fault of the employee.
11. (___ n e ___ p ___ ___ y ___s___ e n ___   i ___ s ___ ___ a ___ c e) is a joint federal-state program that pays a weekly benefit to eligible workers when they are involuntarily unemployed.
12. (___ o ___   ___ e ___ u ___ i ___ y) is protection against loss of employment and earnings.
13. (P ___ ___ k   s ___ i ___) is a common term used by workers to describe a notice of termination.
14. A law passed Congress in 1985 to help certain terminated employees buy group insurance for themselves and their families is commonly referred to as (___ O ___ ___ A).
15. The part of your paycheck that provides you with a source of cash is called (d ___ r ___ c ___

    c ___ m p ___ n s ___ t ___ ___ n).

Name ______________________________ Date ____________________

12.6 Checkpoint

Checking Your Location

1. For each of the following statements, circle **F** if the statement is more false than true. Circle **T** if the statement is more true than false.

T F a. The career path you select will entail numerous personal and occupational changes.

T F b. As you change your role from student to employee, the importance you attach to different aspects of having a job will change.

T F c. Your definition of a satisfying job is usually formed during your high school years and changes very little during your career.

T F d. Family, friends, and social and professional support are all interrelated with job satisfaction in a worker's overall feeling of success.

T F e. Jobs have numerous characteristics that make them desirable or undesirable to workers.

T F f. Most occupations pay similar wage rates. Geographic location has little to do with wage rates.

T F g. The type of job you have and the policy of your company will have a lot to do with when you will receive a pay raise.

T F h. Millions of Americans change jobs each year. Many choose to change; others have no choice.

T F i. If the first job you select is a poor choice, you have made a total waste of your time and education.

T F j. Employers are required by law to provide a minimum package of fringe benefits for their workers.

T F k. If you are asked to submit a letter of resignation, don't be afraid to describe problems created by the organization or your supervisor. Top management will appreciate your information.

T F l. Whatever the cause of unemployment, those who are most highly skilled and trained are most likely to be reemployed.

T F m. A general rule of law states that "no employer shall discharge an employee without good cause."

T F n. Organizations are not consistent in how they lay off or terminate employees.

T F o. In most firings, the employee to be released knows in advance or at least has some suggestion that termination is coming.

continued

2. Use the space below to rewrite the statements you marked **false** and make them **true**. Include the letter of each statement you rewrite.

Name ______________________________ Date ____________________

13.1 Checkpoint

Men's Roles — Women's Roles

Men and women can be discouraged from pursuing certain careers because of stereotypes about the work role. They often do not consider a particular career because they simply do not know anyone like them in that career.

1. a. In the following list of occupations, write an ***M*** next to the occupations you usually associate with men, a ***W*** next to those you usually associate with women, and a ***B*** next to those you usually associate with both sexes.

___ Physician	___ Cashier	___ Pharmacologist	___ Dietician
___ Chemist	___ Teacher	___ Lab technician	___ Computer scientist
___ Engineer	___ Banker	___ Auto mechanic	___ Skilled trades apprentice
___ Secretary	___ Nurse	___ Accountant	___ Technologist
___ Lawyer	___ Architect	___ Fire fighter	___ Executive

b. Is your father's occupation a traditional one for men? ______________

c. Is your mother's occupation a traditional one for women? ______________

d. Why do you believe women enter occupations you indicated with a ***W***?

____

____

e. Why do you believe men enter occupations you indicated with a ***M***?

____

____

2. The following chart lists qualities frequently associated with men or women.

a. In column 1, check (✓) off those qualities that you believe describe you.

b. In column 2, write an ***M*** next to the qualities you most often associate with men, a ***W*** next to those you most often associate with women, and a ***B*** next to those you most often associate with both sexes.

c. In column 3, check off the characteristics you think are representative of a person with a career requiring advanced math or science skills.

Quantities Frequently Associated with Men or Women

Characteristic	Column 1 Me	Column 2 Men/Women/Both	Column 3 Characteristics Needed for Careers Requiring Advanced Math/Science Skills
Analytical	______	______	______
Self-confident	______	______	______
Abstract thinker	______	______	______
Intelligent	______	______	______
A loner	______	______	______
Well read	______	______	______
Independent	______	______	______
Decision maker	______	______	______
Scientific	______	______	______
Creative	______	______	______
Patient	______	______	______
Observant	______	______	______
Studious	______	______	______
Logical	______	______	______
Ambitious	______	______	______
Patient	______	______	______
Responsible	______	______	______

d. How many characteristics did you think applied mostly to men? ________ To women? ________

e. How many characteristics describing yourself, (column 1) did you think applied mostly to men? ________ To Women? ________

f. How many characteristics describing yourself are associated with a nontraditional career for your sex? ________

g. What stereotypical pattern do you see? ________________________________

Career Tip: The characteristics listed are generally associated with a career using advanced math and science skills.

3. The word *man* has for centuries been used as a generic term that includes both men and women. The generic use of masculine gender terms does not convey a female image and actually devalues the actions, contributions, and ultimately the very presence of women. Change the following words from sex-biased to sex-fair. (Your teacher has the answers.)

	Sex-biased	Sex-fair		Sex-biased	Sex-fair
a.	Mankind	____________	j.	Stewardess	____________
b.	Chairman	____________	k.	Workman	____________
c.	Manmade	____________	l.	Policeman	____________
d.	Cleaning lady	____________	m.	Coed	____________
e.	Fireman	____________	n.	Ladylike	____________
f.	Craftsman	____________	o.	Gal Friday	____________
g.	Congressman	____________	p.	Foreman	____________
h.	Salesman	____________	q.	Man-hours	____________
i.	Statesman	____________	r.	Spokesman	____________

4. a. What are your beliefs about the roles of women in the work force and as homemakers? ____________

____

____

____

b. What are your beliefs about the roles of men in the work force and as homemakers? ____________

____

____

____

"MY SISTERS..."

Name ________________________________ Date ____________________

13.2 Checkpoint

Making the Labor Market Fair for *ALL* Workers

Review Figure 13–1 in your textbook. This figure reflects major changes in the makeup of the labor force. More women, minorities, and immigrants will participate in the labor force in the years ahead than ever before. These groups have often been relegated to low-paying, low-status occupations because of long-standing stereotypes and prejudices and limited educational and life experiences. As a result, they have not reaped the full benefits of career fulfillment.

1. If you were a counselor, what career advice would you give an 18-year-old minority or immigrant woman regarding the following problems?

   a. Discrimination: ____________________

   b. Lack of availability of educational opportunities: ____________________

   c. Lack of funds for further education and training: ____________________

   d. Lack of information concerning career options: ____________________

   e. Lack of self-confidence: ____________________

Review Figure 13–3 in your textbook. This figure shows the annual earnings of full-time female workers as a percentage of the earnings of full-time male workers. This earnings gap also exists for minority men. Answer the following questions, and explain your answers.

2. How much of the inequality in earnings do you believe is due to

   a. Differences in the quality of education for women? ____________________

   b. Differences in the quality of education for minority men? ____________________

   c. The career fields chosen by minority men? ____________________

d. The career fields chosen by women? ______

e. Job performance evaluations for minority men? ______

f. Job performance evaluations for women? ______

g. The size and financial strength of the employer? ______

Name ____________________ Date ____________________

13.3 Checkpoint

The Glass Ceiling

1. Damon Farrier is a recent graduate of the Central State School of Automotive Technology. Damon, an African American, hopes to find a job where he will be promoted on the merit of his job performance and where he will not experience limitations because of racial prejudice. He has three summers of work experience as an automobile mechanic.

   Damon interviewed with sixteen potential employers and received two job offers. Review Damon's experience with the two interested employers and help him make a career choice.

   Employer 1: Damon noticed about twelve mechanics working in the garage. Most of the mechanics were black. The shop supervisor, the parts manager, the service manager, and the owner who interviewed Damon were white. The only woman in the garage was employed as a secretary. The owner was overly friendly during the interview.

   Employer 2: Damon noticed about seventeen mechanics working in the garage. The parts manager was a black woman. The shop supervisor, the service manager, and the owner were white males. Four of the mechanics were black. The owner treated Damon in a cordial, businesslike manner but wasn't overly friendly.

   a. What message did Damon receive from each of the two employers?

   b. Which employer would you select if you were Damon? Why?

   c. What message would a female mechanic receive from two similar interviews?

2. Minorities and women continue to represent less than 5 percent of the top management of America's Fortune-1,000 corporations.

   a. Visit your school library, and examine the organizational chart of three major corporations. (Your librarian can help you select a directory with this information.) How many women are listed in top management positions in each company?

      Company 1: ________ Company 2: ________ Company 3: ________

   b. What effect does the glass ceiling have on the quality of leadership in U.S. business?

Name ______________________________ Date ____________________

13.4 Checkpoint — Issues: Sexual Harassment, Pregnancy, Contingent Employment

1. *Sexual harassment:* Ashley is the only female in the junior welding program at Eastern Vocational School. The instructor, Mr. Smith, frequently makes jokes about any mistake she makes in the shop. The male students use Mr. Smith's jokes to tease Ashley. One student in particular makes repeated sexual comments. When Ashley complained to Mr. Smith, she was told she had better get used to it if she planned to work with men.

   a. Is anyone guilty of sexual harassment in this class? If so, who? ______________________________

   ____

   b. How would you handle this problem if you were Ashley? ______________________________

   ____

   ____

   c. What would you do if you were the instructor? ______________________________

   ____

   ____

   d. How would you react if you were a male student in the class and felt that Ashley was being harassed?

   ____

   ____

   ____

2. *Pregnancy:* Five states and Puerto Rico have temporary disability insurance (TDI) laws that provide partial salary replacement for nonwork-related disabilities including childbirth and pregnancy-related conditions. Should all states have these kinds of laws? Explain your answer. ______________________________

   ____

   ____

   ____

3. *Contingent employment:* The contingency (leased) labor force is growing faster than the rest of the labor force. However, only one-third of contingency workers receive health benefits. Should there be a national health-care program to make up for this benefit? If so, how should it be paid for? If not, why not?

   ____

   ____

   ____

   ____

Name ______________________ Date ______________

13.5 Checkpoint

The Past — The Future

The quotation from *Future Shock* at the beginning of Chapter 13 emphasizes the rapid and dramatic changes that have taken place in technology during the past sixty-two years (one person's estimated lifetime).

1. List one advance in technology that has taken place during the past sixty-two years in each of the following occupations. Describe how the advance has affected the occupation. The first one is done for you.

Occupation	Technological Advance	Effect of the Technology on the Occupation
Accountant	Electronic calculator	Bookkeeping can be completed more quickly.
Musician		
Nurse		
Bank teller		
Engineer		
Physicist		
Dentist		
Pharmacist		
Journalist		
Aircraft pilot		
Cashier		
Retail salesperson		
Secretary		
Police officer		
Chef		
Farmer		
Mechanic		
Carpenter		
Assembly line worker		
Truck driver		

2. Overall, have advances in technology been beneficial for these workers? Explain your answer. ________

____

____

Name ____________________ Date ____________________

Checkpoint 13.6

Job Mobility and Adapting to Change

In less than a hundred years, we have gone from a nation of farmers to a highly technical and mobile society. Today, less than 3 percent of Americans are farmers, and 75 percent of us now live on less than 3 percent of the land. Jobs are changing rapidly due to the reorganization of companies, technological changes, and an expanding international economy. Workers of the future can expect at least three to four career changes requiring retraining during their working life.

1. Why is it important to be aware of job trends when planning your future career? ____________________

2. a. What are two occupations you are now considering for your future career?

   Occupation 1: ____________________ Occupation 2: ____________________

   b. What technological changes do you predict for these careers by the year 2000? ____________________

   c. What social, political, and economic changes can you imagine that would alter the future growth of these occupations? ____________________

3. Your lifestyle would be affected by the location of your future career. The house you live in, the car you drive, the activities you do for enjoyment, the type of food you prefer, the friends you have, the family you are a part of, and the way you spend your income are all a part of your lifestyle.

   a. Describe three lifestyle needs that will be important to you as an adult. ____________________

   b. Where do you plan to live? ____________________

   c. Who will live with you? ____________________

   d. What recreational activities will you enjoy? ____________________

4. Consider the reaction of the Catalano family to a recent move. Mr. Catalano took a new job that required relocating the family from Fort Worth, Texas, to Little Rock, Arkansas.

   Mr. Catalano loves his new job. He has made a lot of friends at the plant and is excited about remodeling an older home overlooking the Arkansas River.

   Cheryl Catalano is sixteen years old. She misses her friends in Texas, she's unhappy with her new school, and she feels sad most of the time.

   Angelo Catalano is twelve years old. He made the basketball team at his new school, he loves fishing on the Arkansas River, and he feels great most of the time.

   Mrs. Catalano doesn't say a lot about the move to Arkansas. She misses her family in Texas, but she really likes her new job at Dillard's corporate headquarters.

   a. How do you think things would be for you if you were put in a similar situation this year? ________

   ____

   b. How do you think you would adapt if you were making the move for a career opportunity? ________

   ____

   c. What advice would you offer to Cheryl? ____

   ____

   d. What advice would you offer Mrs. Catalano? ____

   ____

5. At some point in your career, you may need to move to a new job or take a transfer. You may become unemployed and unable to find local employment. You may need to seek employment opportunities in another geographic area, or you may simply wish to move to a different area. This kind of lifestyle change causes emotional highs and lows for most people. Some people cope better than others.

   a. What would you be willing to give up for a job you really wanted?

   _____ Close family ties　　_____ Educational plans　　_____ Place of worship

   _____ Favorite activities　　_____ Familiar restaurants and shopping areas

   _____ Friends

   b. How would you react to these changes in lifestyle? __________________________________

   ____

   ____

   c. Does the occupation you are most seriously considering fit your lifestyle goals? Explain your answer.

   ____

   ____

Name ______________________________ Date ____________________

Checkpoint 13.7

Finding the Right Words

Complete the word-find puzzle by finding and circling the vocabulary terms you learned in this chapter. (They are listed below.) The words appear horizontally and vertically.

acquisitions	divestiture	goods producing	offshore
CBERA	downsizing	maternity leave	stereotype
contingent	glass ceiling	mergers	technological
deregulation	gender identity	nontraditional	urban area

U C S N X X X O S Z C X Y N G G C B N M X V N K W

S T E R E O T Y P E A U G L O O T I Z R C A O N T

E J A C F M E C F N G A B O F O D L J I H Q N N W

A T H Y R L U U Q P L K A Y F D E C X S K K T K R

Q X C Y J Y O Z Q Q A F J V S S R U P N D W R T Q

R U P D B A P M B M S U A T H P E R R C K I A K A

Z L A C R I L Q V D S E A S O R G B C J Z R D X I

V E Y D O W V J B K C Q T Y R O U A Z A M V I G Z

D Y V D Q C M K A Q E W V L E D L N G B Y W T G E

C V A C Q U I S I T I O N S E U A A O U X L I F J

B M A T E R N I T Y L E A V E C T R G J X A O R P

C C I T K R T E Y C I H V U Y I I E E A N W N X L

F F Q Z L B E S W J N S E H W N O A N B B J A Q O

K R C J G I C H F P G Z P R Y G N A D U L X L H S

U E Y E Y M H I V T B G I C W I F Q E J V V C Q O

V X G Q T E N X U D I V E S T I T U R E T G F C L

S L Q W T R O C K O D Z F H C T M E I Q T W I H H

B W Y P C G L L D Z Y X I A H J X K D P U R K F E

X C T T I E O J T O T C V Y I F J O E F V Y E B R

J A B T M R G A D P R V D B B R W X N N G V R G M

N A M V S S I C O N T I N G E N T J T R D C H A K

J O T J D S C G I V E W F U R B S W I M Q B L I O

L T D W T E A U U B D H A W X F S K T A C E S N P

B L Q N M L L N T A C O F Y U S P G Y M T R Y J H

U J H N F P G W U V G D O W N S I Z I N G A I L N

Name ______________________________ Date ____________________

13.8

Checkpoint

Checking Your Location

1. For each of the following statements, circle **F** if the statement is more false than true. Circle **T** if the statement is more true than false.

T F a. By the year 2000, working-age women will constitute 47 percent of the work force, and men will retain a slight majority (54 percent).

T F b. During World War II, women's earnings nearly equaled the average for men.

T F c. The feminist movement grew during the 1960s and 1970s as women were encouraged to seek a larger role in the labor market.

T F d. The opportunities for women in nontraditional occupations have increased significantly in the last fifty years.

T F e. Sex-role stereotypes are based on roles assigned to people because of their relation to personal skills or interests.

T F f. Minorities and women have made significant gains at the entry level of employment and in the first levels of management.

T F g. An employer is responsible for sexual harassment by employees if the employer knew or should have known of the conduct and failed to take immediate and appropriate action.

T F h. More than 60 percent of U.S. children have mothers who are either employed or looking for work.

T F i. Employers rarely include contingent employees in benefit programs, such as health insurance, paid leave, or pensions.

T F j. The U.S. work force will increase 50 percent from 1990 to 2005.

T F k. Service-producing organizations have dominated economic growth over the past several decades.

T F l. The impact of foreign competition can be measured by the loss of domestic and foreign markets and the decline of many basic industries in the U.S.

T F m. Hiring contingent workers is more expensive than maintaining permanent workers.

T F n. More than 350,000 Americans work for Japanese companies in either the service or manufacturing sectors.

T **F** o. In tomorrow's world of work, a worker's job security will depend on his or her marketable skills.

2. Use the space below to rewrite the statements you marked **false** and make them **true**. Include the letter of each statement you rewrite.

Name ______________________ Date ______________

14.1 Checkpoint

The United States— A Global Production System

The production of consumer goods creates profits for employers and jobs for workers. *Helpful hint*: Review section 1 in Chapter 14 of your textbook before beginning this activity.

1. a. List four consumer goods that you purchased during the past six months.

   (1) ______________ (3) ______________

   (2) ______________ (4) ______________

   b. Cross out the consumer good you could most easily give up.

   c. Circle the consumer good you need the most. Why do you need this particular consumer good?

   ____

   ____

   d. Ask your parents which of the four consumer goods on your list was most uncommon when your parents were your age? ______________

   e. How did this affect their life? ______________

   ____

2. a. Name one consumer good that many families purchase today that was uncommon when your parents were your age. ______________

   b. How has the widespread use of this consumer good affected the average American's lifestyle?

   ____

   ____

   c. What occupations were created, increased in number, or eliminated because of this consumer good?

   ____

   ____

3. Industrial products are goods that are produced for and sold to other producers. List one industrial product used to manufacture each of the following.

   a. Tires ______________

   b. Automobiles ______________

   c. Clothing ______________

   d. Donuts ______________

   e. Windows ______________

   f. Trash bags ______________

Name ______________________________ Date ______________

Checkpoint 14.2

The United States— A Global Service System

The provision of consumer services for businesses and consumers creates profits for employers and jobs for workers. *Helpful hint*: Review section 1 in Chapter 14 of your textbook before beginning this activity.

1. a. List four services that your family purchased during the past month.

   (1) ______________________ (3) ______________________

   (2) ______________________ (4) ______________________

   b. Cross out the service your family could most easily give up.

   c. Circle the service your family needs the most. If the service you circled were no longer available, how would it affect your everyday family life? ______________________

   ____

   d. Ask your parents which of the four services on your list was most uncommon when they were your age? ____

   e. How did this affect their life? ______________________

   ____

2. a. Name one service that many families purchase today that was uncommon when your parents were your age. ______________________

   b. How has the widespread use of this service affected the average American's lifestyle?

   ____

   ____

   c. What occupations were created, increased in number, or eliminated because of this service?

   ____

   ____

3. Industrial services are services that are produced for and sold to other businesses. List one industrial service that would be used by each of the following:

   a. A gasoline service station ______________________

   b. A hospital ______________________

   c. A restaurant ______________________

Name ______________________________ Date ______________

Checkpoint 14.3

Consumers See the Light

Producers of goods must recover their cost of production in order to stay in business. They must know how much money they have invested in a certain product before they can establish a selling price. Their goal is to attract the largest number of consumers without reducing the price below their production cost. A graph representing the number of products (goods) or services that suppliers are willing to furnish at different prices, at a certain time, is known as a *supply curve*.

The following supply curve represents the number of circular florescent light blubs produced each day by the B.R. Stolz Corporation. When prices go up, the company increases production. When prices go down, it decreases production.

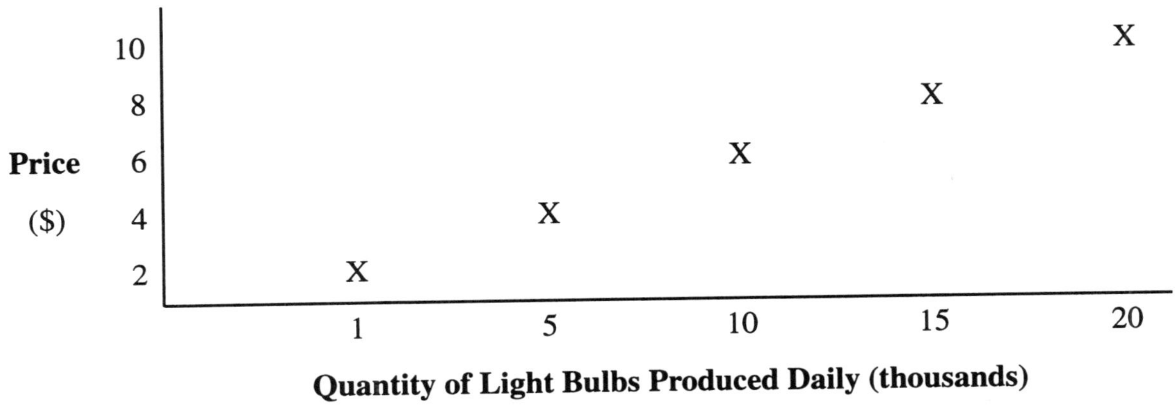

1. The Stolz Corporation normally produces ten thousand bulbs per day and sells them at a price of six dollars.
   a. If the prices rises to eight dollars, how many bulbs would the Stolz Corporation be willing to produce each day? ______________________________
   b. If the price falls to four dollars, how many bulbs would the Stolz Corporation be willing to produce each day? ______________________________
2. During normal production (ten thousand bulbs per day), the Stolz Corporation employs fifteen workers. What would be the effect on Stolz's work force if the long-term demand for bulbs
   a. Increased to eighteen thousand bulbs per day? ______________________________
   b. Decreased to five thousand bulbs per day? ______________________________

Name ______________________________ Date ______________

Checkpoint 14.4

Inflation Affects Everyone

Helpful Hint: Review section 4 in Chapter 14 of your textbook before beginning this activity.

During periods of inflation, the price of goods and services increases. During periods of recession, the price of goods and services decreases. Small price changes toward recession or inflation have little effect on most workers, but large changes can be devastating.

> Imagine that the price of food, clothing, and housing increased 2 percent last month and is expected to increase at this rate for the next two or three years. Wages will rise about half as fast as prices. What lifestyle adjustments will each of the following families need to make in the food, housing, clothing, and transportation categories. Provide specific reasons for each of your answers.

1. A family of four earning $18,000 per year. Both parents are employed. They live and work in a large city and currently spend 35 percent of their income on apartment rent.

   a. Quantity and type of food purchased: ______________________________

   ____

   b. Housing: ______________________________

   ____

   c. Clothing: ______________________________

   ____

   d. Transportation: ______________________________

   ____

2. A family of four earning $85,000 per year. Both parents are employed. They live in a suburban community and commute to work in the city. They currently spend 20 percent of their income on house payments.

   a. Quantity and type of food purchased: ______________________________

   ____

   b. Housing: ______________________________

   ____

   c. Clothing: ______________________________

   ____

   d. Transportation: ______________________________

   ____

continued

3. An elderly couple living on a fixed pension income (income that doesn't change) of $21,000 per year. They own a small house in the city and currently spend 45 percent of their income on housing.

   a. Quantity and type of food purchased: ______________________________

   b. Housing: ______________________________

   c. Clothing: ______________________________

   d. Transportation: ______________________________

"IF WE HIRE MORE WORKERS AND GO TO THESE 'STATE OF THE ART' CHISELS, WE CAN INCREASE PRODUCTION.. WITHIN FIVE YEARS, EVERYONE WILL OWN ONE..."

Name ______________________________ Date ______________

Checkpoint 14.5

Production, Quality , and Price

Helpful hint: Review section 5 in Chapter 14 of your textbook before beginning this activity.

Technology has changed the way we work. When workers are more productive, more goods and services are available at lower prices. Consider the case of Gordon Lee.

> Gordon enjoyed making wooden furniture as a hobby. His specialty was a rocking chair. Several friends and neighbors admired Gordon's work and asked him to build rocking chairs for them. When a local furniture store offered to sell his chairs, Gordon decided to quit his job at the Legion Hall and build chairs full-time.
>
> Working with hand tools in his garage, it takes Gordon three days to build one chair. He has orders for all of the chairs he can build at $150 per chair. Recently, the owner of a furniture store in a nearby city saw one of Gordon's chairs at a friend's house. She has offered to buy six chairs per week at a price of $125 each. Gordon's business is doing very well, but he has a serious problem with productivity. If he can't keep up with the demand for his goods (chairs), he will begin to lose business.

1. What effect would you expect the following decisions to have on the quality and production of Gordon's chairs?

   a. Hiring one or more workers? ______________________________

   ____

   b. Using power tools, such as a table saw and lathe? ______________________________

   ____

2. If you were Gordon, what steps would you take to increase production and maintain the high quality of the chairs you produce? ______________________________

   ____

   ____

   ____

3. What course of action could Gordon follow to lower the price of his chairs and still make a satisfactory profit? ______________________________

   ____

   ____

   ____

Name ______________________________ Date ____________________

14.6 Checkpoint

Machines at Work

We live in an age of machines. Machines mow our grass, cook our food, heat and cool our homes, wake us up in the morning, transport us to our jobs, balance our checkbooks, and entertain us in the evening.

1. Think about the daily events that happen to you from the time you wake up until you go to sleep. Make a list of ten machines and the work they perform for you during your typical day.

Machine	Work the Machine Performs
Example: Alarm clock	Wakes me up at the time I select
a. ____________	____________________
b. ____________	____________________
c. ____________	____________________
d. ____________	____________________
e. ____________	____________________
f. ____________	____________________
g. ____________	____________________
h. ____________	____________________
i. ____________	____________________
j. ____________	____________________

2. You would need a full-time worker to replace many machines. The alarm clock is one example. In addition to waking you up at the time you select, it's always available to provide you with the correct time.
   a. If you need to hire workers to replace the ten machines on your list, how many workers would you need? ____________
   b. What is your estimate of the total number of worker hours required each week? ____________
   c. If you paid each worker $6 per hour, how much would it cost you to replace the ten machines on your list for one week? $____________ For one year? $____________
   d. How many hours would you estimate that the ten machines on your list save you each day? ________ Each year? ________

continued

3. What jobs have been eliminated from the work force because of the machines on your list? What jobs have been created?

	Machine	Job Eliminated	Job Created
a.	______	______	______
b.	______	______	______
c.	______	______	______

Name ______________________________ Date ____________________

14.7 Checkpoint

Stock Ownership— Fuel for the Economy's Furnace

Whether you own one share or one thousand shares, stock ownership makes you a part owner of a business. In both good times and bad times, investors purchase shares of stock with hopes of making a profit. Although many people think of stockholders (owners of stock) as wealthy, the majority are ordinary people. Depending on the type of stock they own, stockholders are entitled to a certain percentage of the profits and are permitted to vote on certain corporate matters.

Most investors—whether they are individuals with a few hundred dollars to invest or large institutions with millions—use securities sales representatives when buying or selling stocks. Securities and financial services sales representatives hold more than 200,000 jobs. Most sales representatives work for a small number of large firms with main offices in big cities (especially in New York) and approximately twenty-five thousand branch offices in other areas.

1. Imagine that you are a securities and financial services sales representative for a large brokerage firm. Research the financial section of your daily newspaper or another newspaper, such as the *Wall Street Journal* or *USA Today*, for lists of businesses that buy and sell on the New York Stock Exchange.
   a. You are to invest $10,000 for a client.
   b. You have three weeks to work with this investment.
   c. You may purchase any number of stocks you choose in blocks of one hundred or more.
   d. You must charge your client $30 for each stock transaction (purchase or sale).
   e. You are limited to ten purchase transactions and ten sales transactions, using daily close price.
   f. Record all of your transactions on charts A and B.

Chart A: Record of Stock Purchases

Date of Stock Purchase	Name of Stock	Number of Shares Purchased	Price per Share	Brokerage Fee ($30)	Total Cost of Stock plus Brokerage Fee

continued

Chart B: Record of Stock Sales

Date of Stock Sale	Name of Stock	Number of Shares Sold	Price per Share	Brokerage Fee ($30)	Total Amount of Sale minus Brokerage Fee

2. What is the differece between the purchase price of the stocks you selected and the price you sold them for? (Note whether the price is up (+) or down (-) from the price you originally paid for each stock.)

   Stock 1 _____ Stock 2 _____ Stock 3 _____ Stock 4 _____ Stock 5 _____

   Stock 6 _____ Stock 7 _____ Stock 8 _____ Stock 9 _____ Stock 10 _____

3. At the end of three weeks, how much did you earn in brokerage fees? (The brokerage fee is charged to pay your commission and salary and the company's costs for doing business.) $________________

4. How much did your client's account earn or lose during this three-week period?

   Profit $________________________ Loss $________________________

continued

Name ______________________________ Date ____________________

14.8

Checkpoint

Pay Cash or Borrow?

Some people refuse to purchase anything unless they can pay cash, and some people purchase almost everything on credit. Most money managers feel that making wise use of a modest amount of credit is the best course of action for most consumers. Consider the case of Dwayne Sells and Marylin Fowler.

> Dwayne is single and earns $22,000 per year. From the time Dwayne was a child, his parents impressed him with the idea that he should never borrow money. Dwayne has decided to buy a new car. The purchase price is $18,700. He has no debts and has $41,000 invested in a savings account, government bonds, and common stocks. Dwayne's investments earned 12 percent last year and are doing a little better this year.
>
> Marylin is single and earns $31,000 per year. She can't remember the last time she bought a large-ticket item for cash. Marylin has also decided to buy a new car that will cost $18,700. She has $4,200 invested through her credit union. It pays her about 9 percent interest. Marylin plans to withdraw $2,500 from her credit union and use it as a down payment on the new car. She presently owes $3,500 on her credit card at an annual rate of 17 percent interest. She also owes a large department store $5,600 at an annual rate of 19 percent interest.
>
> Both Dwayne and Marylin are eligible for the best rate of interest in the area (9.5 percent) if they decide to borrow money to purchase a car. They would be required to make a down payment of at least $2,500.

1. What financial advice would you offer Dwayne? (Provide specific reasons for your advice.)

   a. Borrow as much as possible ____ b. Pay cash____ c. Other:____

   ____

   ____

   ____

2. What financial advice would you offer Marylin? (Provide specific reasons for your advice.)

   a. Borrow as much as possible ____ b. Pay cash____ c. Other:____

   ____

   ____

   ____

3. If interest rates on car loans increased to 13.5 percent, would you change the advice you gave Dwayne? If so, provide your new advice and reasons. If not, why not? ______________________________

   ____

4. If interest rates on car loans increased to 13.5 percent, would you change the advice you gave Marylin? If so, provide your new advice and reasons. If not, why not? ______________________________

   ____

Name ______________________________ Date ____________________

Checkpoint 14.9

Finding the Right Words

Chapter 14 of your textbook contains numerous terms that employers and workers use. Recognizing and understanding these terms will help you make the important career decisions you will soon face.

Fill in the blank spaces in the vocabulary terms to complete the following sentences.

1. E ___ o ___ ___ mi ___ s is the social science concerned with the way a society uses its productive resources to fulfill the needs and wants of each member.

2. A ___ ca ___ cit ___ exists when people have limited resources compared to their wants.

3. ___ e ___ ___ i ___ es are tasks that other people or machines do that cannot be physically weighed or measured.

4. ___ nd ___ str ___ ___ l ___ r ___ d ___ ct ___ are goods that are produced for and sold to other producers.

5. A ___ a ___ ke ___ comprises people or organizations that purchase a particular good or service.

6. Resources or benefits that a business gives up to produce a particular product or provide a particular service, are known as the ___ pp ___ rt ___ n ___ ty c ___ s ___.

7. Natural resources, labor, capital and management are examples of l ___ m ___ t ___ d ___ e ___ ou ___ ___ e ___.

8. An e ___ o ___ o ___ i ___ s ___ s ___ e ___ is the method a society uses to determine how it will use and distribute available resources.

9. In a fr ___ ___ ___ nt ___ rpr ___ s ___ ___ y ___ t ___ m, people may own the means of production, have the freedom to use them as they see fit, and may freely create and operate businesses.

10. ___ ro ___ i ___ is the money left over after all expenses are paid.

11. D ___ m ___ ___ d is the willingness of consumers to buy goods or services at a certain price in the marketplace.

12. A person or group that buys or uses goods or services to satisfy personal needs and wants is a c ___ ns ___ m ___ r.

  continued

13. The total value of goods and services that a nation produces for the marketplace during a specific period ot time, usually a single year, is known as the g ___ o ___ s d ___ m ___ ___ t ___ c p ___ ___ d ___ c ___.

14. T ___ ch ___ ___ l ___ gy is the science of mechanical and industrial arts.

15. S ___ p ___ l ___ is the willingness of producers to produce and sell goods or services at a certain price in the marketplace.

16. C ___ m ___ e ___ i ___ i ___ n means striving against others to win something.

17. The F ___ d ___ r ___ l R ___ s ___ r ___ e S ___ s ___ e ___, a network of twelve regional banks, regulates banking in the United States.

18. The ability of a producer to provide a good or service at a lower opportunity cost than other producers is its c ___ mp ___ r ___ t ___ v ___ ___ dv ___ nt ___ g ___.

Name ______________________ Date ______________

14.10 Checkpoint

Checking Your Location

1. For each of the following statements, circle **F** if the statement is more false than true. Circle **T** if the statement is more true than false.

T F a. The word *economics* comes from the ancient Greek word *oikonomikos*, meaning "the management of a household."

T F b. For most purposes, the terms *capitalist system*, *market system*, and *free enterprise system* have the same meaning.

T F c. Government regulations may limit certain areas of free choice, private ownership, competition between businesses, or the right to make unlimited margins of profit.

T F d. Every time a new idea is turned into a product or a service and a business is formed to produce the product or provide the service, workers are laid off, jobs are eliminated, and profits are restricted.

T F e. Profit is the major motivator of every business.

T F f. Services are usually more difficult to distribute than goods.

T F g. Consumers give little thought to prices if the product is high quality and satisfies a need or a want; producers want to sell the highest possible volume of their products or services without worrying about profits.

T F h. When a business obtains complete control of the supply or demand of a good or service, it becomes a monopoly.

T F i. Early settlers on the American frontier had little need for money.

T F j. The Federal Deposit Insurance Corporation (FDIC) protects banks against losses on real estate mortgages.

T F k. During periods of good times, business peaks, and economic activity reach their highest point in the business cycle.

T F l. Workers are protected, in part, from bad times by unemployment benefits.

T F m. When the average price of goods and services decreases over a prolonged period of time, the economy is in a period of inflation.

T F n. As systems of communication and production technology change at a dizzying pace, the skill requirements for jobs become more sophisticated.

T F o. Ninety-five percent of the customers buying goods in the world economy live outside the United States.

continued

2. Use the space below to rewrite the statements you marked **false** and make them **true**. Include the letter of each statement you rewrite.

Name ______________________ Date ______________

Checkpoint 15.1

Interview a Successful Entrepreneur

Finding out about business from successful entrepreneurs will help you understand what it takes to succeed. Pick an area of business that interests you, and contact a business of that type. Ask to speak with the owner. If the owner is busy, explain the purpose of your call and ask if you can make an appointment to interview the owner at a time that is convenient for the owner.

1. Ask the following questions in your interview.

Name of entrepreneur: ______________ Form of business: ______________

Business name: ______________ Date business was started: ______________

a. When and where did you first get the idea of going into business? ______________

b. What personal interests or hobbies were involved in your decision? ______________

c. What education or training and previous work experience have been helpful in this business? ______________

d. Why did you select your present location for the business? ______________

e. How many hours a week do you work? ______________

f. What are some of the risks and problems you face in operating this business, and how do you handle them? ______________

g. What legal forms must you complete, and how much time do you spend on them? ______________

h. What do you like about having your own business? What don't you like? ______________

continued

2. Answer the following questions after the interview.

   a. What personal characteristics made the entrepreneur successful in business? ______________________

   ____

   ____

   b. Do you have any of these characteristics? If so, which ones? ______________________

   ____

   c. In what ways did this interview convince you that you would or would not like to become an entrepreneur? ______________________

   ____

   ____

"I GOT THE IDEA FOR THE BUSINESS FROM MY CHILDHOOD HOBBY.. COLLECTING COINS.."

Name ______________________________ Date ____________________

15.2 Checkpoint

Follow Your Hobbies to Entrepreneurship

In Chapter 15 of your textbook, you learned that our free enterprise economic system encourages people to become entrepreneurs. Many entrepreneurs began by turning their hobbies and other activities into money-making opportunities.

1. Match the hobbies or activities in column B with the entrepreneurs in column A that are most related.

Column A - Entrepreneurs

a. _____ Owner of an auto repair shop
b. _____ Owner of a photography studio
c. _____ Owner of a lawn and garden store
d. _____ Owner of a health spa
e. _____ Owner of a kennel

Column B - Childhood Hobby or Activity

1. Having pets and caring for them
2. Raising flowers and having a garden
3. Being active in sports activities
4. Riding and repairing bikes and, later driving and repairing automobiles
5. Taking photographs of family and friends

2. What are your two favorite hobbies or activities?

   a. ______________________________

   b. ______________________________

3. What two skills have you developed from these hobbies or activities?

   a. ______________________________

   b. ______________________________

4. a. Name one business that uses these skills. ______________________________

   b. How would an entrepreneur use these skills? ______________________________

   ____

5. What hobbies do you suppose the following entrepreneurs enjoyed?

   a. Elvis Presley (musician) ______________________________

   b. Bill Gates (founder of Microsoft, a computer software company) ______________________________

   c. Liz Clairborne (Liz Claiborne Fashions) ______________________________

   d. Walt Disney (Walt Disney Productions) ______________________________

6. a. Name one new product or service that you would like to have in your community.

   ____

   b. As an entrepreneur, how would you go about making this product or service available in your community. ______________________________

   ____

Name ______________________________ Date ____________________

15.3 Checkpoint

Entrepreneurship — Is It for You?

Outgoing, upbeat, enthusiastic, positive-thinking risk takers are good candidates for entrepreneurship. From each group of three statements below, select one that is most like you. Circle the statements you select.

1. a. I like to play a competitive sport.
   b. I like to watch TV.
   c. I like to go to a party.

2. a. I enjoy adventurous activities.
   b. I enjoy safe activities.
   c. I enjoy routine activities.

3. a. I prefer to organize work tasks my own way.
   b. I prefer to help others to organize tasks.
   c. I prefer to have work tasks organized for me.

4. a. I like being responsible for my actions.
   b. I like sharing responsibility with others.
   c. I like not being responsible for things.

5. a. I know I can succeed at a task.
   b. I am usually able to succeed.
   c. I frequently don't succeed.

6. a. I like new ways to solve problems.
   b. I am cautious in solving problems.
   c. I like proven answers.

7. a. I enjoy organizing people for a purpose.
   b. I enjoy being a useful member of a group.
   c. I don't care for groups of people.

8. a. I don't quit until the problem is solved.
   b. I do it right the first time.
   c. I don't waste time on problems.

9. a. I like to find new ways to do things.
   b. I like to be careful about new ways of doing things.
   c. I like to do things using proven methods.

10. a. I frequently take risks.
    b. I seldom take risks.
    c. I am always sure of what I do.

11. a. I become impatient with delays.
    b. I accept delays without anger.
    c. I am not at all concerned with delays.

12. a. I prefer to plan and make my plan work.
    b. I do good work without planning things.
    c. I prefer to follow plans that are given to me.

13. a. I use my time efficiently.
    b. I spend a lot of time just enjoying whatever I'm doing.
    c. I'm seldom concerned about time.

14. a. I refuse to quit until I succeed.
    b. If it doesn't work, I try something else.
    c. Often times, success isn't worth the trouble it requires.

15. a. I like to learn and improve from my failures.
    b. I like to be cautious and not fail.
    c. Most things don't make a difference to me.

16. a. I would enjoy producing a new product.
    b. I would enjoy producing a proven, quality product.
    c. The type of product is unimportant.

continued

Count the total number of ***a***, ***b***, and ***c*** statements you circled.

Total ***a*** statements: _____ Total ***b*** statements: _____ Total ***c*** statements: _____

Number of *a* Responses	**Similarity to an Entrepreneur**
11 – 16	You have very strong entrepreneurial characteristics.
8 – 10	You have a greater-than-average interest in entrepreneurship.
5 – 7	You have an average interest in entrepreneurship.
0 – 4	You have very little similarity to an entrepreneur.

Review the ***a*** statements that you circled, and give examples of times when you demonstrated these entrepreneurial characteristics.

____

____

____

____

Name ______________________ Date ______________

Checkpoint 15.4

A Franchise Is Best for Some Entrepreneurs

Statistics indicate that nine out of ten franchises succeed during their first year of business. Select a franchise business that interests you, and contact the owner of that business. It may be a McDonalds, I Can't Believe It's Yogurt, H & R Block, Computertots, UniGlobe Travel, Jiffy Lube, or any franchise that you frequent. (For additional names of franchises, review the franchise directory published by the International Franchise Association or Gale Research's *Worldwide Franchise Directory*. Ask to speak with the franchise owner. If the owner is busy, explain the purpose of your call and ask if you can make an appointment to interview the owner at a time that is convenient for the owner. Ask the following questions in your interview.

Name of entrepreneur: ______________________ Name of business: ______________________

1. Why did you choose to be associated with this company and its products and services?

   ____

   ____

2. What kind of training did you receive to operate this franchise? (Did your training include selling, merchandising, advertising, and bookkeeping?) ______________________

   ____

   ____

3. What manuals and sales and marketing aids are available? ______________________
4. Did the franchisor check to see if you have the background experience and financial ability to succeed in the franchise? ______________________
5. Does the franchisor provide continuing assistance? ______________________
6. What were the franchise fees and the initial investment royalities? ______________________

   ____

7. Did the franchisor offer to help finance the franchise? ______________________
8. What are your rights and obligations according to your contract, including any restrictions on business activities if you leave the franchise? ______________________

   ____

9. What inventory, equipment, and working capital did you need to open the franchise? ______________________

   ____

continued

10. Do you have exclusive rights to a certain territory? ______

11. What do you like about having this franchise? What don't you like? ______

______

______

12. Would you buy the franchise again? ______

Why or why not? ______

______

______

Name ______________________________ Date ______________________

15.5

Checkpoint

Select a Business and Develop a Plan for Its Success

When people think about running a business, they frequently think about working for or with people. What about businesses where you spend most of your time working with facts or machines? In fact, an entrepreneur might have a business working with people, facts, or things.

1. Look back at your answers to Checkpoint 2.6. Record your totals here:

   a. People _____ b. Data _____ c. Things _____

2. a. Review the yellow pages of your telephone book. Find four businesses that match your people, data, and things interests. (Some promising fields in the years ahead are energy, environment, hazardous waste handling, robotics, health care, child care, and elder care.)

   (1) ______________________ (2) ______________________

   (3) ______________________ (4) ______________________

   b. Circle the business you would be most interested in owning.

3. Image that you are starting a business of the type you have circled.

   a. What goods or services will you offer? ______________________

   b. Who will be your target market? (Include age, sex, and interests.) ______________________

   ____

   c. What are the positive aspects of this business for you? What are the negative aspects? __________

   ____

   ____

   d. What form of business will you have (sole proprietorship, partnership, franchise, corporation)?

   ____

   e. What are the advantages of this form of business to you? ______________________

   ____

   ____

   f. What are the disadvantages of this form of business to you? ______________________

   ____

   ____

   g. What special licenses or permits will you need to operate legally? ______________________

   ____

continued

h. What will you name your business? ______________________________

i. Where will you locate your business? Why? ______________________________

____

j. What will make your business different from and better than your competition? ______________________________

____

____

k. How will you promote your business so that it is profitable? ______________________________

____

l. What prices will you charge? ______________________________

m. What will you need to learn to be successful in this business? ______________________________

____

n. What resources can you locate to help start and maintain your business? ______________________________

o. What supplies, tools, furniture, special equipment, and inventory will you need to start your business? ______________________________

____

p. How many employees will you need? ______________________________

q. What are their job titles? ______________________________

____

r. What will your business hours be? Opening time: __________ Closing time: __________

s. What days of the week will you be open? ______________________________

t. What is one reason your business might fail? ______________________________

____

u. What entrepreneurial characteristics do you have that will make you succeed? ______________________________

____

4. Write a newspaper advertisement to announce the opening of your business. Consider the image you want to project and the specific customers you are trying to reach.

____

____

____

____

____

Name ______________________ Date ______________

Checkpoint 15.6

Profit or Loss — Income and Expenses

The amount of income received from a business transaction minus the expenses of conducting the transaction equals the profit. If the total cost of the transaction is greater than the amount taken in, there is a loss.

Remember Erica from Chapter 15, She started the Pied Piper Day-Care Center. She will hire extra employees in the summer for children who are in grades 1 through 3.

1. Calculate Erica's daily and weekly profit or loss for the two weeks described below. Use a separate piece of paper for your calculations.

Formula: Total money received – cost = profit
Cost – total money received = loss

Date	Total Receipts	Wages	Rent	Equipment/ Supplies	Profit	Loss
Monday, Dec. 2	$780	$500	$000	$185	$	$
Tuesday, Dec. 3	$1,100	$500	$000	$45	$	$
Wednesday, Dec. 4	$912	$500	$000	$38	$	$
Thursday, Dec. 5	$912	$375	$000	$55	$	$
Friday, Dec. 6	$580	$500	$500	$135	$	$
Weekly Total	$____	$____	$____	$____	$____	$____

Date	Total Receipts	Wages	Rent	Equipment/ Supplies	Profit	Loss
Monday, June 17	$2,200	$850	$000	$295	$	$
Tuesday, June 18	$1,800	$850	$000	$383	$	$
Wednesday, June 19	$2,400	$990	$000	$225	$	$
Thursday, June 20	$2,275	$990	$000	$265	$	$
Friday, June 21	$1,800	$1,075	$550	$445	$	$
Weekly Total	$____	$____	$____	$____	$____	$____

continued

2. Figure the monthly profit or loss for each of the following businesses. First, figure the gross profit by subtracting the cost of goods sold from the net sales. Second, figure the net profit or loss by subtracting the operating expenses from the gross profit.

Company	Sales	Goods Sold	Profit	Expenses	Profit	Loss
J&R Books	$4,790	$2,440		$1,240		
Stolz Personnel	$240,650	$144,067		$76,800		
Waterloo Transmission	$184,400	$136,800		$65,200		

Name ______________________________ Date ______________________

15.7 Checkpoint

The American Dream

1. Jeremy graduated from a vocational high school two years ago. He majored in electronics repair. He has saved almost $4,000 while working as an electronics repairer for a large company. A year ago, Jeremy started a small shop in his parent's basement where he works part-time repairing TVs, VCRs, tape players, and radios. Jeremy has decided that he can't continue to work forty hours per week on his regular job and another twenty in his part-time business. He has decided to select one of the following alternatives.

   - Continue with his regular job. The pay is average, but the work is steady. The fringe benefits are average. He likes his boss, his fellow workers, and his work tasks. The job requires little risk on Jeremy's part.
   - Rent a small store and establish his own sole-proprietorship electronics repair shop. The hours would be long and the income low — for a long time. In fact, Jeremy would need to borrow money from a bank to get started. Jeremy likes being his own boss, and he would enjoy the challenge. He hopes that he will be able to employ other electronics repairers in the future. The potential rewards are high, but the risks are great. Jeremy could lose his savings and end up in debt.

   a. Which of Jeremy's characteristics and experiences would help him succeed in his own business? What advice would you offer him? ______________________________

   b. If Jeremy starts his own business, what business niche would he fill? What community needs would his business serve? ______________________________

   c. What school experience would be helpful to Jeremy as an entrepreneur? ______________________________

   d. For Jeremy, what would be the rewards of owning his own business? ______________________________

   e. What experiences would make Jeremy feel confident that he can succeed as an entrepreneur? ______________________________

f. What type of business ownership is Jeremy considering? __________

g. In what way has Jeremy's family shown support for his potential enterprise? __________

h. Do you believe that Jeremy should learn how to fix computers and fax machines in addition to the electronics repair work he does now? Explain your answer. __________

i. What do you believe will be the key to Jeremy's success or failure in business? __________

2. Look back to Checkpoint 15.5. What business did you decide to start? __________
   a. Estimate the cost of three major items you will need to start up this business. (for example, licenses, franchise fees, insurance, equipment, office supplies, remodeling, advertising, accountant fees, employees wages, building rental.)

Item	Approximate Cost	Company to Purchase item From

   b. Would you be willing to use all or most of your personal assets as collateral against a loan to start a business? Why or why not? __________

3. Lenders will want to know if you have ever borrowed money before, from whom you borrowed, and when you paid it back. Complete the following chart.

When and Why I Borrowed Money Borrowed Money	From Whom?	How Long I Took to Repay the Loan

Were you a good credit risk to the people who loaned you money? Why or why not? __________

Name ______________________________ Date ________________

Checkpoint 15.8

Piles of Paperwork

The Fair Labor Standards Act (FLSA) requires employers to keep records on wages, hours, and other items, as specified in the Department of Labor recordkeeping regulations. Remember Erica and her Pied Piper Day-Care Center? Her sister Lindsay became her business partner and the business became very successful.

1. Name four types of employees that would be needed to operate the Pied Piper Day-Care Center.

	Job Title	**Major Work Task**
a.	____________________	____________________
b.	____________________	____________________
c.	____________________	____________________
d.	____________________	____________________

2. The employees of Erica's day-care center work an eight-hour day with time and a half for all hours over eight per day. Use the following payroll worksheet to calculate the wages the business must pay this week.

Employee	**Hours per Day**					**Hourly Rate**	**Overtime Rate**	**Regular Wages**	**Overtime Wages**	**Total Wages**
	M	**T**	**W**	**T**	**F**					
Barbara Tate	8	12	8	12	8	$6.00	$9.00			
Janet Simms	8	12	8	12	8	$6.20	$9.30			
Alonzo Adams	8	8	8	8	8	$9.50	$14.25			
Trisha Wilson	8	0	8	0	7	$6.00	$9.00			
Mack Johnson	8	8	8	8	10	$15.00	$22.50			
Arnold Smith	8	8	8	8	8	$6.00	$9.00			
Traci Garcia	8	8	8	8	8	$7.00	$10.50			
Akeesha Brown	8	8	8	8	8	$7.00	$10.50			
Total wages for the week										

continued

3. Notice that Trisha Wilson didn't come to work on Tuesday and Thursday. She was an hour late on Friday.

   What effect did this have on the weekly payroll? ______________________________

   ____

4. Which employee would you expect to be the most skilled? ______________________________

   What makes you think so? ______________________________

Name ______________________________ Date ____________________

15.9

Checkpoint

Checking Your Location

1. For each of the following statements, circle **F** if the statement is more false than true. Circle **T** if the statement is more true than false.

T F a. Entrepreneurs see business ownership as the most promising path to financial success, independence, and true job satisfaction.

T F b. The most common types of self-employment are as a small-scale hotelier, beauty shop owner, and car manufacturer.

T F c. Most successful entrepreneurs earn better-than-average wages, and some become wealthy.

T F d. According to the Small Business Association (SBA), most small businesses fail within one year.

T F e. Most small business entrepreneurs acquire business capital by taking out personal loans.

T F f. Luck is the most important factor in building a successful enterprise.

T F g. Most small gas stations, barber shops, restaurants, video stores, and campgrounds are sole proprietorships.

T F h. Like an individual person, a corporation can sue or be sued in a court of law.

T F i. All franchisors are required by law to provide a Uniform Franchise Offering Circular to the Federal Trade Commission.

T F j. Financial institutions rarely require entrepreneurs to provide them with a written business plan before they will consider making a loan.

T F k. Whether large, small, new, or well established, sooner or later every business has problems and the owner needs help.

T F l. Most new enterprises lose money for several months or longer.

T F m. Venture capitalists usually require the business owner to sell them 50 to 90 percent ownership of the new business in return for the capital.

T F n. Only large businesses must have an employer identification number to complete tax forms and other required government information forms during the life of a business.

T F o. Business owners can deduct legal business expenses from their gross income to arrive at their taxable income.

continued

2. Use the space below to rewrite the statements you marked **false** and make them **true**. Include the letter of each statement you rewrite.

Name ______________________ Date ______________

Find and Use Career Information

The satisfaction you receive from your career will depend on how well your choice of an occupation meets your personal, social, and economic needs and expectations. Career information can help you discover several occupations that may meet your needs and expectations.

The library is an excellent place to find up-to-date career information. You will find useful information in occupational information files, audio- and videotapes, films, books, pamphlets, and magazines. Visit your school or public library, and research the following materials.

1. Select a career audio- or videotape or a film to preview. (Circle one.)

   a. What is the title of your selection? ______________________

   b. What specific jobs does it describe? ______________________

   c. List two important facts that you learned from this material. ______________________

   ____

2. Using the *Encyclopedia of Associations*, list three trade and professional publications that you discovered in your library research.

	Title	Publisher	Author
a.			
b.			
c.			

3. If you are not familiar with the computerized career information system in your school or public library, ask your guidance counselor, school librarian, or public librarian to help you access it. What career information were you able to find on the computer? ______________________

   ____

   ____

   ____

4. Using the *Reader's Guide to Periodical Literature*, list three periodicals or magazines that contain career articles.

	Title of Magazine	Title of Article
a.		
b.		
c.		

Name ______________________________ Date ____________________

Checkpoint 16.2

The Occupational Outlook Handbook

Use the *Occupational Outlook Handbook* (OOH) in your school library or in your counselor's office for this activity.

1. Browse through the OOH's table of contents. Notice how related occupations are grouped according to the Standard Occupational Classification System. This system is based on the type of work performed in occupations. Which of the clusters are you considering most seriously for your future occupation?

   ____

2. Read the section "Keys to Understanding What's in the Handbook," and answer the following questions. What will you learn about in each of the following categories when you use the OOH to research occupations?

   a. The nature of the work ______________________________

   b. The working conditions ______________________________

   c. The education and training needed for employment ______________________________

   d. The job outlook ______________________________

   e. The earnings ______________________________

   f. Occupations related to the occupation you are researching ______________________________

   g. Sources of additional occupational information ______________________________

3. Using the table of contents, locate the occupation of engineering technician. It's under the heading 'Technicians and Related Support Occupations.'

   a. List one of the DOT numbers given for this occupation. ______________________________

continued

b. What is the nature of the work for this occupation? ____________________

____

c. What is the job outlook for engineering technicians? ____________________

____

4. Go to the back of the OOH to the section "Dictionary of Occupational Titles Coverage." Locate the DOT number you used for engineering technician in question 3.
   a. What page is this occupation found on in the *Dictionary of Occupational Titles* (DOT)? __________
   b. What is the Standard Occupation Code (SOC)? ____________________

5. Look at the index at the back of the OOH. On what page will you find information about the occupation you are most interested in pursuing? ____________________

"I SEE CLOUDS.. YOU WILL BE PAID TO TAKE A LONG JOURNEY!"

Name ______________________________ Date ____________________

16.3 Checkpoint

Learn to Use the DOT

The *Dictionary of Occupational Titles* (DOT) contains a brief description of job duties for more than twenty-five thousand occupations. The current two-volume set includes definitions and information about occupational requirements, such as interests, body strength, education, and specific vocational preparation.

Occupations in the DOT are assigned a code number based on the occupation's relationship to other occupations and the extent to which the work involves people, data, or things. Use the DOT in your school library for this activity.

There are two easy ways to locate occupational descriptions in the DOT.

1. If you know the title of the occupation you are looking for, turn to the alphabetical index in the back of the DOT. Each occupation listed has a nine-digit code. The first occupational description in the DOT is architect, and the first three digits are 001. The last occupational description is screen printer helper, and the first three digits are 979. All DOT occupational descriptions are found in order of their first three digits. Several occupational descriptions will have the same first three digits, but using this simple technique will enable you to find the occupation you are seeking.

   a. Number the following occupations in the order you would find them in the DOT.

Occupational Title	Nine-Digit Code	Order of Appearance
Sail cutter (canvas goods)	781.384-018	________
Assembler, automobile	806.684-010	________
Bag machine operator	649.685-014	________
Photoengraver	971.381-022	________
Wedding consultant	299.357-018	________

   b. Locate these occupational titles for practice.

2. The occupations in the DOT are divided into nine occupational groups. Locate the index called "Three-Digit Occupational Groups" in the front of the DOT. This index allows you to review occupations in the nine groups and locate them by the first two numbers of their nine-digit code.

   a. Number the following occupational groups in the order you would find them in the DOT.

Three-Digit Occupational Group	Occupational Group	Code	Order of Appearance
Professional, technical, and managerial	Medicine and health	07	________
Structural work occupations	Welders and cutters	81	________
Processing	Processing paper	53	________
Clerical and sales occupations	Production/stock clerks	22	________
Benchwork occupations	Painting and decorating	74	________
Agricultural, fishery, forestry	Forestry occupations	45	________
Service occupations	Protective services	37	________
Machine trades	Printing occupations	65	________

   b. Locate the occupational groups for practice.

continued

3. Each occupation in the DOT has a nine-digit code. To research careers in the DOT, you will need to understand the meaning of the first six digits. You have learned how to use the first three digits to locate careers. The second group of three digits (000.**XXX**-000) tells you how much involvement the occupation has with Data (facts), People, or Things (tools, machines). (Refer to Chapter 3 in your textbook where you learned about data, people, and things involvement.) The level of involvement is designated by the numbers 0 to 8. 0 represents a very high level of involvement, and 8 represents no involvement at all. The following are descriptions of the various levels of involvement.

Digit 4 (Data)	**Digit 5 (People)**	**Digit 6 (Things)**
0 = synthesizing data	0 = Mentoring people	0 = Setting up tools/machines
1 = Coordinating data	1 = Negotiating with people	1 = Doing precision work
2 = Analyzing data	2 = Instructing people	2 = Operating/controlling things
3 = Compiling data	3 = Supervising people	3 = Driving/operating machines
4 = Computing data	4 = Diverting people	4 = Manipulating things
5 = Copying data	5 = Persuading people	5 = Tending machines
6 = Comparing data	6 = Speaking/signaling	6 = Feeding/taking things off
7 = No involvement with data	7 = Serving people	7 = Handling things
8 = No involvement with data	8 = No involvement with people	8 = No involvement with things

a. What levels of data, people, and things involvement would you like to have on your ideal job?

Data ____________________ People ____________________ Things ____________________

b. How much involvement do each of the following occupations have with data, people, things?

	Occupation	**DOT Code**	**Data**	**People**	**Things**
Example:	Architect	001.061-010	0 = Synthesizing	6 = Speaking/Signaling	1 = Precision work
	Accountant	160.167-042	________	________	________
	Geologist	024.061-161	________	________	________
	Counselor	045.107-010	________	________	________
	Mechanic	620.261-010	________	________	________
	Typist	203.362-010			
	________	________	________	________	________
	________	________	________	________	________

c. Use the DOT to complete the chart above for two occupations you are considering.

d. Does the level of data, people, and things involvement for the two occupations you are most seriously considering match with your answer to question 1? ____________________

e. How would you like to spend your time on the job? Record the percentage of work time you would spend in each of the following areas on your ideal job. Be certain that the nine categories total 100 percent.

Working with Data	**Working with People**	**Working with Machines**
___% of time spent analyzing	___% of time spent leading	___% of time spent understanding
___% of time spent organizing	___% of time spent persuading	___% of time spent fixing/adjusting
___% of time spent collecting	___% of time spent helping	___% of time spent using

Name ______________________________ Date ____________________

Checkpoint 16.4

Career Research Report

Use the following outline to write a career research report using the resources described in Chapter 16 of your textbook. Consult several sources of information for your report.

Title of Occupation to be researched: ____________________

I. **Nature of the work**

a. What work tasks are performed? ____________________

b. What equipment or tools are used? ____________________

c. What are the fields of specialization? ____________________

d. What skills are needed? ____________________

II. **Working conditions/surroundings**

a. What are the physical conditions of the work site (noise levels, health hazards, stress level, cleanliness, indoors/outdoors)? ____________________

b. What is the daily and weekly work schedule? ____________________

III. **Projected earnings**

a. What are the beginning, average, and highest earnings a worker can expect? ____________________

b. What are the benefits in addition to earnings, (commissions, tips, overtime bonuses, vacations, medical care, retirement plans)? ____________________

IV. **Where workers are employed**

a. In which career cluster or industry is this occupation usually found? ____________________

continued

b. In what type of establishment and location is the work performed? ______________________

____

V. Employment outlook

a. How many workers are employed in this occupation? ______________________

b. What is the projected number of openings for this occupation in the future? ______________

____

VI. Education and training

a. What are the education and training requirements? ______________________

____

b. What licensing or certification is required? ______________________

____

VII. Career paths

a. What are the usual paths of advancement or movement? ______________________

____

____

VIII. Qualities and rewards that affect success and satisfaction

a. What personal qualities are related to success (interests, values, goals) in this occupation?

____

____

b. What accomplishments or aptitudes demonstrate ability to be successful? ______________

____

____

c. What personal rewards and satisfactions will this occupation provide or not provide? ________

____

____

IX. Related occupations

a. What occupations are related to this occupation? ______________________

____

X. Additional information

a. Where is there additional information about this occupation? ______________________

____

Name ______________________________ Date ____________________

Evaluating Your Occupational Research

Evaluate the information in your occupational report and decide if this occupation be a good choice for you.

1. Number of workers employed in this occupation: ____________________

   Would this provide you with numerous job openings? Yes ________ No ________

2. Education and training required: ____________________

   Does this match with your personal educational goals? Yes ________ No ________

3. Outlook for this occupation: ____________________

   Would you have good employment in the future? Yes ________ No ________

4. Earnings for this occupation: ____________________

   Would the earnings satisfy your lifestyle needs and wants? Yes ________ No ________

5. Nature of the work: ____________________

   Would the job tasks satisfy your interests and values? Yes ________ No ________

6. Working conditions for this job: ____________________

   Would these working conditions satisfy you? Yes ________ No ________

7. Occupations related to this job: ____________________

   Would any of these occupations interest you? Yes ________ No ________

   Total your responses. **Total "yes": _____** **Total "no":_____**

If you have:

0-3 yes answers	You probably wouldn't care for this job area. Use the same activity questions to explore additional occupations.
4 yes answers	You should continue to research this job. With additional research you may increase your interest in this job, or you may discover that it isn't for you.
4-7 yes answers	You probably would enjoy this career area. You would benefit from speaking to workers in this occupation about their work and researching related occupations. Perhaps you can visit a worker in this career area at his or her place of employment.

Name ______________________________ Date ____________________

Checkpoint 16.6

Listen and Observe: Interviewing a Worker

Interview a worker in an occupation that interests you. Use the following interview format to complete this activity. Remember to do research on the occupation before interviewing the worker.

Person interviewed ______________________________ Job title ____________________

Years of experience ____________ Name of employer's business ____________________

Questions to ask:

1. What organizations or industries provide employment for this occupation? ____________________

____

2. Why did you choose this line of work? ______________________________

____

3. In what ways do you find your work satisfying? What has been the highlights of your career so far?

____

____

4. In what way is the work not satisfying? What have been your most unpleasant work experiences?

____

____

5. What skills are needed to perform your daily work tasks? ______________________________

____

6. What personal characteristics are needed to be successful in this career? ____________________

____

7. Please record the percentage of time you spend in each of the following areas on an average workday. (Be certain that the nine areas total 100 percent).

Working with Data	**Working with People**	**Working with Machines**
___% of time spent analyzing	___% of time spent leading	___% of time spent understanding
___% of time spent organizing	___% of time spent persuading	___% of time spent fixing/adjusting
___% of time spent collecting	___% of time spent helping	___% of time spent using

continued

8. What are some characteristics of the people with whom you work? The people for whom you work?

9. What education, training, or certification would I need to qualify for entry into this occupation?

10. Compared to other jobs, what are the advantages and disadvantages of your work?

11. How will changes in technology and world economics affect this occupation?

12. What are the career paths or areas of specialization in your line of work?

13. What are the beginning earnings in this occupation? What are the future earnings?

14. How does this occupation affect your family life? Your leisure activities? Your friendships?

15. What advice would you give a young person who is considering this line of work?

16. If you could do it over, would you choose this same line of work? Why or why not?

After the interview; answer these questions:

1. Did my expectations of the career differ from what I observed and learned during the interview?
2. Which of this occupation's job activities and benefits would I like as part of my future career? Which would I dislike?
3. Which of my personal qualities could cause me to be successful or unsuccessful in this career?
4. Compare how you would like to spend your time and how a real worker in this occupation actually spends his or her time. Were the results very similar, or somewhat similar, or very different?
5. Overall, would you be interested in pursuing the occupation in the future?

Name ______________________________ Date ____________________

16.7 Checkpoint

The Real Thing

You may not earn a lot of money and the working hours may not be perfect in a part-time or summer job, but this is a great way and time to learn about careers and how businesses operate. Remember, legal restrictions that are part of the Fair Labor Standards Act will limit your possibilities for employment.

1. Which of the following part-time or summer jobs are available in your community? Check all that apply.

Entertainment and recreation:

___recreation aide
___arts and crafts counselor
___entertainment at a theme park
___art work in advertising dept. or window trimming
___camp counselor
___nature guide
___modeling
___sightseeing guide
___music counselor
___stage hand
___ticket taker
___golf course attendant
___cabana attendant
___lifeguard

Clerical:

___word processing
___bookkeeping clerk
___receptionist
___typing
___stock clerk
___filing
___message or mail clerk
___cashier
___price marking and tagging on goods

Sales:

___telephone sales
___sporting events vendor
___door-to-door sales
___ice-cream vendor
___store or demonstration sales

Service:

___baby-sitting and child care
___packer or bagger in grocery
___ cook
___waiter/waitress
___dishwasher
___errand and delivery
___locker room attendant
___hostess
___chambermaid or janitor
___car/boat/trailer cleaning

Agriculture:

___greenskeeper
___fish hatchery worker
___landscape laborer
___forester aide
___deckhand
___law-service worker

Construction trades:

___ laborer

2. Which of the jobs that you checked most closely match your personal orientation? (Review Section 2 in Chapter 4 of your textbook)

a. ______________________ c. ______________________

b. ______________________ d. ______________________

3. How could working at a part-time or summer job that closely matches your personal orientation help you make a long-term career decision? ______________________

____

Name ______________________________ Date ______________________________

16.8 Checkpoint

Finding the Right Words

Chapter 16 of your textbook contains numerous terms that employers and workers use. Recognizing and understanding these terms will help you make the important career decisions you will soon face. Unscramble the terms in column **B** and match them to the definitions in column **A**.

Column A

_____ a. a classification system used to faciliatate the collection and presentation of industrial data

_____ b. fifteen groups of careers developed by the U.S. Office of Education

_____ c. a method for exploring occupations using an extensive data base

_____ d. a reference book that focuses on twelve specific interest areas

_____ e. an article written on a particular subject

_____ f. a reference book published every two years by the U.S. Department of Labor that describes in detail about 250 occupations

_____ g. an organizational framework for the OOH that contains twelve categories

_____ h. a Department of Labor production that defines more than 25,000 occupations or groups of occupations

_____ i. future employment trends

_____ j. a meeting to talk over something special

Column B

1. ______________________________
upaccontiola oooklut khanbdoo

2. ______________________________
iidonctyar fo puacontcioal lttise

3. ______________________________
edgui orf accupontiloa oraiontplxe

4. ______________________________
ziedmoctupre iionnformat mtssye

5. ______________________________
eniirtwev

6. ______________________________
aatsddnr apaccontiolu noitacifissalc

7. ______________________________
soeu reacer rustlec

8. ______________________________
asddatnr raidnuslt noacitifislcsa

9. ______________________________
phonogram

10. ______________________________
oymenpteml oooktlu

Name ______________________________ Date ____________________

Checkpoint 16.9

Checking Your Location

1. For each of the following statements, circle **F** if the statement is more false than true. Circle **T** if the statement is more true than false.

T F a. The OOH provides detailed descriptions of more than 85 percent of all jobs in the nation.

T F b. The DOT contains definitions and brief descriptions of more than one hundred thousand occupations.

T F c. The GOE focuses on twelve clearly defined interest areas.

T F d. Computerized career information systems usually contain nationwide as well as state-specific career information.

T F e. Classified newspaper advertisements are a poor source of local employment opportunities.

T F f. Industries that provide services will account for almost one out of every five new jobs by 2005.

T F g. You can learn a lot about careers from speakers and field experience.

T F h. Career exploring, career shadowing, and field experiences are good ways to observe workers in specific occupations.

T F i. Co-op and internship programs are a poor way for students to determine their suitability for an occupation.

T F j. Tech-prep programs offer students a foundation in many job skills and courses that are necessary for a technical education beyond high school.

T F k. Approximately 58 percent of all workplaces employ fewer than two workers.

T F l. Identifying certain occupations, occupational classifications, and career clusters that you dislike is a waste of time.

T F m. Learning how to use occupational information and exploring career choices now will help you make new career decisions in the future.

continued

T **F** n. The SOC divides occupations into groups, according to the type of work performed.

T **F** o. The SIC system answers the question of where people work.

2. Use the space below to rewrite the statements you marked **false** and make them **true**. Include the letter of each statement you rewrite.

Name ______________________ Date ______________

Checkpoint 17.1

Your Paycheck

Look at the sample pay stub shown here, then answer the questions that follow.

Name: Debi R. Mukherjee Social Security #: 274-25-1411 Check No.: 0046271

Payperiod: 9/15/95–9/30/95

Earnings	**This Pay Period**	**Year to Date**	**Deductions**	**This Pay Period**	**Year to Date**
Salary	1,154.25	26,547.75	Federal tax	142.61	3,279.92
Earnings			State tax	35.06	806.27
Hourly rate			City tax	23.09	530.96
Hours paid			FICA	125.02	4,270.80
Overtime rate			Pension	18.00	342.00
O.T. hrs. paid			Bonds		
Sales amount			United Way	5.00	90.00
Commission	480.00	9,500.00	Health Ins.		
			Dues		175.00

Gross Pay 1,634.25

Total Deductions 348.78

Net Pay 1,285.47

Illness Unpaid	**Illness Paid**	**Family Illness**	**Jury Duty**	**Vacation**	**Sick Leave Days Accum**
	2	2		**5 days**	63

1. What are the dates for this pay period? ______________
2. What is the amount of Debi's gross pay for this pay period? ______________
3. How much was taken our for the United Way? ______ For federal taxes? ______ For city tax? ______
4. What is the amount of Debi's take-home pay? ______________
5. Debi was paid for five vacation days. How much was this benefit worth to Debi if his annual salary is $46,535? ______________
6. If Debi earns a 6 percent commission on sales of chemicals, what would his commission be on sales of $75,400? ______________ On sales of $876.00? ______________
7. Your Social Security number is used to track your earnings while you're working and to track your benefits when you're receiving Social Security. How much was deducted from Debi's pay this period for Social Security/FICA? ______________

continued

8. Most people need forty credits (10 years of earnings) to qualify for Social Security benefits. Younger people need fewer credits to be eligible for disability benefits or for their family members to be eligible for survivors' benefits if they should die. A person with a forty-year work life who has contributed to the Social Security fund will find that at retirement, a total of five years of lowest earnings or no earnings are dropped in figuring their retirement benefits. Do you believe Social Security is a good idea? Explain your answer. ______________________________

____

____

____

____

____

____

____

____

____

"FORGET WHAT YOU LEARNED IN HIGH SCHOOL.. THIS IS CONGRESS AND WE ALWAYS SPEND MORE MONEY THAN WE HAVE!"

Name ______________________________ Date ____________________

17.2 Checkpoint

The W-2 Tax Form

Your employer will withhold (take out) taxes from your paycheck during the year and will deposit them in a federal bank. The amount your employer deducts is determined by how many dependents you tell your employer you have when you fill out your W-4 Form. By the end of the year, you should have paid all or almost all of the income tax due on your yearly income.

Soon after the end of the calender year in which you are employed, your employer will send you a W-2 form. This form shows how much you earned and how much income tax, Social Security, and Medicare was withheld from your earnings during the preceding year. Your withholding probably won't match your tax exactly. So when you report your income and figure your tax return for the year, you will usually have underpaid or overpaid your tax. If you owe money for taxes, you pay the balance due when you file your income tax return after the end of the year. If you paid too much, the IRS will send you a refund check after you file your return.

a Control number		OMB No. 1545-0008	
001			

b Employer's identification number 00-0000001	1 Wages, tips, other compensation 18,900.00	2 Federal income tax withheld 2,839.00
c Employer's name, address, and ZIP code CRS Sailing School 2001 Dolphin Way Seaside, HI 00111	3 Social security wages 18,900.00	4 Social security tax withheld 1,171.18
	5 Medicare wages and tips 274.05	6 Medicare tax withheld 274.05
	7 Social security tips	8 Allocated tips
d Employee's social security number 080-01-0404	9 Advance EIC payment	10 Dependent care benefits
e Employee's name, address, and ZIP code Lindsay M. Millard 700 Oceanview Drive Seaside, HI 00111	11 Nonqualified plans	12 Benefits included in box 1
	13 See Instrs. for box 13	14 Other
	15 Statutory employee ☐ Deceased ☐ Pension plan ☐ Legal rep. ☐ Hshld. emp. ☐ Subtotal ☐ Deferred compensation ☐	

16 State	Employer's state I.D. No.	17 State wages, tips, etc.	18 State income tax	19 Locality name	20 Local wages, tips, etc.	21 Local income tax
HI	XXX		HI			

Department of the Treasury—Internal Revenue Service

Form **W-2** Wage and Tax Statement **1995**

This information is being furnished to the Internal Revenue Service.

Copy B To Be Filed With Employee's FEDERAL Tax Return

continued

Examine the sample W-2 form on the previous page, then answer the questions that follow.

1. How much did Lindsay earn during the tax year? ________________
2. Who is her employer? ________________
3. How much was withheld for federal income taxes? ________________
4. How much was withheld for Social Security? ________________
5. How much was withheld for Medicare? ________________
6. What is Lindsay's Social Security number? ________________ (If your Form W-2 shows an incorrect Social Security number or name, notify your employer or the form-issuing agent as soon as possible to make sure your earnings are credited to your Social Security record.)

Name ______________________________ Date ______________________

17.3 Checkpoint

Filing Your Income Tax (Form 1040EZ)

According to the law, every taxpayer must file an income tax return no later than midnight on April 15, for the preceding calendar year. At this time, an adjustment is made for any overpayment or underpayment of the total tax due. Instructions for the tax form that you will complete will come to you in the mail in late December or early January. Once you receive your W-2 form, you will be able to fill out your income tax return.

In this activity, you will practice filling out a sample 1040EZ tax form. Form 1040 EZ is the shortest, simplest tax form. Read and follow the instructions below and on the form.

1. **Name and address**. Fill in your name, address, and Social Security number. For this activity, assume that you are single, have no dependents, and no one can claim you for a dependent.
2. **Presidential Election Campaign Fund**. If you wish to contribute to this fund, check the "yes" box. If you do not, check the "no" box.
3. **Report Your Income**. On line 1, enter the total wages from the sample W-2 form in Checkpoint 17.2.
4. The interest you receive from bank accounts and certain other investments is income and is therefore taxable. Assume that you had earned $220 in interest on your educational savings account. On line 2, enter interest income of $220.
5. On line 3, add your wages and interest together to figure your adjusted gross income.
6. **Standard Deduction and Personal Exemption**. Use the worksheet on the second page of Form 1040 EZ to figure the amount to enter on line 4. Assume that you lived on your own during the preceding year. Take a standard deduction of $3,800 and a personal exemption of $2,450 for a total of $6,250.
7. **Figure Your Payments and Tax**. Subtract line 4 from line 3, and enter the result on line 5. This is the amount of your taxable income. Your income tax is based on this amount.
8. On line 6, enter the amount of federal income tax withheld, as reported on the sample W-2 form in Checkpoint 17.2.
9. Line 7. Assume that you are not eligible for earned income credit.
10. Add the amounts on lines 6 and 7 (you will have nothing for line 7) and enter the total payments on line 8.
11. Look up your taxable income in the tax table shown below. Read down the income column until you find the line that includes your **taxable income**, shown on line 5. Read across the line to the tax column for a single person to find your tax. Enter this amount on line 9.
12. **Refund or Amount You Owe**. Compare lines 8 and 9. In this case, line 8 is larger than line 9. Subtract line 9 from line 8. Enter this amount on line 10. This is the amount of your tax refund.
13. If your employer had not withheld enough federal income tax from your wages, you would have had to enter that amount on line 11 and attach a check or money order for the amount due.
14. **Sign the Return**. Check your return, and make sure that the numbers are clear and correct and that the math is correct. Enter your occupation, and sign and date your return at the bottom of the form.

If Form 1040EZ, line 5, is—

At least	But less than	Single	Married filing jointly
		Your tax is—	
12,000	12,050	1,804	1,804
12,050	12,100	1,811	1,811
12,100	12,150	1,819	1,819
12,150	12,200	1,826	1,826
12,200	12,250	1,834	1,834
12,250	12,300	1,841	1,841
12,300	12,350	1,849	1,849
12,350	12,400	1,856	1,856
12,400	12,450	1,864	1,864
12,450	12,500	1,871	1,871
12,500	12,550	1,879	1,879
12,550	12,600	1,886	1,886
12,600	12,650	1,894	1,894
12,650	12,700	1,901	1,901
12,700	12,750	1,909	1,909
12,750	12,800	1,916	1,916
12,800	12,850	1,924	1,924
12,850	12,900	1,931	1,931

continued

Department of the Treasury—Internal Revenue Service

Form **1040EZ** **Income Tax Return for Single and Joint Filers With No Dependents** **1994** (L)

OMB No. 1545-0675

Use the IRS label (See page 12.) Otherwise, please print.

LABEL HERE

Print your name (first, initial, last)

If a joint return, print spouse's name (first, initial, last)

Home address (number and street). If you have a P.O. box, see page 12. Apt. no.

City, town or post office, state and ZIP code. If you have a foreign address, see page 12.

Your social security number

Spouse's social security number

See instructions on back and in Form 1040EZ booklet.

Presidential Election Campaign (See page 12.)

Note: *Checking "Yes" will not change your tax or reduce your refund.*

Do you want $3 to go to this fund? ▶ Yes No

If a joint return, does your spouse want $3 to go to this fund? ▶ Yes No

Dollars Cents

Income

Attach Copy B of Form(s) W-2 here. Enclose, but do not attach, any payment with your return.

1 Total wages, salaries, and tips. This should be shown in box 1 of your W-2 form(s). Attach your W-2 form(s). 1

2 Taxable interest income of $400 or less. If the total is over $400, you cannot use Form 1040EZ. 2

3 Add lines 1 and 2. This is your **adjusted gross income.** If less than $9,000, see page 15 to find out if you can claim the earned income credit on line 7. 3

Note: *You **must** check Yes or No.*

4 Can your parents (or someone else) claim you on their return?

Yes. Do worksheet on back; enter amount from line G here.

No. If **single,** enter 6,250.00. If **married,** enter 11,250.00. For an explanation of these amounts, see back of form. 4

5 Subtract line 4 from line 3. If line 4 is larger than line 3, enter 0. This is your **taxable income.** ▶ 5

Payments and tax

6 Enter your Federal income tax withheld from box 2 of your W-2 form(s). 6

7 **Earned income credit** (see page 15). Enter type and amount of nontaxable earned income below. 7

8 Add lines 6 and 7 (don't include nontaxable earned income). These are your **total payments.** 8

9 **Tax.** Use the amount on **line 5** to find your tax in the tax table on pages 28–32 of the booklet. Then, enter the tax from the table on this line. 9

Refund or amount you owe

10 If line 8 is larger than line 9, subtract line 9 from line 8. This is your **refund.** 10

11 If line 9 is larger than line 8, subtract line 8 from line 9. This is the **amount you owe.** See page 20 for details on how to pay and what to write on your payment. 11

Sign your return

Keep a copy of this form for your records.

I have read this return. Under penalties of perjury, I declare that to the best of my knowledge and belief, the return is true, correct, and accurately lists all amounts and sources of income I received during the tax year.

Your signature		Spouse's signature if joint return	
Date	Your occupation	Date	Spouse's occupation

For IRS Use Only — Please do not write in boxes below

For Privacy Act and Paperwork Reduction Act Notice, see page 4. Cat. No. 12617R Form 1040EZ (1994)

Name ______________________________ Date ______________________

17.4 Checkpoint

Checking Accounts

In this activity, you will learn how to keep accurate records of a checking account.

1. Fill out the following checking account deposit slip for Denise Wong.

   a. Denise's paycheck totals $343.85. Deposit $125.00 of this into her checking account. The date is September 24, 1996.
   b. Keep $40.00 in cash for Denise.
   c. How much does Denise have left to deposit into her savings account? ______________________

DEPOSIT TICKET

Denise Wong
711 Adolph St.
Denver, CO

Date __________________ 19_____
Deposits may not be available for immediate withdrawl

____
Sign here for cash received (if requested)

National City Bank
Denver, CO
0100 330: 010000 069

CURRENCY		
CASH COIN		
LIST CHECKS		
SEPARATELY		
TOTAL		
LESS CASH RECEIVED		
NET DEPOSIT		

2. Make out the following check to Sunrise Gardens Apartments in the amount of $425.00 to pay for Denise's rent. The date is September 25, 1996.

Denise Wong (1)
711 Adolph St.
Denver, CO

(2) 170
(3) 33-1/100
(4) ____________________ 19 ____

(5) Pay To The
Order Of ____(6) $ ____________

(6) ____ DOLLARS

(7) National City Bank
Denver, CO
- NOW -
(8) For ______________________________(9) Signature____________________________

(10):0100 330: 010000 0170

continued

3. How well do you know the parts of a check? Match the parts of Denise's check to the Sunrise Gardens Apartments to the definitions below.
   a. _____ The person or business to whom the payment is being made.
   b. _____ The number of the check.
   c. _____ The name of the bank and the type of account.
   d. _____ The current month, day, and year.
   e. _____ The amount of the check. (The amount is written twice — once in numerical figures and once in words. Write to the far left in each space so that no figures can be inserted.
   f. _____ The electronic coding number, account number, and number of the check.
   g. _____ The name of person or business who draws on the account.
   h. _____ The purpose of the payment. (This notation is important for budget records.)
   i. _____ The signature of the person writing the check. (Sign all of your checks using the form of your name that appears on the account signature card.
   j. _____ The bank transit number.
4. On Thursday, September 26, Denise received a bill from Lindsay's Trend Setter Shop for $39.63 for a sweater she purchased last month. Write a check to pay for this bill.

Denise Wong   171
711 Adolph St.   33-1/100
Denver, CO   ______________ 19 ____

Pay To The
Order Of ________________________________ $ __________
____ DOLLARS

National City Bank
Denver, CO
- NOW -
For ____________________ Signature ____________________

:0100 330: 010000 0170

5. On Friday, September 7, Denise mailed a check for her monthly electric bill to the Rocky Mountain Electric Company. The check was for $63.75. Write a check for this bill.

Denise Wong   172
711 Adolph St.   33-1/100
Denver, CO   ______________ 19 ____

Pay To The
Order Of ________________________________ $ __________
____ DOLLARS

National City Bank
Denver, CO
- NOW -
For ____________________ Signature ____________________

:0100 330: 010000 0170

continued

6. Bring Denise's check register up-to-date.

   a. Record the checking account deposit she made on September 24 (see question 1).

   b. Record the checks she wrote (questions 2 to 4). Include the bank charge of $.35 for each check written.

   c. Balance the check register. (Add the amount of the deposits and subtract the amount of the checks written to figure the balance.) What is the balance in this account? ________________

   d. How often should you balance your check register? ____

RECORD ALL CHARGES OR CREDITS THAT AFFECT YOUR ACCOUNT

Number	Date	Description of Transaction	Payment Debit	✓	Fee (If any)	Deposit/ Credit	Balance
168	9/5/96	Myer's Shoe Store	$36.76		$.35		$677.76
169	9/21/96	Delchamps Grocery Store	59.88		.35		617.53
	9/22/96	Deposit				$55.37	672.90

7. At regular intervals, the bank sends Denise a bank statement. When she receives her bank statement, she puts her canceled checks in order by number, then goes through the canceled checks one by one to check her records against the bank's record.

   a. The following checks were returned: numbers 168, 169, 170, and 172. Check them off in Denise's check register in the correct box (✓).

   b. Which check or checks were not returned? __________

   c. Denise's deposits of 9/22/96 and 9/24/96 were recorded. Check these off on her check register.

   d. According to the bank, what is Denise's final balance? __________

Helpful Hint: Look at the back of a bank statement. Most bank statements have a printed format to assist you in balancing your account. Ask a family member if you can help balance his or her account.

Name ______________________________ Date ________________

Checkpoint 17.5

Savings Accounts

Your savings can be used for future purchases, education, or retirement. Regular saving is an important part of wise money management.

1. a. Write each of the following entries in the correct column of the passbook savings account below.

Date	Entry	Amount
May 7	Deposit	$125.00
May 15	Deposit	66.00
May 21	Withdrawl	98.00
May 30	Withdrawl	50.00
June 7	Withdrawl	75.00
June 18	Deposit	190.00
June 22	Deposit	96.00
June 30	Deposit	25.00

b. Figure the new balance after each entry.

c. Figure the interest on this account at the end of each month. Assume that the account earns 5 percent interest a year, compounded monthly (.05 x monthly balance ÷ 12 = monthly interest). Interest will be credited May 30 and June 30.

Date	Withdrawal	Deposit	Interest Credited	Balance
April 30				$430.00
May 30				
June 30				

continued

2. Imagine that you start a savings account when you are 17 and deposit $800.00 a year to the account. Assume that the account has an interest rate of 3.92 percent but actually yields 4 percent a year. Solve the following percentage problems to figure the amount the account will be worth in four years.

Year 1: 199__ $800.00 x .04 (4%)	Year 2: 199__ $1,632.00 x .04 (4%)
Year 3: 199__ x .04 (4%)	Year 4: 199__ x .04 (4%)

a. How much will the account be worth in four years?______________________________

Name ______________________________ Date ____________________

17.6 Checkpoint

Buying on Credit

Your first credit account will be the beginning of your credit record. It will form the basis for future credit. Shop for the best value.

All creditors — whether banks, stores, credit card companies, or others — must state the cost of their credit in terms of the finance charge (which includes interest charges and other costs, such as service charges or credit-related insurance premiums) and the APR (the percentage cost of credit on a yearly basis). Federal law does not set interest rates or other credit charges, but it does require their disclosure so that consumers can compare credit costs. The law requires that these two pieces of information be shown to you before you sign a credit contract or use a credit card.

1. Use the yellow pages of your telephone book to identify a bank, a finance company, an auto dealer, and a credit union to call or visit regarding a consumer loan for a used car. Ask to speak with a loan officer. Ask the loan officer the following questions, and record your findings on the chart below.

   a. What is the current annual percentage rate (APR) for a $5,000 loan on a five-year-old car?
   b. What is the length of the loan? What is the monthly payment?
   c. What will the interest and finance charges be over the total period of the loan?
   d. What is the true annual percentage rate of the loan?

	Current APR	Length of Loan	Monthly Payment	Total Finance Charge	Total Payments
Bank					
Finance company					
Auto dealer					
Credit union					

2. What are the important differences between the four lenders? ______________________________

____

____

3. What will be the total cost of the credit at each lender?

   a. Bank __________ b. Finance company __________
   c. Auto dealer __________ d. Credit union __________

continued

4. What percentage of a monthly income of $1,600 will the payments take at each lender's institution? (Divide $1,600 by the monthly payment.)

a. Bank ___________

b. Finance company ___________

c. Auto dealer ___________

d. Credit union ___________

5. Which lender is the best choice for this loan? Why? ___________

____

____

Name ______________________________ Date ____________________

17.7 Checkpoint

Credit Card Applications

1. Use the yellow pages of your telephone book to contact two banks. Ask to speak with a bank officer about acquiring a Visa or MasterCard charge card. Ask the following questions.

	Bank 1	Bank 2
a. What is the annual fee for use of the card?		
b. What is the bank card's APR? (APRs can vary from 12 to 22 percent.)		
c. How is the interest calculated?		
d. What rebates or discounts are offered?		
e. What is the amount of the late fee?		
f. What is the over-the-line fee? (The fee you are charged if you exceed your maximum line of credit.)		
g. What is the grace period for repayment?		

2. Learn to fill out applications accurately and completely. Complete the credit card application on the next page with the care you would use if you were submitting the completed application to the lending institution for approval. Imagine that you are filling out this form two years from now.

3. Much of the information on this application has to do with *the three C's of credit*.
   a. Which information on this application involves *character*? ______________________
   b. Which information on this application involves *capacity*? ______________________
   c. Which information on this application involves *capital*? ______________________

continued

Card Application

CHECK ONE

☐ VISA
☐ MasterCard
☐ Application For Both

Salesperson Code __ - __ - __ - __ - __ - __

IMPORTANT: Read the following instructions and indicate the kind of account you desire.

☐ Individual account (one card—one person is responsible)
Complete Sections A,C,D,E,F, and G.

☐ Joint account (one card in each name—both persons are responsible)
Complolo all sections.

☐ Check here if you are applying as a guarantor. See your local branch for a Guarantor Form.
(Complete Sections B,C, and G.)

OVERDRAFT PROTECTION

☐ Overdraft Protection Requested

No. ________

Section A Primary Applicant Please tell us about yourself

Last Name | First | Initial | Birthdate

Present Street Address | City | State | Zip | How long

☐ Own
☐ Rent
☐ Other

Monthly Rent or Mortgage Payment $ | Mortgage Holder/Landlord | Purchase Price $ | Mortgage Balance $

No.of dependents (Include yourself) | Social Security Number | Area code – Home phone number ( )

Previous Address (If less than 3 yrs.) | City | State | Zip | How long

Present Employer | Occupation | How long | Gross Monthly Wage $

Street Address | City | State | Employer's phone ( )

Previous Employer (Or School attended If less than 3 yrs. at present employer) | How long

Income from alimony, child support or separate maintenance payments need not be revealed if you do not choose to have it considered as a basis for repaying this obligation.

Source of other income | Amount $ | ☐ Monthly ☐ Yearly

Name of nearest relative not living with you | Relationship | Street Address | City | State | Zip

Section C Tell us about your existing accounts

The following constitute all debts owed by applicant and joint applicant (if no debts, list 2 former institutional references). Be sure to include other names under which your credit references or credit history may be verif ed.	Payment	Balance
Creditors		

Checking Account with:	Number	Balance	Savings Account with:	Number	Balance

Section D Select your personal identification code

Select four letters and/or numbers for your Personal Identification Code: ☐ ☐ ☐ ☐

Section E

Check here if you are currently a member of: ☐ CheckIt ☐ Group Banking ☐ Prime Advantage

Section F Credit Card Insurance

☐ Yes, Please initial here ______. Please enroll me in the Group Credit Card Insurance Program described in this brochure.
I understand enrollment is voluntary and I am free to cancel at any time.
Print name of co-cardholder for joint life coverage. ________

☐ No, Please initial here ______. I waive my right to enroll at this time.

Section G Please sign here

The undersigned hereby applies for a MasterCard or VISA card as indicated above to be issued by National Bank. The undersigned further authorizes Society, its affiliates and agents, to check credit and employment history and acknowledges that the undersigned's acceptance and/or use of the credit card will confirm agreement to the terms and conditions of the Cardholder Agreement to be delivered with the credit card, and the undersigned's signature on this application will be considered the undersigned's signature on such Cardholder Agreement.

X ____________ Date ______
Applicant's Signature (Required for Processing)

X ____________ Date ______
Joint Applicant's Signature (If Second Card Requested)

X ____________ Date ______
Guarantor's Signature (If Applicable)

NOTICE: The laws against discrimination require that all creditors make credit equally available to all creditworthy customers, and that credit reporting agencies maintain separate credit histories on each individual upon request. The Civil Rights Commission administers compliance with this law.

FOR INTERNAL USE ONLY—DO NOT WRITE BELOW THIS LINE

1	2	3	4	5	6	7	8	9	10	11	12	13	14	15	16

Name ______________________________ Date ____________________

17.8 Checkpoint: Understanding Customer Statements

Carefully read the following customer statement from Lindsay's Trend Setter Shop.

LINDSAY'S TREND SETTER SHOP	Please mail payment at least 5 days before this date in order to reach our office by the payment due date 3/22/96	CUSTOMER STATEMENT		
		Bill closing date 3/2/96	Account # 00765400	Type 4 REVOLVING
	Total amount due if payment received by due date $92.58	Minimum payment now due $10.00	Indicate amount paid	

DETACH HERE - RETURN TOP PORTION WITH YOUR PAYMENT

Date	Store	Reference Number	Dept.	Description of Transaction	Charges	Payments and Credits
2/4	3	NYF32784	12	New York Fashion slacks	35.73	
		PT3491	7	Paris Trends accessories	12.48	
2/16	1	RF16811	3	Roman Footware	38.61	
2/24	3	PT3491	7	Paris Trends accessories		CR 12.48

Previous Balance	Total Purchases and Other Charges	Total Credits	Total Payments	Finance Charge	Your New Balance	Minimum Now Due
23.07	86.82	12.48	10.00	5.17	92.58	10.00

At Lindsay's Trend Setter Shop " We Appreciate Your Patronage"	Average daily balance	Periodic rate	Annual Percentage rate
	87.41	.05918	21.6

1. What is the finance charge on this customer statement? ____________
2. How many days does the customer have until the payment must be made? ____________
3. What is the annual percentage rate the customer pays for purchases not paid in full on the day the payment is due? ____________

   What is the periodic rate? ____________
4. How much did the customer pay in total payments last month? ____________

continued

5. Why was the customer's account credited for $12.48 on 2/24? ______________________________

____

6. What is the balance the customer owes as of 3/2/96 ____________________

7. How much did the customer charge on 2/16? ____________________

8. What was the previous balance from the month of January? ____________________

9. What indication do you have that the customer has reached or passed his or her credit-debit limit?

____

____

____

10. How much of the customer's previous balance was carried over to this bill? ____________________

11. How did Lindsay's Trend Setter Shop arrive at the total amount due? ____________________________

____

____

Name ______________________________ Date ____________________

17.9 Checkpoint
Develop a Successful Budget

Before you declare your independence and decide to make it on your own, you will need a realistic financial game plan — a budget. A budget will help you gain a sense of financial confidence and control. A budget will show you how much is coming in and how much is being paid out. The money coming in must be more than the money being paid out or you'll be in debt.

1. In this activity, assume that you are living on your own and have a job that pays $1,600 a month. With this income, establish a realistic budget, using the following categories.

Source of Income	**Monthly Estimate**	**Yearly Estimate**
Wages/salary (after taxes)	________	________
Bonuses/commissions	________	________
Interest on savings	________	________
Dividends on investments	________	________
Other (alimony, AFDC)	________	________
Income totals	________	________
Estimate Expenses		
Set-asides		
Savings accounts, investments	________	________
Emergency fund	________	________
Education (tuition, books)	________	________
Fixed Expenses		
Insurance (life, health, auto, property, rental)	________	________
Property taxes	________	________
Rent or mortgage payment	________	________
Loan payments, debt (car, furniture, student loans)	________	________

	Monthly Estimate	**Yearly Estimate**
Relatively Fixed Expenses		
Food (at home, away from home)	________	________
Utilities (phone, fuel, trash, electricity	________	________
Transportation (fuel, bus, car repairs, parking)	________	________
Child care	________	________
Variable Expenses		
Clothing	________	________
Household repairs	________	________
Dry cleaning	________	________
Health care (doctors, dentist, other)	________	________
Entertainment (vacations and recreation)	________	________
Gifts/contributions	________	________
Personal care (beauty/ barbershop, etc.)	________	________
Other	________	________

continued

	Monthly Estimate	Yearly Estimate
Summary of Income		
Total income (after tax deductions	________	________
Total savings and investments	________	________
Total funds available Each Month	________	________

Summary of Expenses		
Total set-asides	________	________
Total fixed expenses	________	________
Total relatively fixed expenses	________	________
Total variable expenses	________	________
Total Expenses	________	________
Difference between available funds and expenses	________	________

2. List the six most expensive things you have to pay for when you are living on your own.

   a. ____________________ d. ____________________

   b. ____________________ e. ____________________

   c. ____________________ f. ____________________

3. How well does your budget cover your expenses? ____________________

   ____

4. Which two of the expenses listed will be most difficult to meet? Why? ____________________

   ____

5. Which six of the expenses listed are the most important to you?

   a. ____________________ d. ____________________

   b. ____________________ e. ____________________

   c. ____________________ f. ____________________

6. Which six of the items listed would you be willing to give up first?

   a. ____________________ d. ____________________

   b. ____________________ e. ____________________

   c. ____________________ f. ____________________

7. What is the least amount you must earn, after taxes, to live on your own? ________

8. Imagine that you want to have a new car and an apartment, but you can only budget for one at this time. Your wants exceed your resources. Use the rational decision-making plan described in Chapter 4 to make a decision.

   a. Analyze the alternatives: ______________________________

   b. Check each alternative against personal attitudes, values, and culture: ______________________________

   ____

   c. Make the decision: ______________________________

   d. What is the opportunity cost of your decision? ______________________________

   e. What values influenced your decision? ______________________________

   ____

9. How much consumer credit can you afford? (Consumer credit is short-term debt with a payback term of five years or less. It does not include a home mortgage.) This will be one of the key questions to managing your credit obligations. As a quick estimate, some financial advisers recommend limiting your consumer credit use to 15 to 20 percent of your current take-home pay.

In the *credit capacity analysis* that follows, use information from the budget you just completed. Write the amount of your take-home pay ($1,600) in (a). Write the amount of your total monthly expenses in (b). Subract (b) from (a), and write the result in (c).

<u>Credit Compacity Analysis</u>

(a) Total take home pay $__________

(b) Total expenses $__________

(c) Balance for credit, savings, etc. $__________

Income that exceeds expenses can be used for savings, additional spending, or credit repayments. If your expenses exceed $1,600, the balance is negative. This means that additional credit obligations should be avoided, and you should rework your budget so that it balances. How did you do? ______________

10. Financial advisers recommend limiting your consumer credit use to 15 to 20 percent of your current take-home-pay. The credit signal light is when your consumer credit use exceeds 15 percent. This is a signal to let you know that you should not make any more credit purchases until your lower your consumer debt.

    Use information from your budget to decide if you have reached your limit on consumer debt.

    a. Total take-home pay __________

    b. Total consumer debt owed __________
       (excluding rent/home mortgage)

    c. 10 percent of take-home pay = ______

    d. 20 percent of take-home pay = ______

    e. Is the amount owed in your budget more than 20 percent of your take-home pay? __________

    f. Is the amount owed 10 to 15 percent of your take-home pay? ______________

    If your answer is no, proceed carefully with buying on credit.

Name ______________________________ Date ____________________

17.10 Checkpoint

Finding the Right Words

Complete the word-find puzzle by finding and circling the vocabulary terms you learned in this chapter. (They are listed below.) The words appear horizontally, vertically, and diagonally.

APR	ATM	bank statement	bounced check
budget	canceled check	check	check register
clearinghouse	collateral	commission	credit
capacity	credit history	creditor	deposit slip
EFTS	electronic fund	deductions	FDIC
FSLIC	gross earnings	endorsement	interest rate
manage finances	Mastercard	income tax	open-end credit
overtime work	piecework	net pay	salary
savings account	Social Security	quarterly	VISA
wages		taxes	

H R R G C E B N B B D B C Q J M X A E B S C H R B A M Z M Q

R G H J J S J T E E B O F Q U U A R Q Q G A Y X A A P L S J

O P C R E D I T H I S T O R Y F O J V B C M E F W T B R U U

Q U Q I T W I U Z B K C E Z D T H V F K S A T A H N U U K X

Q A U U G N C Z P U Q F F F N W H U S Q X U E Y C X W N M J

R G A P U N E P Q D Z N M T R J O V K L N E T P A Y G V A B

C X R B C Y L H T G V G E I M B K J A A V I W S N D C P S A

R R T A M O E I T E T S S A V I N G S A C C O U N T T Z T N

E C E F G K C L W T U R I A E R G E S A A Z S N L I T E E K

D O R B J Q T D L O P F S M I N O F P V T A J U D K M K R S

I L L N I L R N H Z A G J W M K D A C K M F Z E E K I M C T

T L Y I H R O G W S A E F H W A C O K O Q V R K C X Q I A A

O A C E I X N C I I Q X A P E T N C R X M C Z E W S I J R T

R T E A P I I V O K H N C E I L E A F S D M H I U L I U D E

B E C S R F C F T U W O T D T H O S G N E C I T S H U Z G M

Z R Y A P E F L F V D A E H C S T C E E D M E S A V O V G E

D A E S I S V E M Y R R J D E N C N Q E F T E J S X Y Q R N

O L X F G R N K V T C K E Y B W E W L M J I Z N Z I E W O T

C V H X C L D I S X R C R O I P Z E K V P K N P T H O S S Y

D M E I V S C E A O N A I G O Y C W A G E S G A E T R N S S

B E D R C A R Z W U L U J O I N C O M E T A X H N Y I Q E C

C F D F T E G E O A S O C I A L S E C U R I T Y N C B A A H

Y H I U T I C B S C C H E C K R E G I S T E R D U A E D R F

D V E N C E M D E P O S I T S L I P P F M W E G X H E S N W

Z C I C I T E E X L B J I W N F K O X S E Y H W F B A H I T

Y E Z P K E I D W T Y Z Y W P A G T L L M Y R L H L C M N C

N Z I S H S V O G O X K R R Q J R T Q I C A A S Q F C G G K

E Z T C G X K Q N W R B A F Q V I Y I C L U U C Z Y N B S C

K F W H R F X X P S M K Y U S H D P I M X L Y Q H Q O B J G

E H M F V O D C P Y N Y K P C U P V M H C Z A K D W D D P K

Name ______________________________ Date ____________________

Checkpoint 17.11

Checking Your Location

1. For each of the following statements, circle **F** if the statement is more false than true. Circle **T** if the statement is more true than false.

T F a. Financial goals are influenced by personal interests and values, and they never change as a person's needs and situation change.

T F b. Your employer is legally responsible for withholding local, state, and federal taxes from your earnings.

T F c. Income tax returns must be filed by April 15 for the preceding calendar year.

T F d. A checking account is a useful financial-management tool.

T F e. The amount of interest a savings account earns depends on the amount of money deposited and the rate of interest being paid but not on how often the interest is paid.

T F f. A savings account can be opened in a number of financial institutions — including banks, savings and loan associations, credit unions, brokerages, and other financial services companies — and with the federal government.

T F g. A good credit rating is one of the most valuable financial tools you have.

T F h. Credit worthiness revolves around the three C's of credit: character, capacity, and capital.

T F i. People with previous credit problems rarely pay a higher interest rate than people with good credit.

T F j. A bank's lending requirements are usually the same as those of other types of lending institutions.

T F k. Banks join the Mastercard or Visa multipurpose credit card system to earn money.

T F l. Federal law sets interest rates and other credit charges.

T F m. A finance charge is the interest charge paid to use credit.

T F n. If you are refused credit for a specific reason related to your credit report, the Fair Credit Reporting Act requires that the credit agency show you your file — or at least discuss its contents with you — and disclose the agency's information sources.

T F o. A well-planned budget lets you know where you stand financially and helps prevent emergencies from causing a financial strain.

2. Use the space below to rewrite the statements you marked **false** and make them **true**. Include the letter of each statement you rewrite.

Name ______________________ Date ______________

Checkpoint 18.1

How Do You Manage Money?

Financial management is a key to reaching your life goals. It is also a method of meeting future financial crises. In this activity, you will evaluate how you spend your money.

1. a. In column 1, list twelve goods or services that you have frequently purchased with your money.
   b. In column 2, rank the ways you spent money in the order of their importance to you. Let 1 be the most important, and 12 the least important.
   c. Review the decision-making styles described in Chapter 4 (authority, fatalistic, intuitive, impulsive, rational). Then in column 3, write the style of decision making you used for each purchase listed in column 1.

Column 1 **Ways I Spent Money**	**Column 2** **Importance Ranking**	**Column 3** **Decision-Making Style Used**

2. Total the number of spending decisions you made using each decision making style.

   a. Authority ___ b. Fatalistic ___ c. Intuitive ___ d. Impulsive ___ e. Rational ___

3. Which of your decisions and decision-making styles are you most satisfied with? Why?

4. Which of your decisions and decision-making styles are you least satisfied with? Why?

Name ______________________________ Date ______________________

Checkpoint 18.2

Necessities and Frills

An important part of a successful budget is being a prudent consumer—getting the most for your money, recognizing quality, avoiding waste, and realizing time cost as well as money cost in making consumer decisions.

1. Refer to Checkpoint 17.9, the activity in which you developed a successful budget. In that activity, you assumed that you were living on your own and had a job that paid $1,600 a month ($19,200 a year). These earnings would equal $369.23 a week.

   a. How much did you allow for food at home and away from home per month? ______ Per year? ______

   What would be your average weekly food costs? (Divide your yearly food budget by 52.) ______

2. a. In Figure 18.1 in the textbook, you learned that the average amount allotted to food purchases, both at home and away from home, equals 15.1 percent of spending per year. Using the income from Checkpoint 17.9 figure out the average amount allotted to total food expenses for the following:

   - The average yearly amount allotted to total food expenses for yearly earnings of $19,200

     ____

   - The average monthly amount allotted to total food expenses for monthly earnings of $1,600

     ____

   - The average weekly amount allotted to food expenses for weekly earnings of $369.23

     ____

   b. Was the amount of money you allotted in your budget for food more, less, or nearly the same as this?

   ____

   c. In Figure 18.1, the average amount spent on food at home is 8.8 percent. What is 8.8 percent of $369.23? ____________________

   d. The average amount spent on food away from home is 6.4 percent. What is 6.4 percent of $369.23?

   ____

3. Assume you are living on your own and have $32.49 to spend on food you will eat at home and $23.63 to spend on food you will eat away from home. Use the format on the next page and write a menu for each meal you will eat during the week. Mark the meals you plan to eat at home with a (**H**). Mark those you plan to eat away from home with a (**R**).

continued

Weekly Menu Plan for ___________________

(your name)

	Breakfast	**Lunch**	**Dinner**	**Snacks**
Monday	( )	( )	( )	( )
Tuesday	( )	( )	( )	( )
Wednesday	( )	( )	( )	( )
Thursday	( )	( )	( )	( )
Friday	( )	( )	( )	( )
Saturday	( )	( )	( )	( )
Sunday	( )	( )	( )	( )

4. Use the chart on the next page to make a shopping list for the groceries you would need to purchase with your weekly eat-at-home budget of $32.49. Read the food ads in the newspaper before deciding which store to go to because you can save money on sale items.

   a. Compare the prices of the items on your shopping list of different brands, including house brands to see how much you can save by purchasing one brand rather than another. Compare products that satisfy similar dietary needs such as fruits, fresh vegetables, different cuts of meat, and so on.

   b. Clip food coupons from the Sunday newspaper before you shop. (Some stores offer double coupons. In these stores, the coupons are worth twice their printed value.)

   c. When possible, use unit pricing information (the price per measure or unit in weight, volume, count, or area) to make comparisons. Unit pricing information is usually located on the shelf edge, directly below the item.

continued

d. What is the total cost of all of the food items in column 4? ____________________

e. What is the total cost of all of the food items in column 7? ____________________

f. What is the difference in cost between columns 4 and 7? ____________________

A weekly Grocery List for ____________________
(your name)

Column 1 Food Item	Column 2 #1 Choice Unit Price	Column 3 #1 Choice Coupon Savings	Column 4 #1 Choice Total Price	Column 5 #2 Choice Unit Price	Column 6 #2 Choice Coupon Savings	Column 7 #2 Choice Total Price

Total cost for column 4 = __________ Total cost for column 7 = __________

continued

5. a. Were you able to stay within the $32.49 budget for food you will eat at home? ______

b. If you went over the $32.49 budget, redo your weekly menu and grocery list and shop again for the items you need.

c. Would you be able to plan a menu and meet this food budget for a family of four? Explain your answer.

____

____

____

d. What are three food shopping tips you learned from this experience? ______________________

____

____

____

6. a. List the meals in your menu that you plan to eat away from home. Using the following chart, check restaurant prices for those meals.

b. Were you able to stay within the $23.63 budget for food eaten away from home? __________

c. Some people use part of their entertainment budget for eating in restaurants. Would you use some of the money from your entertainment budget for eating away from home, if so, how much? __________

Weekly Restaurant Budget for ________________
(your name)

	Sunday	**Monday**	**Tuesday**	**Wednesday**	**Thursday**	**Friday**	**Saturday**
Breakfast	$	$	$	$	$	$	$
Lunch	$	$	$	$	$	$	$
Dinner	$	$	$	$	$	$	$

Total cost = $__________

Name ______________________ Date ______________

18.3 Checkpoint

Advertisements in the Media

Advertising is communicated to us through newspapers, magazines, billboards, radio, television, junk mail, and motion pictures. Each year, businesses spend large sums of money to determine what will cause consumers to buy a particular product. Advertisements teach us what to want. They are a powerful influence on our attitudes toward a product or service.

1. Cut out at least fifteen newspaper and magazine ads that appeal to you. The ads should describe products that you would like to purchase now or in the future. Use the ads to answer the following questions.

   a. Which ads appeal to your self-esteem and your desire for social approval?

Name of product	**How the ad makes its appeal**

   b. Which ads appeal to your desire for romance and affection?

Name of product	**How the ad makes its appeal**

   c. Which ads appeal to your desire for good health and long life?

Name of product	**How the ad makes its appeal**

   d. Which ads appeal to your desire to make a lot of money and be wealthy?

Name of product	**How the ad makes its appeal**

   e. Which ads appeal to your intellect?

Name of product	**How the ad makes its appeal**

continued

f. Which ads appeal to your desire to be happy and enjoy life?

Name of product	How the ad makes its appeal
____________	____________________
____________	____________________

2. a. List *all* of the brand names of clothes and shoes in your closet.

____________ ____________ ____________ ____________

____________ ____________ ____________ ____________

____________ ____________ ____________ ____________

____________ ____________ ____________ ____________

b. What advertisements influenced you to buy those particular brands?

____

____

____

____

c. Which brand names lived up to their advertising claims?

____

____

____

____

3. What is most influential in making you choose one product over another? Why?

____

____

____

____

Name ______________________________ Date ____________________

18.4 Checkpoint

Finding a Place to Live

Housing costs will probably make up the largest part of your budget.

1. a. Refer again to Checkpoint 17.9. How much did you allow for rent or mortgage payment per month? ____________ Per year? ____________

   b. In Figure 18.1 in your textbook, you learned that the average amount allotted to housing averages 31.3 percent of spending. (This includes utilities, insurance, furnishings, and maintenance costs.) Using the income from Checkpoint 17.9 figure out the average amount allotted to total housing expenses for average monthly earnings of $1,600. ____________

   c. Was the amount of money you allotted in your budget for housing (including utilities, insurance, furnishings, and maintenance costs) more, less, or nearly the same as this? ____________

2. a. In this activity, assume that you are getting ready to rent an apartment on your own and have $500.80 to spend on housing. How much of your housing budget will you allow for utilities, insurance, furnishings, and maintenance costs? ____________

   b. How much does that leave for the rent on the apartment? (If you are going to have a roommate, you will be able to share the rental expenses and might possibly afford a more expensive apartment.)

3. a. Check the classified advertisements in your newspaper for apartments or houses for rent. Look until you find a rental that fits your budget.

   b. Arrange to visit an apartment you are interested in and evaluate its features. (If possible, visit three apartments and compare the features of all three.) Use the following checklist to evaluate the apartment.

Apartment # __________ Address ____________________ Date viewed ____________

Rent $ __________ Approximate utility costs $ __________ Deposit $ ________

Length of lease ___________ Date available _____ Rental agent fee ______________

Rental agent or owner name ________________________ Phone number __________

Number of rooms _______ Bedrooms _______ Baths _______ Type of heat/air ________

continued

c. Rate each of the items listed below according to the following scale:

1 = not acceptable
2 = below average
3 = average
4 = above average
5 = very exceptional

Interior	Rating
Number of rooms	_____
Condition of interior walls	_____
Closet/storage space	_____
Cable TV	_____
Screens, storm windows	_____
Air conditioning	_____
Carpeting, blinds, drapes	_____
Laundry facilities	_____
Soundproof to noises in other apartments	_____
Appliances	_____
Smoke detector/fire alarm	_____
Fire escape/fire exit	_____
Door and window locks	_____
Security system	_____
Furniture (if furnished)	_____
Kitchen and bathroom	_____
Soundproof to outside noises	_____
Odors from other apartments	_____
Restrictions on children/pets	_____
Age mix of renters	_____
Repairs and maintenance	_____
Mailbox	_____

Interior	Rating
Trash/garbage collection	_____
Exterior	
Neighborhood	_____
Condition of grounds	_____
Recreation facilities	_____
Security at night	_____
Parking facilities	_____
Neighborhood traffic	_____
Convenience to	
Work	_____
Public transportation	_____
Supermarket	_____
Shopping	_____
Child care	_____
Hospitals	_____
Recreation/parks	_____
Restaurants/entertainment	_____
Place of worship	_____
School/college	_____
Monthly expenses	
Rent	_____
Utilities	_____

4. You have rated forty-one important areas related to the apartment.
   a. Total all of your forty-one ratings _____
   b. A perfect rating would be 205, average would be 123. If your overall satisfaction with the apartment is less than 123, you will probably be dissatisfied with the apartment.
5. Before you sign a lease to rent an apartment, it is a good idea to evaluate it in terms of your personal lifestyle.
   a. Review your forty-one total ratings. Circle the ten ratings that are most important to you in terms of your personal values and lifestyle.
   b. Total your ten most important ratings. _____
   c. A perfect rating would be 50, average would be 30. If the ten ratings that are most important to you total less than 30, continue searching for a suitable apartment. If they total 30 or more, use the rational approach to decision making before signing a lease.

Name ______________________________ Date ____________________

18.5 Checkpoint

Purchasing Your First Automobile

Buying a new car is usually the second most expensive purchase consumers make. Refer to Checkpoint 17.9. Total the amounts you budgeted for monthly transportation expenses, including the loan payment on a vehicle, fuel, repairs, auto insurance, parking, and public transportation.

1. How much did you allow for transportation expenses per month? $______________
2. In Figure 18.1 in your textbook, you learned that the average amount allotted to transportation, not including auto insurance, equals 18.1 percent of spending. (This includes private vehicles, gasoline and motor oil, and other forms of transportation.)
   a. Using the income from your Checkpoint 17.9 budget, figure out the average amount allotted to total transportation expenses for average monthly earnings of $1,600. ______________
   b. Was this amount of money more, less, or nearly the same as the amount that you budgeted in Checkpoint 17.9? __________
3. Most new car dealers will negotiate on price and bargain on their profit margin, which is generally between 15 and 20 percent. This is usually the difference between the manufacturer's suggested retail price and the invoice price. (You can find invoice price by looking at the dealer's invoice or by reviewing new car publications.)

Helpful Hints: When buying a new or used car, remember that you are in charge of the sale, not the dealer. Don't be afraid to walk away.

If you shop at several dealerships, you might save a small percentage but that small percentage could amount to a lot of money on this big-ticket item.

Visit a new car dealer, and use the following worksheet to compare the invoice price and the retail price of a new car of your choice. Reread the section, "I Really Want a New Car," in Chapter 18 before you visit the dealer to make certain you understand how automobiles are priced.

continued

Worksheet for Buying a New Car

Car Make and Model ____________________ Dealer ____________________

	Invoice Price	Retail Price
Base Price:	________	________
Options:		
Transmission:		
Automatic	________	________
Stick	________	________
Sound System:		
AM-FM	________	________
AM-FM cassette	________	________
Power brakes	________	________
Rear window defogger	________	________
Tires:		
Full-size spare	________	________
Steel-belted radials	________	________
Other	________	________

	Invoice Price	Retail Price
Other	________	________
Other	________	________
Air conditioning	________	________
Engine:		
Size	________	________
Diesel	________	________
Power steering	________	________
Power locks	________	________
Power seats	________	________
Rear window wiper/washer	________	________
Luggage rack	________	________
Mirrors:		
Dual	________	________
Dual remote	________	________
Passenger visor	________	________
Other	________	________
Other	________	________

4. Consumers frequently purchase expensive but unimportant options.

   a. Review the options listed on your worksheet. Circle the four that are most important to you. Draw a line through the four that are least important to you.

   b. Show the dealer the options you consider important and those you consider unimportant. New car options are usually sold in groups. Ask your dealer to show you prices on option groups as well as individual option prices. Can you save money this way? ________

5. As a first-time car buyer, you are beginning your "right of passage" from childhood to being a full-fledged American adult. You have examined the sticker price and invoice cost with and without certain options, kicked all four tires, and opened and closed all of the doors at least twenty times (including a minimum of four slams). You have placed your head under the hood with your nose no more than four inches from the stranger-looking metal things and have impressed the dealer with your knowledgeable grunts and humming noises. Now it is time to "dicker" (negotiate a price).

   a. Total the dealer's invoice cost and the options you want $________

   b. Calculate 15 percent of the total. (The dealer expects to make a profit of 15 to 20 percent.) ________

   c. Total the invoice cost plus 15 percent. $________
   This is your offer.

Name ______________________________ Date ____________________

Checkpoint 18.6

Finding the Right Words

Chapter 18 of your textbook contains numerous terms that employers and workers use. Recognizing and understanding these terms will help you make the important career decisions you will soon face. Unscramble the jumbled vocabulary terms in column **B** and match them to the definitions in column **A**.

Column A

1. _____ rompooitnal lase ____________________
2. _____ iutn pirec ____________________
3. _____ lanoitinutr ingbella ____________________
4. _____ gicener dnabr ____________________
5. _____ antnet ____________________
6. _____ cuitryes itdeops ____________________
7. _____ tendrup ____________________
8. _____ eeasl ____________________
9. _____ incevoi icerp ____________________
10. _____ sureinanc ____________________
11. _____ mmrepui ____________________
12. _____ abitilyli agecovre ____________________
13. _____ hypsilac agecovre ____________________
14. _____ ranwarty ____________________
15. _____ reynonmo erickst ____________________

Column B

a. having no trademark

b. a statement of the various nutrients in a product and the percentages it provides of the U.S. Department of Agriculture's recommended daily requirements.

c. a person paying rent for the temporary use of the building or land of another person

d. the cost of one standard measure of a product

e. a sale in which regular merchandise is promoted by temporary price reductions

f. a contract that involves financial commitment for a specific period of time

g. money you entrust with your landloard to cover any damage you may cause to your rental unit

h. the guaranteeing (insuring) of property, life, or person against loss or harm arising in specified occurrences

i. insurance coverage for damage to your vehicle caused by collision, fire, or theft

j. cautious, careful, wise, and not extravagant

k. insurance coverage for bodily injuries, property damages, and medical expenses for others when you are at fault

l. the manufacturer's initial charge to the dealer

m. the payment a policyholder makes to own an insurance policy

n. a guarantee that a product is of a certain qualify or that defective parts will be replaced

o. the label affixed to a new car window, as required by federal law

Name ______________________________ Date ____________________

Checkpoint 18.7

Checking Your Location

1. For each of the following statements, circle **F** if the statement is more false than true. Circle **T** if the statement is more true than false.

T F a. You share responsibility for final decisions about your consumer purchases with your friends and family.

T F b. Merchants do not have to honor your request for a rain check for an advertised product.

T F c. The unit price can help you compare the price of products that have different weights or volumes.

T F d. The type of store where you shop has little to do with the prices you pay.

T F e. Conspicuous consumption can be very costly if you are living on a tight budget.

T F f. Promotional sales promote regular merchandise through temporary price reductions.

T F g. Advertising is intended to promote the sale of a product or service, to advance an idea, or to bring about some other effect that the advertiser desires.

T F h. Beware of products or services if the manufacturer or service provider will not back its claims with a written guarantee.

T F i. Food costs will probably make up the largest part of your living expenses.

T F j. A general rule is to allow no more than one-half of your take-home pay for housing.

T F k. It is wise to talk with other residents in a rental complex about their likes and dislikes before you make a final decision.

T F l. Before moving into an apartment, it is a good consumer practice to make an inventory of all items furnished in the rental unit, to rate the condition of the furnishings and the overall condition of the unit, and to have the inventory signed and dated by you and the landlord.

T F m. The responsibility of both the tenant and the landlord are defined in a lease, both parties are legally required to live up to the signed agreement.

continued

T F n. As a general rule, financial planners recommend that your mortgage payments not exceed 28 or 29 percent of your gross income.

T F o. As a consumer, you cannot expect quality products and services at fair prices.

2. Use the space below to rewrite the statements you marked **false** and make them **true**. Include the letter of each statement you rewrite.

____

____

____

____

____

____

"THIS IS MY NEWEST FINANCIAL MANAGEMENT SYSTEM..."

Name ____________________ Date ____________

Checkpoint 19.1

How Are You Doing?

Good health is one of our most precious possessions. At least 65 percent of all illnesses are related to lifestyle practices that we can control. In the introduction in Chapter 19, you were asked ten questions about your health habits. The questions have been rewritten for this activity. Answer them again, this time with more than a "yes" or "no".

1. a. When did you last eat a well-balanced nutritious meal? ____________________
   b. What did you eat that was nutritious? ____________________
   ____
   c. Was the meal low in fat or high in fiber? ____________________
2. a. When did you last get at least eight hours of sleep at night? ____________________
   b. Between 20 and 30 percent of Americans suffer from nearly one hundred known sleep disorders. How can you tell when you have gotten a good night's sleep? ____________________
   ____
3. a. When did you last get a checkup from your doctor? ____________________
   b. What did the doctor say about your health? ____________________
   ____
4. a. When did a social or school pressure get you down? ____________________
   b. What got you down? ____________________
   c. What kind of support did you get from family, friends, or an organized support group? ____________________
   ____
   ____
5. a. When did you most recently practice something in a safe manner? ____________________
   b. What did you do? ____________________
   ____
6. a. When did you last turn down an offer of tobacco, alcohol, or drugs? ____________________
   b. Explain the situation and your reason for turning down the offer. ____________________
   ____
   ____

continued

7. a. When did you most recently display a positive mental attitude toward yourself or someone else?

____

b. Describe the situation. ____

____

c. How does a sense of humor contribute to good mental health? ____

____

8. a When did you last participate in sports or exercise? ____

b. What did you do? ____

9. a. When did you most recently make an effort to keep informed about infectious diseases, environmental hazards, or other health risks? ____

b. Describe the situation. ____

____

c. How does this risk endanger your health? ____

____

10. a. When did you most recently avoid a person, thing, or situation that you knew would be a risk to your health? ____

b. What was the situation? ____

____

11. Which of your answers reflect the good health habits of a wellness-oriented lifestyle? ____

12. Which of your answers do not reflect the good health habits of a wellness-oriented lifestyle? ____

13. What steps should you take to have a completely wellness-oriented lifestyle? ____

____

____

____

____

Name ______________________________ Date ____________________

19.2 Checkpoint

You Are What You Eat

Learn to read the facts on the nutrition labels before you decide which products to purchase. This information can help you select a healthy diet.

1. Select two different brands of cereal to compare and evaluate for nutritive value.

   a. Product 1: ____________________ Manufacturer: ____________________

   b. Product 2: ____________________ Manufacturer: ____________________

2. Using the following chart, compare and evaluate the nutritional information on the label of the two cereals you chose. Record the percent daily value (% D.V.) you need of this in your diet (if this information is given on the label.).

	Cereal 1 __________ Name	**% D.V.**	**Cereal 2** __________ Name	**% D.V.**
What is the serving size?				
How many calories in a serving?				
How much total fat?				
How much saturated fat?				
How much cholesterol?				
How much sodium?				
How many total carbohydrates?				
How much dietary fiber?				
How much sugar?				
How much protein?				
Which vitamins and minerals?				

continued

	Cereal 1	% D.V.	Cereal 2	% D.V.
Vitamin _____				
Vitamin _____				
Vitamin _____				
Vitamin _____				
Vitamin _____				
Vitamin _____				
Mineral _____				
Mineral _____				
Mineral _____				
Mineral _____				

3. Review Figure 19.1 showing recommended daily allowance for teenagers in your textbook. Locate your age range on the figure. Compare the recommended dietary allowance you need in each of the vitamins and minerals listed. (The weights and heights are medians for the population of the designated age. This does not mean that the height-to-weight ratios are ideal.)
   a. Which cereal comes closest to meeting your daily dietary needs in the vitamins listed in the box?

   ____

   b. Which cereal comes closest to meeting your daily dietary needs in the minerals listed in the box?

   ____

   c. What vitamins and minerals do you need each day that are not listed on the cereal boxes?

   ____

4. The American Heart Association recommends that your total fat intake be less than 30 percent of your total calories. So, if you consume 2,500 calories per day, you should eat less than 80 grams of fat per day. If you consume 2,000 calories or less per day, you should eat less than 65 grams of fat per day. Which cereal would be most healthful in terms of fat content? ______________________

5. Complete the following chart.
   a. Select one day from the menu you planned in Checkpoint 18.2 , and record how many servings of each of the food groups you had in your menu that day.

continued

b. Review the dietary guidelines illustrated in Figure 19.2. Record how many servings of each food group are recommended.

Food Group	Number of Servings for One-Day of Your Menu	Number of Servings Recommended for One Day
Fats, oils, sweets		
Milk group		
Meat group		
Vegetable group		
Fruit group		
Bread group		

c. Did your menu have the recommended number of servings of the five major food groups? ______________

d. In what food groups were you lacking? ______________________________

e. In what food groups were you about right? ______________________________

f. What changes do you need to make for a healthier diet? ______________________________

____

g. Rewrite your menu to reflect these changes. Mark those you plan to eat away from home with a (**R**). Mark the meals you plan to eat at home with a (**H**).

Weekly Menu Plan for ____________________
(your name)

	Breakfast	**Lunch**	**Dinner**	**Snacks**
Monday	( )	( )	( )	( )
Tuesday	( )	( )	( )	( )
Wednesday	( )	( )	( )	( )
Thursday	( )	( )	( )	( )
Friday	( )	( )	( )	( )
Saturday	( )	( )	( )	( )
Sunday	( )	( )	( )	( )

continued

Name ______________________________ Date ____________________

Checkpoint 19.3

Too Much Stress

We experience stress all the time, but too much stress can seriously affect our physical and mental well-being. Consider the situation of Marcee Jahonovich.

> Marcee is sixteen years old and in the eleventh grade of Harborview High School. Marcee's parents divorced four years ago. She lives with her mother during the school year and spends vacations and summers with her father. Her mother plans to remarry next summer. Her father remarried three years ago and has two stepchildren from his second marriage.
>
> Marcee has gone steady with Perry for over a year. Perry and her best friend, Janet, have helped her deal with the stress in her family life.
>
> Last month, Perry broke up with Marcee. She has been very depressed, and last week she told Janet that she has even considered suicide. Janet spent the night with Marcee and convinced her to get professional help. The next morning, Marcee and Janet visited their school counselor. The counselor convinced Marcee to visit a clinical psychologist.
>
> Marcee is lucky. She had a good friend to help her with a personal crisis. The school counselor brought Marcee and her mother together to face the situation, and the psychologist is helping all of them deal with the problems that caused Marcee's depression.
>
> At first, Marcee blamed her depression on Perry for breaking off their relationship. Now she understands that a lot of factors were involved in her depression. She is rapidly learning life skills that are helping her improve her mental health.
>
> Marcee has learned to get her daily tasks done without making other people angry. This life skill has helped her improve her relationship with her mother and some of her teachers. She has learned to recognize her personal feelings and to express them in a way that is acceptable to others. Getting her feelings out in the open has relieved a lot of Marcee's depression and anger.
>
> When Marcee is unhappy, she has learned to do something positive to solve her problem rather than going to her room and brooding about it. Sometimes, a simple change of pace takes her out of the unhappy mood.
>
> Marcee isn't trying to regain her mental health overnight. Instead, she is moving ahead one step at a time. She has discovered that the slow process of working toward solutions gives her a strong feeling of hope for her future. Even on a bad day, she no longer feels trapped.

1. We all need to love and be loved.

   a. What situations in Marcee's life might have caused her to feel unloved? ______________________

   ____

   b. What situations might have caused her to feel loved? ______________________

   ____

continued

2. We all need to belong and to be acccepted by others.

   a. What situations in Marcee's life might have caused her to feel alone or rejected? ____________________

   ____

   b. What situations might have caused her to feel as though she belonged and was accepted? ____________

   ____

3. We all need to feel we are worthwhile.

   a. What situations in Marcee's life might have caused her to feel hopeless and sad? ____________________

   ____

   b. What situations in Marcee's life caused her to feel she was important to someone? ________________

   ____

4. For what emotional needs did Marcee rely on Janet? ____

5. For what emotional needs did Marcee rely on Perry? ____

6. a. Who makes you feel worthwhile and special? ____

   b. Who feels worthwhile and special because of you? ____

7. a. Who makes you feel lovable? ____

   b. Who feels lovable because of you? ____

8. a. Who accepts you for who you are? ____

   b. Who feels accepted because of you? ____

9. Marcee has discovered that she has feelings of love, self-worth, being accepted, and being special and that they are important to her. She has also discovered that other people have the same feelings. Marcee understands that having her feelings ignored made her feel angry and depressed. Now, when her feelings are hurt by the important people in her life, she still feels sad, but instead of being angry or depressed, Marcee trys to say or do something to let the other person know that she understands their anger and loves them. The more she helps and understands others, the easier it is to ignore her feelings of anger and depression.

   a. Briefly describe a recent situation in which you felt angry or depressed because your feelings were hurt.

   ____

   ____

   ____

   ____

   b. Did you like your reaction? If so, why? If not, describe a better reaction for a similar situation.

   ____

   ____

   ____

   ____

Name ______________________ Date ______________

Checkpoint 19.4

Read the Instructions Carefully

The label on a bottle of prescription medicine is an important source of information for the patient.

1. Read the information on a bottle of prescription medicine from your home. (If there is no prescription medicine at your home, ask the pharmacist at your local pharmacy to help you complete this activity when he or she has time.)
   a. What dosage is prescribed (liquid, capsules, tablets)? ______________
   b. What is the strength of the medication (usually given in milligrams or mgs)? ______________
   c. What is the total amount the patient will receive (15 capsules, 5 fluid ounces)? ______________
   d. What are the directions for use? (These are often abbreviations of Latin words. For instance, *terin die*, written *t.i.d.*, means three times a day.) ______________
   e. How many times can the prescription be refilled? ______________

2. Surveys show that in nine out of ten cases, we take care of our everyday aches and pains without going to a health professional. We tough it out, use a home remedy, or buy an over-the-counter (OTC) product. These medications range from allergy medicine to antacids, painkillers, and laxatives.

   The Federal Drug Administration requires that OTC labels be much more detailed than prescription drug labels so that consumers can properly use the products without the advice of a health professional. It is the consumer's responsibility to read the label and follow the instructions.

   Read the information on a bottle of OTC medication from your home. (If there is none at your home, ask the pharmacist at your local pharmacy to help you complete this activity when he or she has time.)
   a. What is the name of the OTC medication? ______________
   b. What are the suggested uses? ______________
   c. Is the product sealed for your protection? ______________
   d. Describe the tamper-resistant feature? ______________
   e. What are the active ingredients? ______________
   f. What are the inactive ingredients? ______________
   g. What is the net quantity of the contents? ______________
   h. What is the name and address of the manufacturer, packer, or distributor? ______________

      ____
   i. What are the directions and dosage instructions? (Summarize these.) ______________

      ____
   j. What are the warnings, cautionary statements, and drug interaction precautions (if any)? ______________

      ____
   k. What is the expiration date and the lot or batch code of the medication? ______________

      ____

Name ______________________________ Date ______________________

Checkpoint 19.5

The Surgeon General Warns

The following information about the negative effect of tabacco products and alcoholic beverages is common knowledge to most teenagers and adults. Review the information, then complete the activity that follows.

The smoking of tobacco products is the chief avoidable cause of death in our society. Smokers are more likely than nonsmokers to contract heart disease. Indeed, some 170,000 die each year from smoking-related coronary heart disease. Lung, larynx, esophageal, bladder, pancreatic, and kidney cancers also strike smokers at increased rates.

This information is taught to students from the time they are in the intermediate grades of elementary school, yet too many young people ignore the dangers and start to smoke. The following reasons are frequently given for why young people smoke: peer pressure, increased popularity, family problems, home smoking habits, "for kicks," to appear grown up, and lack of knowledge of smoking's effect on the human body.

Imagine that you work on the Surgeon General's staff and are assigned to develop a campaign to keep teenagers from smoking. What would you do? Use the information in this activity to develop a successful campaign. ______________________________

Name ______________________ Date ______________

19.6 Checkpoint

Finding the Right Words

Chapter 19 of your textbook contains numerous terms that employers and workers use. Recognizing and understanding these terms will help you make the important career decisions you will soon face.

Write a short story using the following vocabulary terms. Make certain that you understand the definition of each term before you use it in your story.

surgical insurance
health maintenance organization
drug
drug abuse
mandated

calorie
diet
nutrients
Recommended Daily Allowances
Food Guide Pyramid
ATP

aerobic
cardiorespiratory endurance
muscular strength
muscular endurance
flexibility
hospitalization insurance

Title: ______________________

Name ______________________________ Date ____________________

19.7 Checkpoint

Checking Your Location

1. For each of the following statements, circle **F** if the statement is more false than true. Circle **T** if the statement is more true than false.

T F a. The quality of all aspects of your life is affected by your physical and mental condition.

T F b. If you eat more food than your body requires, the extra food may be changed into fat tissue, which does not promote good health.

T F c. The precise nutrients needed for different age, sex, and weight groups are the same.

T F d. Fat contains less calories than an equal amount of carbohydrates or protein.

T F e. The Food Guide Pyramid recommends eating more servings of meat in a day than vegetables.

T F f. When you exercise, the body converts carbohydrates and fat from food into energy.

T F g. It will probably take a week or two of regular exercise to realize the benefits of a fitness program.

T F h. The chief villain of skin cancer is the sun's ultraviolet rays.

T F i. Drugs are the number one killer of children in America.

T F j. You probably have good mental health if you truthfully consider yourself to be competent, loved, and liked.

T F k. An HMO provides coverage for your medical bills and health-care services.

T F l. It is legal to possess drugs of abuse at the workplace as long as you do not sell them to others at the workplace.

T F m. The drug most frequently involved in work-related fatalities is alcohol.

T F n. When people exhibit sudden negative changes in their behavior, it should be a matter of concern.

T F o. Self-confidence and a positive attitude toward other people and situations play an important role in avoiding the temptation to abuse drugs.

continued

2. Use the space below to rewrite the statements you marked **false** and make them **true**. Include the letter of each statement you rewrite.

____

____

____

____

____

____

Name ____________________ Date ____________________

Checkpoint 20.1

Rate Your Date

Dating provides two people with an opportunity to discover and understand each other's interests, values, and attitudes. If they identify several similarities, they may wish to continue dating and eventually enter a period of courtship.

1. Use the following scale to rate each of the ten dating activities listed in the chart below.
2. Ask the person you are dating, or a good friend, to rate the ten activities. Read the statements to your date or friend and record his or her answers. Don't reveal your answers until your date or friend has completed his or her responses.
3. Read the results together.

Rating Scale

1 = I would enjoy this activity very much.
2 = I would enjoy this activity.
3 = I have no strong feelings about this activity.
4 = I would dislike this activity.
5 = I would dislike this activity very much.

Dating Activity	Your Rating	Your Date's Rating
Going to a school dance	______	______
Relaxing and cruising around in a car	______	______
Attending a musical program	______	______
Eating dinner at a nice restaurant	______	______
Attending a friend's party without parental supervision	______	______
Having a picnic and swimming	______	______
Double-dating with good friends	______	______
Attending a friend's party with parental supervision	______	______
Attending a youth program at your house of worship	______	______
Going to a sports event	______	______

Scoring

For ***each*** activity, determine the difference between you and your date or friend by subtracting the highest score from the lowest score. Record the results below.

Total 0s_____ Total 1s_____ Total 2s _____ Total 3s _____ Total 4s _____

continued

1. If you have identified *six* or more dating activities with a difference of 0 or 1, you have several similarities and will probably enjoy dating. Discuss with your date the activities you both enjoy, and share your reasons for enjoying these activities.
2. If you have identified *four* or *five* activities with a difference of 0 or 1, discuss with your date the activities you both enjoy. You will probably enjoy occasional dates in areas of common interest.
3. If you have identified *fewer than four* activities with a difference of 0 or 1, your differences are far more numerous than your similarities. It is unlikely that you will enjoy spending a lot of time together.
4. In all cases, discuss with your date your areas of similarity and difference and why each of you feels the way you do.

"WHERE WOULD YOU LIKE TO GO?"

Name ______________________________ Date ____________________

Checkpoint 20.2

Marriage

From the time you were a small child, many of the stories you read probably taught the importance of marriage and living "happily ever after." Read the case study, and answer the questions that follow.

> Mario Santos and Ashley Pritchard are both seniors at Manchester High School. Mario and Ashley have dated since the 10th grade, and they have been going steady for the past six months. They have even discussed getting married.
>
> Mario will soon complete a tech-prep program in business education. Following graduation, Mario plans to enter a one-year data-processing program at Fairpoint Community College. He presently works part-time and has saved $2,800 for tuition and books. Mario plans to live at home while attending Fairpoint, and his parents have agreed to provide some financial assistance.
>
> Ashley is in a college-preparatory program but has decided that she doesn't want to continue her education after high school. She works part-time and has $3,500 in her savings account. She would like to get married, buy a couple of motorcycles, and travel around the country for a year or two.
>
> Mario thinks they would be better off postponing the wedding until he gets his associate's degree from Fairpoint. However, he is worried that Ashley will breakup with him if he doesn't do what she wants.

1. a. Do you think Mario and Ashley will live "*happily ever after*" if they get married after they graduate from high school? Explain your answer. ______________________________

   ____

   ____

   b. What responsible behaviors is Ashley demonstrating? ______________________________

   ____

   ____

   c. What irresponsible behaviors is Ashley demonstrating? ______________________________

   ____

   ____

   d. What responsible behaviors is Mario demonstrating? ______________________________

   ____

   ____

continued

e. What irresponsible behaviors is Mario demonstrating? ____________________

____

____

f. How would you handle this situation if you were Mario? ____________________

____

____

g. How would you handle this situation if you were Ashley? ____________________

____

____

2. a. Think of twelve qualities of your ideal marriage partner, and write them in the spaces below.

________(___)	________(___)	________(___)	________(___)
________(___)	________(___)	________(___)	________(___)
________(___)	________(___)	________(___)	________(___)

b. Rank the twelve qualities in order of importance to you let **1** be the most important, and **12** the least important. Number them in the brackets.

c. List, in order of strength, the qualities you feel you possess.

________(___)	________(___)	________(___)	________(___)
________(___)	________(___)	________(___)	________(___)
________(___)	________(___)	________(___)	________(___)

3. What would you seek in a marriage partner that you have or have not had with a serious dating partner?

____

____

____

4. By entering the work force, many wives have become financially independent of or less dependent on their husbands than in the past. Are the benefits of dual-career marriages good or bad for the well-being of a marriage? Explain your answer. ____________________

____

____

____

____

____

Name ______________________________ Date ____________________

Checkpoint 20.3

Parenting and Work

Having a child can have a dramatic effect on a couple. One partner may want to drop out of the work force to care for the family, yet more income will now be needed. On the other hand, both partners may prefer to continue working outside the home. Learning to accommodate the responsbilities and expenses of child care when both parents continue to work outside the home dictates changes in lifestyle as well as marital and family adjustments.

1. One survey found that two out of five husbands almost never do the family cooking, wash dishes after meals, clean the house, or shop for food. Better than three out of five "rarely" or "never" do the laundry; 86 percent almost never iron. Seven out of ten women "almost always" or "often" pay the household bills. Almost half take out the garbage a good part of the time; and about one-fourth make arrangements for car repairs. Three out of ten do a great deal of painting and wallpapering.

   If you become a working parent, with a working spouse, which of the home tasks, listed below, do you expect to do to help with the responsibility of raising children? Rate each activity using the following scale.

1. = Never **2 = Rarely** **3 = Sometimes** **4 = Frequently** **5 = Always**

Parenting Home Tasks

_____Participating in children's activities	_____ Reading to the children	_____ Gardening
_____Driving children to activities	_____ Cooking family meals	_____ Ironing
_____Scrubbing walls or floors	_____ Washing dishes	_____ Baking
_____Bathing the baby	_____ Feeding the baby	_____ Sewing
_____Rocking the baby	_____ Repairing the car	_____ Doing laundry
_____Buying family presents	_____ Cleaning house	_____ Repairing toys
_____Paying household bills	_____ Grocery shopping	_____ Changing diapers
_____Painting the house	_____ Doing household repairs	_____ Washing windows

2. Total your scores for the Parenting Home Tasks and write that number here. __________

3. Using your total score, circle the degree of responsibility you expect to share for the parenting home tasks.

Total Score	**Degree of Responsibility**
24 - 48	Little or none
48 -72	Less than your spouse
72 - 96	More than your spouse
96 - 120	Most or all

continued

4. When both parents work and are tired, how can they still be effective parents and effective employees?

5. If you were the father of a small child, would you prefer that your wife have a career outside the home or be a "*stay-at-home*" mom? Explain your answer.

6. If you were the mother of a small child, would you prefer to have a career outside the home or be a "*stay-at-home*" mom? Explain your answer.

7. Do you believe the father of a child should stay at home and raise the child or be employed? Explain your answer.

8. a. The Family and Medical Leave Act of 1993 ensures millions of employees up to twelve weeks of unpaid leave from their job to deal with a birth, adoption, or medical emergency in the family. Does this law ask too much of employers? Explain your answer.

   b. How far should an employer go in helping resolve an employee's conflicts between work and family?

9. a. A major concern for working parents with school-age children is having them come home to an empty house while the parents are still at work. If you were a latchkey child, how did your parents solve the problem?

   b. How did you feel about coming home to an empty house?

10. Almost 90 percent of children living with a single parent live with their mothers. As a group these women often have lower-than-average incomes. As a result many of the nation's children live in poverty and the consequences of that poverty for many years. Women's career choices often don't pay enough to support a family. Review the occupations listed in the *Occupational Outlook Handbook*, and select five jobs that a woman could do that would enable her to support herself and her children and that do not require a 4-year college degree. Look particularly at nontraditional careers for women in the trades.

    a.

    b.

    c.

    d.

    e.

continued

11. *Working Mother* magazine annually lists the best companies for working mothers. Using the OOH, list three careers that would be available in each of the following industries that were on *Working Mothers*'s list of the top one-hundred employers in the early 1990s.

Industry	**Careers in This Industry**		
Insurance (11 companies)	______	______	______
Pharmaceuticals (7 companies)	______	______	______
Banking (7 companies)	______	______	______
Computers/software (6 companies)	______	______	______
Telecommunications (5 companies)	______	______	______
Chemicals (4 companies)	______	______	______
Publishing (4 companies)	______	______	______

12. Many parents decide to work out of their home when their children are small. Scan the OOH and Chapter 15, and select four careers that lend themselves to "homesite-worksites."

a. ______ c. ______

b. ______ d. ______

13. a. What career could you see yourself operating from home? ______

b. How would you juggle the demands of a crying baby and an impatient customer? ______

______

14. There were 1,351,000 one-parent family groups maintained by men in 1990. This was more than a three-fold increase since 1970, when there were only 393,000 one-parent family groups maintained by men. Do you believe fathers can raise their children as well as mothers? Explain your answer. ______

______

15. Financial support for children who live apart from their fathers, and the lack of it, is of increasing concern. The Child Support Enforcement program is an effort to collect child support from parents who are legally obligated to pay. Is this a good idea? Explain your answer. ______

______

16. Many high-school-age mothers do not establish the paternity of their child because the father has no money. However, as the father gets older and starts working, he will be able to support the child and provide such benefits as health care. If paternity is established legally, even if the order for support is delayed, it means that collecting child support will be easier later on. Is this fair? Explain your answer. ______

______

17. In one year, income received by never-married mothers was $9,820, whereas families maintained by married couples averaged $43,130. Should the wages of the fathers of these children be garnished? (Garnishing is a legal proceeding whereby a portion of a person's wages or other assets are withheld and applied to payment of a debt.) Explain your answer. ______

______

Name ______________________________ Date ____________________

20.4 Checkpoint

Who Will Care for Your Child?

For single parents with incomes slightly above or below the poverty level, a lack of child care is a serious obstacle in obtaining and keeping a job. The vast majority of parents in this category have inadequate education, job training, and work experience. The mood of the U.S. Congress and many voters is to reduce or eliminate welfare payments and child-care support provided through federal legislation such as the Omnibus Budget Reconciliation Act of 1990. (See the section "Financial Support and Single Parents" in Chapter 20.)

1. Imagine yourself as a single teenage parent without welfare payments or child-care support.
   a. Name two occupations you would qualify for without education and training skills beyond your present level. ______________________________
   b. If you accepted a full-time job in one of these occupations, how much money could you expect to earn per day? ______________________________
   c. If you hired a friend or neighbor to baby-sit, what would he or she charge per day? ____________
   What would a professional child-care center charge per day? ______________
   d. What percentage of your daily income would you need to budget for child-care services from a friend or neighbor? __________ From a child-care center? __________

2. Use the following categories to make a time schedule for your typical workday. Activities other than your job schedule may be scheduled at any time you wish.

Activity	Time Frame	Hours Spent
Sleeping	_____ p.m. to _____ a.m.	_____
Preparing breakfast for you and your child	_____ a.m. to _____ a.m.	_____
Eating breakfast with your child	_____ a.m. to _____ a.m.	_____
Dressing and preparing for work	_____ a.m. to _____ a.m.	_____
Dressing child and packing child's bag for the day	_____ to _____	_____
Bathing self	_____ to _____	_____
Bathing child	_____ to _____	_____
Taking child to baby-sitter or daycare	_____ a.m. to _____ a.m.	_____
Traveling from child's daycare to job	_____ a.m. to _____ a.m.	_____
Job schedule (includes one-hour lunch)	8:00 a.m. to 5:00 p.m.	_____
Getting child and returning home after work	5:00 p.m. to _____ p.m.	_____

continued

Activity	Time Frame	Hours Spent
Preparing dinner for you and your child	_____ p.m. to _____ p.m.	_____
Eating dinner with your child	_____ p.m. to _____ p.m.	_____
Shopping for groceries or other necessities	_____ to _____	_____
Entertaining and teaching your child	_____ to _____	_____
Cleaning your home	_____ to _____	_____
Doing laundry and ironing	_____ to _____	_____
Talking on your home telephone	_____ to _____	_____
Watching television	_____ to _____	_____
	Total number of hours budgeted	_____

3. a. How much of the time in your daily schedule is spent communicating with your child? ____________

   b. How much time is spent communicating with other adults? ____________________________________

4. What affect will being a single parent have on your career opportunities? ____________________________

____

____

____

5. In your opinion, what are the major advantages or disadvantages of being a single parent? ____________

____

____

____

6. In your opinion, what are the major advantages or disadvantages of being the child of a single parent?

____

____

____

____

Name ______________________________ Date ______________________

20.5 Checkpoint

Finding the Right Words

Chapter 20 of your textbook contains numerous terms that employers and workers use. Recognizing and understanding these terms will help you make the important career decisions you will soon face.

Fill in the blank spaces in the vocabulary terms to complete the following sentences.

1. D ___ t ___ ng is the process of having social engagements with a member of the opposite sex.

2. The Pr ___ gn ___ ncy D ___ scr ___ m ___ n ___ t ___ ___ n ___ ct specifically prohibits companies with fifteen or more employees from discriminating against pregnant women.

3. A p ___ d ___ ___ tr ___ c ___ ___ n is a physician who specializes in children's medical care and diseases.

4. When a woman changes her work schedule to accommodate her young child or children she is said to be on the m ___ mmy tr ___ c ___.

5. The F ___ m ___ ly ___ nd M ___ d ___ c ___ l L ___ ___ v ___ ___ ct provides workers with twelve weeks of unpaid leave from their job to deal with a birth, adoption, or medical emergency in the family.

6. The process of seeking someone's affections is know as c ___ ___ rtsh ___ p.

7. L ___ ve involves having deep affection for someone.

8. ___ ccr ___ ___d is another word for accumulated.

9. When a person is ___ x ___ mpt, he or she is free from the rule.

10. Thr ___ ___ ___'cl___ck syndr ___ m ___ is the time during during the workday when parents' thoughts turn to their children who are getting out of school.

11. The ___ mn ___ b ___ s B ___ dg ___ t R ___ c ___ nc ___ l ___ ___ t ___ ___ n ___ ct concerns child-care policy and the earned income tax credit.

12. W ___ rk ___ h ___ l ___ cs are compulsive workers.

13. The parent who does not have primary custody of the child but has a responsibility for financial support is the n ___ nc ___ st ___ d ___ ___ l p ___ r ___ nt.

continued

Name ______________________ Date ______________

20.6 Checkpoint

Checking Your Location

1. For each of the following statements, circle **F** if the statement is more false than true. Circle **T** if the statement is more true than false.

T F a. Almost 95 percent of all working mothers return to their jobs before their children reach the age of one year.

T F b. Lasting relationships begin with people who make you feel lovable and capable.

T F c. The kind of love that leads to marriage and family responsibilities affects career roles and goals.

T F d. Approximately 75 percent of all divorced people marry again.

T F e. Opposites attract and strengthen personal attraction, whereas similarities provide opportunity for argument.

T F f. Most women who have education and training in specific career skills expect to work outside the home, even if they take time off from their careers to have children.

T F g. Almost 90 percent of young couples in the United States earn two salaries.

T F h. Statistics show a lower failure rate for teenage marriages than for those who marry after the teen age years.

T F i. With federal and state laws barring discrimination against pregnant women, it is no longer a concern.

T F j. The price tag for raising the average child born in 1991 is estimated to be somewhere between $89,580 and $175,380.

T F k. Employers use work and family policies as a competitive tool to recruit and keep skilled workers.

T F l. The term *mommy track* refers to the time when a woman changes her work schedule to accommodate her young child or children.

T F m. In the late 1980s fewer than 10 percent of the nation's children under 18 lived with only one parent.

T F n. Almost 90 percent of all children living with a single parent live with their fathers. As a group, these fathers have below-average income.

T F o. Almost half of all preschoolers spend at least part of their day in the care of adults other than their parents.

continued

2. Use the space below to rewrite the statements you marked **false** and make them **true**. Include the letter of each statement you rewrite.

Name ______________________ Date ______________

Checkpoint 21.1

Being a Responsible Citizen

"And for the support of this Declaration, with a firm reliance on the protection of divine providence, we mutually pledge to each other our lives, our fortunes, and our sacred honor." As the closing statement to the Declaration of Independence, this pledge of civic responsibility is as true today as it was when it was written.

1. Whether at home or overseas, thousands of living Americans have pledged their lives during local and national emergencies caused by criminal activities, fires, wars, floods, famines, storms, and earthquakes. List six occupations that require workers to pledge their lives, and write down the services these workers provide.

	Occupational Title	**Service Provided**
a.	______	______
b.	______	______
c.	______	______
d.	______	______
e.	______	______
f.	______	______

2. In the modern world, fortunes in the form of taxes must be pledged by responsible citizens to provide many of the services they have come to expect. Review your list of workers and the services they provide. Draw a line through the occupations and services that are funded with tax revenue.

3. Review the tax-funded occupations and services you have identified. How will each of these occupations effect your future?

   a. Occupation: ______ Expected effect on my lifestyle and career: ______

   b. Occupation: ______ Expected effect on my lifestyle and career: ______

   c. Occupation: ______ Expected effect on my lifestyle and career: ______

continued

4. Imagine that it is twenty years from now and you have achieved your major personal and career goals. List some ways you can demonstrate your civic responsibility by doing each of the following?

   a. Pledging your personal involvement (time) ______________________________

   ____

   ____

   b. Contributing money ______________________________

   ____

   ____

   c. Being honest and ethical (honorable) ______________________________

   ____

   ____

Name ______________________________ Date ____________________

21.2 Checkpoint

What's Your Opinion

Most citizens agree on what the major social problems are, but they frequently disagree on the "right" way to solve them.

1. In this activity, you will poll at least five people regarding the following social problem and ask them the question that follows. Use the chart below to record the information from your poll.

The issue: violent crime in America

The facts:

* Crimes of violence increased from 597 per 100,000 people in 1980 to an estimated 758 per 100,000 in 1993.
* The Oklahoma City bombing in May 1995 killed innocent men, women, and children because the murderer was angry at the government.
* In a scientific sampling of hospital emergency departments from June 1, 1992, to May 31, 1993, it was estimated 99,025 people were treated for nonfatal gun injuries.
* Firearms are the second leading cause of injury deaths. If the trend continues, firearm injuries could surpass motor vehicle injuries.

The question: Would harsher punishment for violent offenders slow down the increase in violent crime in America? Why or why not?

Respondent 1

Name ______________________ Age __________ Sex __________

Occupation ______________________ Counselor ______________________

Reason ____

____

____

Respondent 2

Name ______________________ Age __________ Sex __________

Occupation ______________________ Counselor ______________________

Reason ____

____

____

continued

Respondent 3

Name ______________________ Age __________ Sex __________

Occupation ______________________ Counselor ______________________

Reason ____

____

____

Respondent 4

Name ______________________ Age __________ Sex __________

Occupation ______________________ Counselor ______________________

Reason ____

____

____

Respondent 5

Name ______________________ Age __________ Sex __________

Occupation ______________________ Counselor ______________________

Reason ____

____

____

2. Assume that your poll is representative of all of the citizens in the United States. What would your survey report as the perceived solution to the problem? ______________________

____

____

3. Which of your respondents had the most facts or evidence to support his or her opinion? __________
4. Who had the strongest feelings about this problem? ______________________
5. Had any of your respondents ever been the victim of a violent crime? If so, how did this influence his or her opinion? ______________________
6. In your opinion, what is the cause of the increase in violent crime in the United States? __________

____

____

____

7. What do you believe is the solution to this problem? ______________________

____

____

____

8. What are the benefits of your solution for you and your friends? ______________________

____

____

____

9. What consequences must we face if we do not resolve this problem? ______________________

____

____

____

Name ______________________________ Date ____________________

Checkpoint 21.3

Finding the Right Words

Chapter 21 of your textbook contains numerous terms that employers and workers use. Recognizing and understanding these terms will help you make the important career decisions you will soon face.

Unscramble the terms in column B and match them with the definitions in column A. (Some terms contain two or more words.)

Column A

Example: __a__ an independent government agency that is responsible for enforcing federal laws and regulations regarding the environment

1. _____ a citizens' duties to the laws and policies of their community, state, and nation
2. _____ indifference
3. _____ newspapers, magazines, radio, and television
4. _____ an appealing leadership quality
5. _____ the highest law in the country
6. _____ income levels used to determine poverty
7. _____ a tax that depends on property ownership
8. _____ seeing one side of an issue as totally right or wrong
9. _____ income
10. _____ laws, edicts, or decrees enacted by a local government
11. _____ the population of an area divided by its square miles
12. _____ a body of rules that a nation, state, or community recognizes as binding on its citizens
13. _____ a tax based on a citizen's earnings
14. _____ lacking individuality
15. _____ damaging
16. _____ death rate

Column B

a. ENVIRONMENTAL PROTECTION AGENCY
RENTALIVENOMN TONEPITROC CANYEG

b. ______________________
CIICV YESNOLIPSITBIR

c. ______________
HAMISARC

d. ____________
HAYTAP

e. ______________________
VERYTOP SOLDTHERSH

f. __________
ADIME

g. ________________
ROPERTY AXT

h. ____________
UREEVEN

i ______________________
S.U. NONOITITSTUC

j. ______________________________
NOIIRATAZLOP FO SUEISS

k. ________________
CANSORDINE

l. ________________
COMEIN XAT

m. ________
SLAW

n. ______________
TOTALYIRM

o. ________________
TRAINMEETLD

p. ______________________
CIALOS YYNOTIMNA

q. ______________________
PLANOIPOUT YTNEDIS

Name ______________________________ Date ____________________

Checkpoint 21.4

Checking Your Location

1. For each of the following statements, circle **F** if the statement is more false than true. Circle **T** if the statement is more true than false.

T F a. The United States has the most restrictions on voting of any country in the world.

T F b. The U.S. government is the largest employer and purchaser of goods and services in our economy.

T F c. Most registered voters inform themselves equally about all sides of an issue or about all of the political viewpoints on an issue.

T F d. Public services are paid for through taxes.

T F e. Most of the taxes you will pay during your working years will go to the state government.

T F f. The federal government makes decisions with which each citizen must live.

T F g. Registration for selective service is a required citizenship responsibility for men and women.

T F h. Each citizen's rights and privileges end where his or her neighbor's begin.

T F i. The average new job (in terms of earnings) created in the United States requires a high school diploma plus a college degree.

T F j. Families maintained solely by women make up most of the families living in poverty.

T F k. Unmarried teenage mothers are the least likely to be long-term welfare recipients.

T F l. Worldwide, contaminated water causes the death of five million children under five every year.

T F m. Two major reasons for the population shift from mostly rural to mostly urban in the United States are job opportunities and lifestyles.

T F n. An estimated two million Native Americans from approximately 350 federally recognized tribes live in the United States.

T F o. An atitude becomes a prejudice when an individual's thoughts, feelings, and behaviors are open to new information and experiences.

continued

2. Use the space below to rewrite the statements you marked **false** and make them **true**. Include the letter of each statement you rewrite.

Name ______________________________ Date ______________________

22.1 Checkpoint

Going through the Stages

Every basic life skill you learn paves the way for further learning. You probably learned the life skills listed below before you were seven years old. In each case, what further learning did you accomplish? Describe two specific job skills that are directly related to this life skill.

Example: Learning to walk lead to running, skipping, riding a bicycle, skating, hiking, and athletic skills

Two related job skills are 1. A construction worker on a scaffold. 2. A hospital attendant escorting a patient to an examing room.

1. a. Learning to talk led to ______________________________

   b. Two related job skills are ______________________________

2. a. Learning to trust others led to ______________________________

   b. Two related job skills are ______________________________

3. a. Learning to manipulate objects led to ______________________________

   b. Two related job skills are ______________________________

"DON'T WORRY, DEAR... It's JUST A Stage THEY'RE GOING THROUGH..."

Name ______________________ Date ______________

22.2 Checkpoint

The Working Years

People frequently refer to the broad range of time between the late twenties and the middle sixties as *the working years*. Before you answer the following questions, think of the personal and career roles you would like to have during your working years.

1. a. What career role would you like? ______________________

   b. Would this role make you feel like a productive member of society? Why or why not? ______________________

2. a. What family roles would you like (parent, son, daughter, aunt, uncle)? ______________________

   b. Which of these roles would be most important to you? Why? ______________________

3. What will you do to help prepare the next generation for family responsibilities and future careers?

   ____

4. Will you help society to protect the knowledge and products of past generations? If so, how? If not, why not? ______________________

5. List three actions you are presently involved in or have completed to prepare yourself for the working years.

   a. ______________________

   b. ______________________

   c. ______________________

6. List three actions you are planning to begin during the next two years to prepare yourself for the working years.

   a. ______________________

   b. ______________________

   c. ______________________

Name ______________________ Date ______________________

22.3 Checkpoint

Plan Number Two

Murphy's Law states, "Anything that *can* go wrong *will* go wrong." Most people would disagree with Murphy, but it is true that a good plan doesn't always work. Situations change, and plans must be adjusted. Having a backup plan (plan number two) is always a good idea. Consider the case of Jim Stolz.

> Jim is married and has two small children. He is a college graduate with a major in social work. Jim likes to help people solve their problems, but he also enjoys working outdoors. He is considering two job offers.
>
> The first job offer is from the Green Mist Lawn and Tree Service, a locally owned company. After six weeks of training, Jim would be a crew leader in the tree division. The beginning salary is $1,833 per month. During the busy summer season, Jim would be expected to work longer hours and some Saturdays. As a supervisor, he would not be paid overtime.
>
> The second job offer is from a government-funded social agency. Jim would interview elderly clients who are experiencing financial and medical problems. His hours of work would be 8:00 a.m. until 5:00 p.m. Monday through Friday. The beginning salary is $1,575 per month. Jim's opportunity for promotion is very good.
>
> If Jim accepts the job with Green Mist Lawn and Tree Service, he wants to be involved in some type of leisure-time activity helping people. If he accepts the job with the social acency, he wants to be involved in some type of leisure-time activity in the outdoors.

1. Write a brief plan for Jim that includes the job he should accept, the reason it should be his first choice, and plan for his leisure-time activities. ______________________

2. Write a backup plan for Jim. Assume that the second job offer is still open. ______________________

3. What adjustments will Jim need to make if plan 1 doesn't work out and he decides to follow plan 2?

Name ______________________________ Date ____________________

Checkpoint 22.4

Finding the Right Words

Chapter 22 of your textbook contains numerous terms that employers and workers use. Recognizing and understanding these terms will help you make the important career decisions you will soon face.

Fill in the blank spaces in the vocabulary terms to complete the following sentences.

1. During the ___ nt ___ m ___ cy stage of life, most adults establish a unique sense of self that is separate from their original families.

2. D ___ l ___ b ___ r ___ t ___ is another word for "carefully considered."

3. The ___ g ___ ___ nt ___ gr ___ ty stage of life occurs when the working years are over.

4. The g ___ n ___ r ___ t ___ v ___ ty stage of life occurs during the working years.

5. The word ph ___ l ___ s ___ phy comes from a Greek noun that means "the pursuit of wisdom."

6. Your c ___ r ___ ___ r ph ___ l ___ s ___ phy is the carefully considered involvement of your personal beliefs and behaviors in choosing an occupation, acquiring the necessary education, performing day-to-day work tasks, and planning a career that might include several occupations.

7. Something that is d ___ st ___ nct is easy to recognize.

8. D ___ m ___ n ___ nt means "most influential."

9. The ideas and feelings within you that give you a sense of right and wrong make up your c ___ nsc ___ ___ nc ___.

Name ______________________________ Date ______________

Checkpoint 22.5

Checking Your Location

1. For each of the following statements, circle **F** if the statement is more false than true. Circle **T** if the statement is more true than false.

T F a. In the future world of work, new technology will eliminate most companies.

T F b. Being aware of likely changes will help you prepare for them in a positive way.

T F c. Certain parts of each developmental stage will be dominant at various times in your life.

T F d. Although the characteristics of each person are different, many of the changes that take place during the adult years are predictable.

T F e. The responsibility for your friendships, love relationships, and career path is shared with your friends, parents, teachers, and employers.

T F f. A person who is unable to find satisfaction during the working years will accept mediocrity, boredom, and self-interest.

T F g. It is important that your career philosophy take into account your personal limitations and ambitions.

T F h. Realistic expectations can be a source of discouragement and underachievement.

T F i. Mature adults remain firm and unchanged in the face of events that are beyond their control.

T F j. The last stage of life is called *despair*. During this stage, it is normal for older people to be suspicious of others, lacking in faith and confidence, and without meaningful work, love, or friends.

T F k. Learning certain life skills at each stage of your development will help you grow into a mature person and be successful in your chosen career.

T F l. Getting a reprimand instead of approval helps a child learn what is ethically and morally accepted as right or wrong.

continued

T F m. Recognizing that you are an independent, responsible, productive adult should provide satisfaction for you and your parents.

T F n. The mature adult has a sense of caring, purpose, and confidence in the next generation.

T F o. Being actively involved in selecting a career and exploring the necessary education and training requirements will help you establish realistic career expectations.

2. Use the space below to rewrite the statements you marked **false** and make them **true**. Include the letter of each statement you rewrite.

____

____

____

____

____

____